2 THE FUNCTIONS OF

English Grammar

2

THE FUNCTIONS OF

English Grammar

LOUIS W. HOLSCHUH
The Ohio State University

ST. MARTIN'S PRESS
New York

Editor: Kathleen Keller
Development editor: Bob Weber
Project editor: Erica Townsend
Production supervisor: Alan Fischer
Text design: Butler/Udell Design
Cover design: Celine Brandes

Library of Congress Catalog Card Number: 89–64015

Manufactured in the United States of America.
543
fedc

For information, write:
St. Martin's Press, Inc.
175 Fifth Avenue
New York, NY 10010

ISBN: 0-312-01999-8

To Nathan

Preface

2. The Functions of English Grammar is the second level of three grammar texts for adult students of English as a second or foreign language. It is intended for students in the TOEFL range of 440 to 500. Such students are already familiar with basic English structure and are somewhat fluent, but they need to increase their understanding of structure and improve their ability to use English in academic and professional situations. A companion volume, *1. The Elements of English Grammar*, is available for students in the TOEFL range of 390 to 440, and *3. The Applications of English Grammar* will be published in 1992.

THE GOALS

2. The Functions of English Grammar takes an analytical approach based on clear explanations and a wide variety of exercise material to address a broad range of goals—from mastering form, to understanding and controlling grammatical meaning, and ultimately to productive fluency. The book has been carefully structured to help students improve their command of English and to extend it outside the grammar classroom. Specifically, the book:

- **Presents the formation of basic grammatical structures and provides practice in using them**. As students develop greater grammatical accuracy, they also develop the analytical skills needed to edit their own English production—and to respond correctly on objective proficiency examinations.

- **Presents the meanings and functions of basic grammatical structures and provides practice in controlling their use.** Exercise sequences include practice in discriminating among different structures based on appropriate usage and in expressing core meanings in alternate ways. In this manner, students develop a wider range of expression as well as a finer focus on meaning.

- **Provides opportunities for students to create language, not simply fill in blanks and edit mistakes.** Practice material throughout the book helps students to apply their understanding of grammatical form and function in producing real language. This approach encourages the development of fluency along with accuracy by challenging students to express their own ideas as they respond to academic subject matter.

THE APPROACH

This text has been written for adult students who have previously studied basic English grammar and who are now ready for more advanced structures and a comprehensive overview of the English grammatical system. Such students generally feel comfortable with formal rules and with grammar terminology. This text accommodates such learners by providing an analytical approach that is transparent, flexible, and interesting:

- **A transparent grammar text.** The structure and format of this text are clear and reliable. Numbered sections and exercises make it easy to assign and refer to specific material; example sentences are displayed in a box and are followed immediately by explanatory notes; and each exercise is labeled to identify which grammatical feature is to be practiced and in what manner. In class or out, these consistent signals and patterns guide students quickly to the relevant material.

- **A flexible grammar text.** A teacher's overall goals and an individual student's most pressing needs are easily accommodated by the features that make this text transparent—simply assign, omit, reorganize, or insert content by referring to section and exercise numbers. Even greater flexibility is achieved by the diversity of exercises in each section: some focus on form, some on discriminating among meanings, and some on productive fluency. By selecting which type of material to emphasize, teachers can meet course goals and also guide the progress of individual students.

- **A high-interest grammar text.** The analysis of formal grammar is a means, not an end, and students should be encouraged to create language that lets them express themselves. Exercise sequences in this text begin by emphasizing form and then move quickly to practice material that teaches students to consider context and situation when making grammatical choices. The final exercises in most sections promote productive fluency by focusing on self-expression and on interaction with academic subject matter.

Students enjoy going beyond formal analysis to apply what they've learned—both in the English classroom and in their other courses. While the approach of this text is clearly analytical, the range of practice material it offers can help students become self-sufficient and expressive in both academic and professional settings.

THE ORGANIZATION   The completeness of explanations and the diversity of practice material make this text different from many basic grammars, but its enrichment and interest are made manageable by a consistent organization within each numbered section. Every chapter consists of three to five sections, each focusing on a particular structure or feature of grammar. In turn, each section includes the following elements:

- **Example sentences.**   Boxed displays present a variety of examples to demonstrate important aspects of the grammatical point under discussion. Each example sentence is identified by a letter (A, B, and so on) to tie the examples to the explanatory notes and to ease discussion of the examples in class.

- **Explanatory notes.**   Each box of examples is followed directly by numbered notes that explain the formation and use of the targeted structure. Additional examples within the numbered notes further illustrate the forms and meanings of that structure. Common errors are explained, and structures of similar form or usage are noted.

- **Exercises that focus on form.**   The first exercises in a sequence, both oral and written, focus on mechanics and are intended to check students' understanding of the targeted structure and their ability to produce it accurately. This material can be skimmed or omitted when it is apparent that students understand and control form.

- **Exercises that focus on meanings.**   These exercises, usually written, follow up the formal practice. They teach students to make grammatical decisions based on meaning distinctions, to create sentences from given elements, and to rephrase information using the targeted structure. This practice material strengthens students' formal abilities while refining their control of grammatical meaning.

- **Exercises that focus on productive fluency.**   To encourage language production, the concluding exercises of a sequence give students opportunities to create original language by sharing personal information and by responding to and manipulating information of an academic nature. For example, students restate information provided in tables and time lines, react to situations, and gather information from one another and report it to the class—always with a focus on the target structures.

ACKNOWLEDGMENTS   The following reviewers offered valuable comments and suggestions during the various stages in developing this text: Gloria Jones, Youngstown State University; Margaret Lindstrom, Colorado State University; Charles Mickelson, Ohio University; Amy Sales, Boston University; Joy S. Tesh, University of Houston; Stephen Thewlis, San Francisco State University; William C.

VanderWerf, City College of San Francisco; and especially Robert Kantor, The Ohio State University. I also want to thank the staff and students of the American Language Program at The Ohio State Univeristy for field-testing the various drafts of manuscript.

The staff of St. Martin's Press have done everything possible to make this project pleasant and rewarding for me. Bob Weber, development editor, has done a remarkable job coordinating all the pieces and all the people involved in the production of this project, and I also deeply appreciate the guidance, encouragement, and efforts of Susan Anker, Kathleen Keller, and Erica Townsend.

I could not have completed this project without my family's encouragement. Thanks, Mary Ann, Nathan, and Eric, for your understanding and patience.

Louis W. Holschuh

Contents

2 THE FUNCTIONS OF
English Grammar

1 Basic Sentence Types

In this chapter you will review basic grammar terminology, and you will practice applying grammatical labels as you analyze English sentences. Understanding grammar terminology will help you to understand the explanations in later chapters. You will also examine basic sentence patterns and how they can be expanded.

SECTION 1.1 Basic Components of Sentences: Subject and Predicate

SECTION 1.2 Parts of Speech

SECTION 1.3 Expanding Basic Sentences with Adjectives and Phrases

SECTION 1.4 Expanding Basic Sentences with Adjective Clauses and Adverb Clauses

SECTION 1.1 Basic Components of Sentences: Subject and Predicate

English sentences have two basic components: a subject and a predicate.

BASIC COMPONENTS OF SENTENCES	
Subject	*Predicate*
A. Winters in Maine	can be extremely difficult.
B. Temperatures	frequently drop below zero.
C. Heavy snowfalls	make travel risky.
D. Being self-reliant and resourceful	helps a person to survive through the winter.

1. Basic components: Most English sentences must have a subject and a predicate. Sentences A through D have been divided into these two basic components.

1

2. The subject: The subject of a sentence generally tells what the topic of the sentence is. It is usually at the beginning of the sentence. The subject can be one word (*Temperatures*) or several words (*Winters in Maine; Being self-reliant and resourceful*).

3. The predicate: The predicate of a sentence generally follows the subject; it describes the subject or an activity performed by the subject. The predicate consists of a verb phrase and all the words and phrases that follow it (*can be extremely difficult; frequently drop below zero; make travel risky*).

EXERCISE 1.1-A   ANALYZING FORM

subjects and predicates

Read the following sentences. Identify the subjects and predicates, and draw a slash between them.

Example: *Summers in southern Texas / are usually hot and dry.*

1.   Bevis Hall was closed for repairs during most of October.

2.   The headlights of an oncoming car blinded me.

3.   Reference materials may not be taken out of the library.

4.   Identifying subjects and predicates is the focus of this exercise.

5.   Martha's roommate has decided to leave school.

6.   Restrictions on automobile imports go into effect next month.

7.   The population of the inner city has been decreasing for the past fifteen years.

EXERCISE 1.1-B   COMPLETING SENTENCES

adding predicates

Complete each sentence by adding a predicate. Use your own ideas, and try to create meaningful sentences.

1.   Poverty in some developing nations _____

_____

2.   My friends and I _____

_____

3.   Talking with Americans _____

_____

4.   Space exploration _____

_____

5.   The Soviet Union and the United States _____

_____

6.   English grammar _____

_____

EXERCISE 1.1-C   COMPLETING SENTENCES

● ·

adding subjects

Complete each sentence by adding a subject. Use your own ideas, and try to create meaningful sentences.

1.   _____ are sometimes ignored.

2.   _____ like to sit in the back of the room.

3.   _____ don't enjoy studying English.

4.   _____ upsets my parents.

5.   _____ is rude in my country.

6.   _____ is my most difficult class.

Refer to box   As we have seen, the predicate usually follows the subject and consists of a
on page 4.   verb phrase and the words that follow it. The words that come after the verb phrase are called the complement. Different types of verbs can be followed by different types of complements.

4. Activity verbs: Activity verbs show some type of action, either mental or physical. The verbs in sentences E through I on page 4 are all activity verbs.

5. Objects: Activity verbs are often followed by a noun phrase called an object. An activity verb is called transitive when it has an object. Sentences E, F, and G on page 4 each contain a transitive verb (*received; had sent; put*) and an object (*Laura's letter; it; it*). Notice the relationship between the verb and the object: The verb acts on the object, and its action ties the subject and the object together.

> What did we receive only yesterday? *Laura's letter*
> What had she sent over a week ago? *It (her letter)*
> What had the letter carrier put in the wrong mailbox? *It (Laura's letter)*

COMPLEMENTS OF ACTIVITY VERBS

	Subject	Verb	Predicate	
			Complement	
			Object	Adverb
E.	We	received	Laura's letter	only yesterday.
F.	She	had sent	it	over a week ago.
G.	The letter carrier	put	it	in the wrong mailbox.
H.	We	complained		loudly.
I.	The letter carrier	apologized.		

Activity verbs that are *not* followed by an object are called intransitive. Sentences H and I contain intransitive verbs (*complained; apologized*).

6. Adverb phrases: The complement of a sentence may also contain an adverb phrase. Sentences E through H each have an adverb phrase (*only yesterday; over a week ago; in the wrong mailbox; loudly*). The adverb phrase adds information about time, place, or manner. Note that an adverb can follow either a transitive verb or an intransitive verb.

EXERCISE 1.1-D   ANALYZING FORM

complements of activity verbs

Read each sentence, and identify the parts of the complement. Underline the verb once. Circle the object (if any). Underline the adverb (if any) twice. Is the verb transitive or intransitive?

> **Example:** *The librarians* sorted (all the new books) *last week. (transitive)*

1. Janet plans the office party every year.

2. The boys are walking to the gym.

3. Professor Naumoff teaches an eight o'clock class each semester.

4. Our team won the state championship tournament last year.

5. Our team will not win this year.

COMPLEMENTS OF LINKING VERBS			
Subject		*─────Predicate─────*	
	Linking Verb	*────Complement────*	
		Noun or Adjective	*Adverb*
J. New Mexico	is	a state	in the Southwest.
K. It	is		north of Mexico.
L. Its climate	is	hot and dry.	
M. New Mexico	became	a state	in 1912.
N. Its economy	seems	healthy.	
O. Its cities	look	new and clean.	

7. Linking verbs: Linking verbs do not show activity like activity verbs. The verbs in sentences J through O are all linking verbs. Linking verbs are followed by either a noun (sentences J and M) or an adjective (sentences L, N, and O). The linking verb BE can be followed by an adverb of place, without an adjective or noun (sentence K).

When an adjective follows a linking verb, the adjective describes the subject of the sentence.

> *Linking Verb + Adjective*
>
> Its climate is hot and dry. (Its climate = hot and dry)
> Its economy seems healthy. (Its economy = healthy)
> Its cities look new and clean. (Its cities = new and clean)

When a noun follows a linking verb, the noun restates the subject of the sentence.

> *Linking Verb + Noun*
>
> New Mexico is a state. (New Mexico = a state)
> New Mexico became a state in 1912. (New Mexico = a state in 1912)

Remember that a noun that follows an activity verb is called an object. An object does not restate the subject; instead, it receives the action of the verb.

> *Activity Verb + Object*
>
> Laura sent the letter last week. (Laura ≠ the letter)

8. Common linking verbs: The verb BE is the most common of the linking verbs. Other linking verbs include *appear, seem, feel, taste, become, sound, look,* and *smell.* Some verbs are linking verbs if their meaning in the sentence is the same as *become*; in other instances, they may be activity verbs.

Linking Usage	*Activity Usage*
The teacher *fell* ill.	The teacher *fell* down the steps.
The child *grew* restless.	The child *grew* three inches.
The audience *went* wild.	The audience *went* to the lobby.

9. Choosing an adjective or an adverb after the verb: Notice that a regular verb can be followed directly by an adverb of manner and that a linking verb can be followed directly by an adjective. Some adjectives can be changed to adverbs of manner by adding the suffix *-ly*.

Linking Verb + Adjective	*Activity Verb + Adverb of Manner*
George is *loud*.	He talks *loudly*.
Martha's pronunciation is *good*.	She speaks *well*.
Sam appears *confident*.	He moves *confidently*.

EXERCISE 1.1-E   ANALYZING FORM

complements of linking verbs

The following sentences contain linking verbs. Read each sentence to identify the parts of the complement. Underline the verb once. Circle the adjective or noun that follows the linking verb (if any). Underline the adverb (if any) twice.

Example: *The cafeteria food tasted (awful) last night.*

1.   Columbus is in the center of Ohio.

2.   The fumes from the chemical plant smell horrible in the morning.

3.   Mr. Mathers appeared upset at the end of our discussion.

4.   Georgine became a stockbroker after college.

5.   Denmark is the smallest Scandinavian country.

6.   The exam questions seemed easy at first glance.

7.   The children became restless toward the end of the class.

8.   The index is in the back of the book.

EXERCISE 1.1-F   ANALYZING FORM

complements of activity verbs and linking verbs

Decide whether the verb in each sentence is an activity verb or a linking verb. What does the complement consist of? Label the parts of the complement as follows: *OBJ* = object, *ADJ* = adjective, *N* = noun, *ADV* = adverb.

ADJ   ADV

Example: *The children seemed happy yesterday. (linking)*

1.   The building on the corner of Main Street and Fifth Avenue appears empty.

2.   The new laboratory equipment arrived yesterday.

3.   We studied the effect of computers in everyday life.

4.   The clerks reported the mistake immediately.

5.   Our wish will come true someday.

EXERCISE 1.1-G   DISCRIMINATING FORM

adjectives and adverbs of manner

Decide whether each sentence requires an adverb of manner or an adjective in the blank space. Then complete each sentence by adding an appropriate adjective or adverb from the list.

Adjectives	*Adverbs*
crazy	crazily
loud	loudly
timid	timidly
terrible	terribly
inconsolable	inconsolably

1.   Herman's ideas seem _____ to me.

2.   Mary's parents cried _____ when they learned of the accident.

3.   The children walked _____ down the street.

4.   This soup tasted _____ when I tried it earlier.

5.   He tasted his soup _____, and everyone in the restaurant turned around and looked at him.

6.   The car's engine sounds _____ today. Do you think something is wrong?

SUMMARY: BASIC SENTENCE PATTERNS

A. *Pattern 1:* Subject + Linking Verb + Adjective (+ Adverb)
The building looked empty last night.

B. *Pattern 2:* Subject + Linking Verb + Noun (+ Adverb)
The building is a museum now.

C. *Pattern 3:* Subject + BE + Adverb of Place
The building is on Fifth Avenue.

D. *Pattern 4:* Subject + Activity Verb (+ Adverb)
The child cried loudly.

E. *Pattern 5:* Subject + Activity Verb + Object (+ Adverb)
The child understood my question easily.

EXERCISE 1.1-H   ANALYZING FORM

basic sentence patterns

Use the summary chart above to identify the pattern that each sentence
follows. Write the number of the pattern in the blank.

Example: *The cat eats in the kitchen.* _____4_____

1. I buy a newspaper every morning. _____

2. Janet became a chemical engineer. _____

3. Sean speaks fluently. _____

4. The class grew restless by the end of the hour. _____

5. We need to write a letter to him every week. _____

6. The dictionary is on the top shelf. _____

EXERCISE 1.1-I   ANALYZING FORM

basic sentence patterns

Read the paragraph. Then use the summary chart to identify the basic
pattern of each sentence. Write the number of the pattern in the blank.

(1) The abacus is the earliest mechanical computer. (2) The Chinese invented it
more than 5,000 years ago. (3) It has a wooden frame with wires and beads.
(4) The beads represent the ones units, tens units, hundreds units, and so forth.
(5) The operator moves beads on the wires very quickly. (6) Using an abacus

looks very difficult. (7) But even young children can master it. (8) Skilled opera-
tors make calculations as fast as on a calculator. (9) People continue to use the
abacus in the Soviet Union and the Far East.

Sentence 1: _____   Sentence 6: _____

Sentence 2: _____   Sentence 7: _____

Sentence 3: _____   Sentence 8: _____

Sentence 4: _____   Sentence 9: _____

Sentence 5: _____

EXERCISE 1.1-J   UNSCRAMBLING SENTENCES

basic sentence patterns

Rearrange each group of words and phrases to form a meaningful sentence.
Then use the summary chart to identify which basic sentence pattern you
have used.

> **Example:** mailed – my office – last week – the letter
> *My office mailed the letter last week. (pattern 5)*

1. weak – during the past several years – has grown – his eyesight

   _____

2. will explain – tomorrow – the manufacturers – their new products

   _____

3. for years – the same crop – in this region – have grown – farmers

   _____

4. quickly – the professor – since his wife's death – has aged

   _____

5. mild – the weather – in May – turns

   _____

6. was – Hollywood – the film capital of the world – for many years

   _____

EXERCISE 1.1-K   COMPLETING SENTENCES

complements

Each item on page 10 gives you a subject and a verb phrase. Add a complement that will make a meaningful sentence. Then use the summary chart to
identify which basic sentence pattern you have used.

Example: *The letter carrier took the package this morning. (pattern 5)*

1. The people in that neighborhood will receive _____

_____

2. The students in this class have become _____

_____

3. The computer revolution is _____

_____

4. The master of ceremonies introduced _____

_____

5. This building looks _____

_____

SECTION 1.2   Parts of Speech

To understand the grammar of a sentence, it is useful to classify words into groups and to give labels, or names, to these groups of words.

IDENTIFYING PARTS OF SPEECH

A. Severe winter storms in the Northeast have caused several deaths and many injuries during the past week.

B. Telephone service was frequently out, and most areas lost electric service.

C. New York City closed its enormous public school system for three days.

D. Governor Cuomo declared a state of emergency immediately because conditions were extremely dangerous.

E. The storm was a disaster, and it will probably not be forgotten soon.

---

1. Nouns: Nouns are words that name persons, animals, places, objects, ideas, and institutions. Proper nouns name particular people, places, or things. Proper nouns are capitalized. All other nouns are called common nouns. Some of the nouns found in sentences A through E are listed here. Can you identify the others?

Proper Nouns	*Common Nouns*
Northeast	storms
New York City	deaths
Governor Cuomo	service

Nouns can have several functions in a sentence; for example:

Subject of the sentence — *storms* in sentence A
Object of the verb — *system* in sentence C
Complement of a linking verb — *disaster* in sentence E
Object of a preposition — *week* in sentence A
Modifier of another noun — *telephone* in sentence B

2. Pronouns: A pronoun is a word that can take the place of a noun or a noun phrase; for example:

its refers to *New York City* in sentence C
it refers to *storm* in sentence E

Pronouns have different forms, depending on their function in the sentence.

Subject Pronouns	*Object Pronouns*	*Possessive Pronouns*
I	me	my, mine
you	you	your, yours
he	him	his, his
she	her	her, hers
it	it	its, its
we	us	our, ours
they	them	their, theirs

3. Verbs: Verbs are words which express activity or a state of being. Every sentence has a main verb; a sentence may also have one or more auxiliary, or helping, verbs to add to the meaning of the main verb.

	Auxiliary Verb	*Main Verb*
Sentence A:	have	caused
Sentence B:	—	was
	—	lost
Sentence E:	—	was
	will (not) be	forgotten

4. Adjectives: Adjectives describe nouns. *Severe* is an adjective in sentence A, describing the noun *storms*. *Enormous* is an adjective in sentence C, describing the noun *system*. What are the other adjectives in sentences A through E?

Notice that nouns can also describe other nouns; in that case, they function as adjectives, for example:

> winter storms (sentence A)
> Telephone service (sentence B)

5. Determiners: Determiners (words like *some, every, this, that, these,* and *those*) also modify nouns. Numbers are determiners when they modify a noun (*one book; two tables*). Possessive nouns and pronouns are another group of determiners (*my car; John's class*). Can you identify the determiners in sentences A through E?

6. Articles: Articles are the words *a, an,* and *the.* They are a special type of determiner. Find the articles in sentences A through E.

7. Adverbs: An adverb can modify a verb or an entire complement. Phrases can also function as adverbs. Adverbs often answer the questions *how, where, when,* and *why.* Adverbs in sentences A through E include *during the past week, frequently, for three days,* and *immediately.*

Adverbs can also modify an adjective or another adverb, for example:

> They are *extremely* dangerous conditions. (Adverb + Adjective)
> Cars have to move *very slowly*. (Adverb + Adverb)

8. Prepositions: Prepositions show relationships of time and location and relationships between ideas. Common prepositions of time include *after, during, in, on,* and *before.* Common prepositions of location include *in, on, under, above,* and *inside.* What prepositions are used in sentences A through E?

9. Conjunctions: Conjunctions are words that join ideas by joining together grammatical units. The coordinating conjunctions are *and, but, for, or, nor,* and *yet.* Subordinating conjunctions are words like *because, although,* and *while.* Can you find any conjunctions in sentences A through E?

EXERCISE 1.2-A   ANALYZING FORM

● ·

parts of speech

Identify the parts of speech of the words in the following sentences.

1. The Great Sphinx is one of the wonders of ancient architecture.
    The _____
    Great Sphinx _____
    is _____
    one _____

of _____
the _____
wonders _____
of _____
ancient _____
architecture _____

2. Fire destroyed St. Mark's Cathedral in Venice in 976, but it was rebuilt later.
Fire _____
destroyed _____
St. Mark's Cathedral _____
in _____
Venice _____
in _____
976 _____
but _____
it _____
was _____
rebuilt _____
later _____

3. Notre-Dame de Paris is a twin-towered church with a steeple over the crossing and immense flying buttresses.
Notre-Dame de Paris _____
is _____
a _____
twin-towered _____
church _____
with _____
a _____
steeple _____
over _____
the _____
crossing _____
and _____
immense _____
flying _____
buttresses _____

EXERCISE 1.2-B CORRECTING ERRORS

sentence patterns and parts of speech

Each sentence on page 14 has one or more mistakes. Read the sentences carefully; then write the correct form for each one.

1. Summers in Arizona very hot.

_____

2. She smiled sweet.

_____

3. Speaks well but slow.

_____

4. He kissed on her forehead.

_____

5. The teacher grew very angrily.

_____

6. Her is getting better.

_____

7. Sitting at home alone not much fun.

_____

SECTION 1.3   Expanding Basic Sentences with Adjectives and Phrases

Information can be added to a sentence by using adjectives and phrases. Examine how the basic sentence patterns from the summary chart in the box on page 15 have been expanded.

1. Using adjectives: Adjectives have been added before nouns in sentences A, B, D, and E. What are the adjectives that have been added? Notice that adjectives are placed before the nouns that they modify.

2. Using nouns as adjectives: In sentence B, the noun _government_ has been placed before the noun _building_. Remember that a noun can function as an adjective to describe another noun.

3. Using prepositional phrases: Prepositional phrases have been added to each of the sample sentences. Most of them describe nouns. In sentence A, the phrase _by the river_ shows the location of the noun _building_, and it has been placed immediately after the noun it describes. Identify the other prepositional phrases that show location. Which noun does each describe?

In sentence B, the prepositional phrase _for modern art_ describes the purpose of the noun _museum_.

In sentence C, the phrase _with the Department of Education office_ describes the noun _building_ more precisely. What other sentence has a similar type of phrase?

BASIC SENTENCES WITH ADJECTIVES AND PHRASES

A. *Pattern 1:* Subject + Linking Verb + Adjective (+ Adverb)
The building looked empty last night.
The **old** building **by the river** looked empty last night.

B. *Pattern 2:* Subject + Linking Verb + Noun (+ Adverb)
The building is a museum now.
The **old government** building is a museum **for modern art** now.

C. *Pattern 3:* Subject + BE + Adverb of Place
The building is on Fifth Avenue.
The building **with the Department of Education office** is on Fifth Avenue **near the park**.

D. *Pattern 4:* Subject + Activity Verb (+ Adverb)
The child cried loudly.
The **small** child **in the back of the room** cried loudly.

E. *Pattern 5:* Subject + Activity Verb + Object (+ Adverb)
The child understood my question easily.
The **alert** child **in the red sweater** understood my question **about states' rights** without difficulty.

In sentence E, the phrase *without difficulty* has been substituted for the single-word adverb *easily*. In this case, the prepositional phrase does not describe a noun; instead, it functions as an adverb to describe the verb *understood*.

EXERCISE 1.3-A   ANALYZING FORM

identifying the basic sentence

The following sentences are expansions of the basic sentence patterns that have been discussed. In each sentence, circle the adjectives and prepositional phrases that expand the basic sentence.

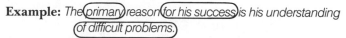

Example: The (primary) reason (for his success) is his understanding (of difficult problems.)

1. A company in Atlanta will provide the necessary equipment for our lab.

2. The clerk in the store recommended a typewriter with an easier self-correction feature.

3. The old lobby in the girls' dormitory should look beautiful by the end of the week.

4. Cars with front-wheel drive are safe on icy or snowy roads.

5. The final chapter in the book describes the latest methods in experimental design.

6. A feast with all the relatives was a family tradition during the holidays.

EXERCISE 1.3-B   EXPANDING SENTENCES

adding adjectives and prepositional phrases

Eight basic sentences are given. Expand each one by adding adjectives and prepositional phrases. You may want to add adverbs to some of the sentences.

> **Example:** A ship collided with a boat.
> *A large cruise ship from Panama collided with a small fishing boat in the San Francisco Bay yesterday afternoon.*

1. The explanation is clear.

_____

_____

2. The student provided an answer.

_____

_____

3. The car hit a pedestrian.

_____

_____

4. The construction company will finish the building.

_____

_____

5. The mayor gave an order.

_____

_____

SECTION 1.4   Expanding Basic Sentences with Adjective Clauses and Adverb Clauses

Section 1.3 discussed how to add information to basic sentences by using adjectives and prepositonal phrases. Basic sentences can also be expanded by using clauses that function as adjectives and adverbs.

The grammar of adjective clauses and adverb clauses will be presented later. For the time being, it is important that you be able to read a sentence and identify its basic pattern. To do this, you must also be able to identify dependent clauses and to understand what type of information they provide.

Examine how the basic sentence patterns from the summary chart on page 8 have been expanded in the box below.

BASIC SENTENCES WITH CLAUSES

A. The building looked empty last night.
The building **that sits across from the park** looked empty **when we drove past it**.

B. The building is a museum now.
The building **that used to belong to the Briggs family** has been a museum **since Mr. Briggs died in 1986**.

C. The building is on Fifth Avenue.
The building **which contains the legislative offices** is on Fifth Avenue **because the senators need to be able to walk to the State Building across the street**.

D. The child cried loudly.
The child **who was sitting in the back of the room** cried loudly **so that the teacher could hear him**.

E. The child understood my question easily.
The child **who was wearing a red sweater** understood my question **although it was very difficult**.

---

1. Clauses: A clause is a group of words that has a subject and a verb. Clauses are either independent or dependent.

Independent clauses are meaningful by themselves and can stand alone as sentences. In fact, each of the sample sentences A through E is a single independent clause.

Dependent clauses cannot stand alone as sentences. They must be attached to an independent clause. Each of the expanded sample sentences contains two dependent clauses. The dependent clauses are printed in bold type.

A dependent clause can function as an adjective or as an adverb. Each of the expanded sample sentences contains one clause of each type. Dependent clauses that function as adjectives describe nouns, and those that function as adverbs modify verbs and their complements by answering such questions as *when, where,* and *why.*

2. Adjective clauses: An adjective clause functions as an adjective to describe a noun. It is usually placed immediately after the noun it describes. In sentence A, the adjective clause *that sits across from the park* describes the noun *building.* In sentence D, the adjective clause *who was sitting in the back of the room* describes the noun *child.* What are the other adjective clauses in the example sentences? Which noun does each one describe? Can you identify the subject and the verb in each of the adjective clauses?

3. Adverb clauses: Adverb clauses function as adverbs to modify verbs and their complements. They begin with words such as *because* (to show cause or reason); *when, while,* or *since* (to show time relationships); *so that* (to show purpose); and *although* (to show a certain type of contrast). Identify the adverb clauses in the sample sentences. What is the subject and what is the verb of each one? What word is used to introduce each adverb clause? What type of meaning does each clause give to the basic sentence?

EXERCISE 1.4-A ANALYZING FORM

identifying the basic sentence

The following sentences contain dependent clauses that function as adjectives and as adverbs. Circle those clauses. What is the basic sentence (the independent clause) that remains?

> **Example:** *Cars (which were produced before the mid-1960s) didn't have emission controls (because federal law had not yet required them.)*

1. The law should protect animals which are endangered species so that they won't become extinct.

2. The building that we entered didn't have any elevators that worked.

3. I visited my friend who was in the hospital because I thought it might cheer her up.

4. The scientists who had been working on the project made a breakthrough when they identified the missing element.

5. The huge building which NASA is constructing is a giant wind tunnel that will be used to test new aircraft.

6. An oil spill that occurred near Pittsburgh has endangered thousands of people because the drinking water has been contaminated.

EXERCISE 1.4-B ANALYZING FORM

. . . .

identifying the basic sentence

Examine each of the following expanded sentences. Circle each adjective clause, and place an X over each noun that it modifies. Underline each adverb clause. What is the basic sentence (the independent clause) that remains?

> X
> **Example:** *Many students who have weak backgrounds in mathematics avoid the various majors in the sciences because they are afraid of math-oriented courses.*

1. The last words that he said to me before he left were a sharp criticism of my work on the project.

2. The book that I have been reading for my history class explains the complex origins of war in an understandable manner.

3. Because he was so busy, the mechanic at the service station that I go to couldn't repair my car immediately.

4. Since customers started complaining, the restaurant on the first floor has been offering a better variety of health food.

5. The computers that have been placed in the engineering labs in Watts Hall use a new operating system that is not compatible with the old software.

6. The elderly woman whose home was vandalized is extremely upset because she feels that the police haven't given her adequate protection.

EXERCISE 1.4-C ANALYZING FORM

. . . .

identifying the basic sentence

Read the paragraph. Examine each sentence carefully. Circle any adjectives or prepositional phrases that are used to expand the basic sentence. Underline any adjective clauses or adverb clauses.

> (1) The world's first public telegraph system, which the British erected in 1843, helped to catch a murderer. (2) The builders placed it along a railway track between London and West Drayton, Middlesex, because it was intended to control train movements. (3) In 1845, police spotted a murder suspect by the name of John Tawell on a train at Slough. (4) The police could not stop the train, so they telegraphed a message to London. (5) London police arrested Tawell near Paddington Station. (6) The government tried, convicted, and hanged him after his arrest.

2   The Simple Present Tense

This chapter examines the formation and use of the simple present tense. You will practice making statements in the present tense and forming different types of questions. You will also practice using adverbs of frequency with present tense verbs.

SECTION 2.1   The Simple Present Tense

SECTION 2.2   Asking Questions in the Simple Present Tense

SECTION 2.3   Adverbs of Frequency

SECTION 2.1   The Simple Present Tense

PRESENT TENSE OF THE VERB *BE*	
A. I **am** tired today.	And I **am not** happy.
B. You **are** correct about the date.	But you **are not** right about the location.
C. Martha **is** in the next room.	She **is not** in the library.
George **is** upstairs now.	He **is not** downstairs.
The report **is** on the table.	It **is not** on the counter.
D. We **are** freshmen.	We **are not** sophomores.
E. The new students **are** from Brazil.	They **are not** from Argentina.

1. Affirmative statements with BE: The present tense of the verb BE has three forms: *am, is,* and *are.* Remember that BE is one of the linking verbs. It can be used in three of the basic sentence patterns that were reviewed in Chapter 1 (see page 8):

Subject + BE + Adjective (basic sentence pattern 1)
Subject + BE + Noun (basic sentence pattern 2)
Subject + BE + Adverb of Place (basic sentence pattern 3)

Which of the sample sentences use pattern 1? Which use pattern 2? Which use pattern 3?

2. Negative statements and contractions: Use *not* after the verb BE to make the verb phrase negative, as in the sample sentences in the right column of the box. In speech and in informal writing, we often use a contraction of the verb BE and *not*.

Green *isn't* a primary color, but red is.
These chairs *aren't* very comfortable.

There is no contraction for *am + not*.

3. Other contractions: The present tense forms of BE are often contracted with a pronoun subject in speech and informal writing.

I + am	*I'm* ready now.
you + are	*You're* wrong about the requirements.
she + is	*She's* in the language lab right now.
he + is	*He's* a physics major.
it + is	*It's* a form of carbon.
we + are	*We're* late for class.
they + are	*They're* in the gym every morning.

EXERCISE 2.1-A   CHECKING FORM (ORAL)

BE in the present tense

Answer each question with a complete negative statement. Then make a truthful statement in the affirmative.

Example: Is (student X) from Japan?
No, he's not from Japan. He's from Malaysia.

1.   Is (student X) from (name of country)?

2.   Are (students X and Y) from (name of country)?

3.   Are you from (name of country)?

4.   Am I from (name of country)?

5.   Is the earth flat?

THERE AS AN INTRODUCTORY WORD

F. **There is** a phone in the next room.   **There is not** one in this office.

G. **There are** some pencils on the table.   But **there are not** any pens.

---

4. Use of *there* as an introductory word: Another sentence pattern with the verb BE uses *there* at the beginning of the sentence, as in sentences F and G.

> *there* + BE + Noun

In these sentences, *there* does not really have any meaning. It merely announces that the noun follows. The verb must agree with the noun that follows. In sentence F, the verb *is* agrees with the noun *phone*. In sentence G, the verb *are* agrees with the noun *pencils*.

> A concert *is* on Friday.   *There is* a concert on Friday.
> Several children *are* in the car.   *There are* several children in the car.

5. Contractions: *There* can be contracted with *is* but not with *are*.

> there + is   *There's* a phone in the next room.

6. *There* versus *they*:   Do not confuse *there are* with *they are*. *They* always refers to people or things that have already been identified. *There* simply shows that something exists.

> Mr. and Mrs. Caywood are my new neighbors. *They* are from Dallas.
>   (*They* refers back to Mr. and Mrs. Caywood.)

> *There* are new tenants in the apartment above us.
>   (*There* points ahead to *new tenants*.)

EXERCISE 2.1-B   CHECKING FORM (ORAL)

there as an introductory word

Look around your classroom; then answer each question truthfully in either the affirmative or the negative. Use complete sentences.

> **Example:** Are there any windows in this room?
>   *Yes. There are three windows in this room.*

1.   Are there any desks in this room?

   2.   Is there a table in this room?

   3.   Are there any chalkboards in this room?

   4.   Is there a tape recorder in this room?

   5.   Are there any students from (name of country) in this room?

   6.   Are there curtains in this room?

   7.   Are there any pictures on the walls?

EXERCISE 2.1-C   FOCUSING ON THE VERB

BE in the present tense

Fill in each blank with the appropriate form of BE in the simple present tense.

   1.   Although John and George _____ ready to begin the project, we _____ (negative) sure if they _____ capable of doing a good job. John _____ (negative) a very careful worker, and George _____ often sloppy, too.

   2.   There _____ several ways to interpret these data. Professor Naumoff _____ doubtful that any meaningful conclusions can be made. I _____ (negative) in agreement with her view, however.

   3.   Asking for advice _____ a good idea when you _____ uncertain about how to do something. It _____ (negative) smart to waste your time doing things incorrectly.

   4.   These reports _____ from the Energy Council, so I _____ confident about their accuracy. The information in them _____ usually from the best sources.

   5.   I _____ (negative) a very effective speaker because I _____ afraid when I have to speak in front of people. If the audience _____ large, I _____ even more nervous.

EXERCISE 2.1-D   MAKING PHRASES INTO SENTENCES

BE in the present tense

Make a complete sentence from each group of words and phrases.

   Example: your pronunciation – BE – better – every day
   Your pronunciation is better every day.

1. I – BE – tired – of spending time in the language lab

    _____

2. diamonds – BE – extremely valuable gemstones

    _____

3. we – BE (negative) – ready – to go now

    _____

4. the students – in this school – BE – very capable

    _____

5. you – BE – intelligent – but – you – BE (negative) – very ambitious

    _____

EXERCISE 2.1-E   COMPLETING SENTENCES
● ·
BE in the present tense

Complete each sentence, using your own ideas.

1. Some of the students in this class are _____

2. Only one of the students in this class is _____

3. _____ is easy to understand.

4. There are _____ in this city.

5. I _____ angry about _____

EXERCISE 2.1-F   EXPRESSING YOUR OWN IDEAS
● ·
BE in the present tense

For this exercise, you need to work with two other students in your class.
Interview one another to gather information that describes each of you. Ask
about these topics. Be sure to take notes.

> Native country
> Native city
> Height
> Major or profession
> Personal traits (adjectives, such as _ambitious_; _hardworking_; _intelligent_)
> Physical characteristics (adjectives, such as _thin_; _heavy_; _beautiful_)

Now report the information you have gathered. On the next page, write at
least two sentences about each person in your group, including yourself.

Examples: *I am from Genoa, Italy. I am a mechanical engineer. I am easygoing but ambitious.*
Gary is over six feet tall. He is very thin but quite strong.

1. About yourself:

_____

_____

2. About _____ :

_____

_____

3. About _____ :

_____

_____

EXERCISE 2.1-G   RESPONDING TO INFORMATION

BE in the present tense

Here is information about the major geological layers of the earth. Read the information carefully. Then write a paragraph that reports this information. Use the present tense of the verb BE.

The Crust:	on the surface of the earth depth: about 20 miles
The Mantle:	really three separate layers 1,780 miles deep in total
The Outer Core:	liquid molten iron depth: 1,300 miles
The Inner Core:	solid an iron ball 1,700 miles deep 9,000 degrees Fahrenheit

---

THE PRESENT TENSE OF OTHER VERBS

H.	I **understand** the first problem now.	But I **do not understand** the second one.
I.	You **arrive** at nine o'clock every day.	You **do not arrive** on time.
J.	Debra **likes** her art courses.	But she **does not like** her history courses.
	Fred **gets up** late on weekends.	He **does not get up** late on weekdays.
	The sun **rises** in the east.	It **does not rise** in the west.
K.	We **do** our math assignments every night.	We **do not do** our sociology reading.
L.	Adjectives **modify** nouns.	They **do not modify** verbs.

---

7. Use of the simple present tense: The simple present tense is used to indicate habitual activity, present state or condition, and eternal truth or law.

Habitual activity: Actions that take place on a regular basis are usually described with the simple present tense. Adverbs of time, such as *every day*, *at night*, and *each year*, indicate habitual activity.

> I *read* the newspaper every morning.

Sentence I expresses this type of meaning. Which other sample sentences also indicate habitual activity?

Present state or condition: Sentences that express a state or condition, including mental activity, generally use the simple present tense. Adverbs of time, such as *now*, *today*, *this year*, and *at this time*, are often used.

> I *see* what you mean now.

Sentence H demonstrates this type of meaning. Which other sample sentences also do?

Eternal truth or natural law: Sentences that express truths or laws that do not change use the simple present tense.

> Most coal *contains* high amounts of sulfur.

Which sample sentences also have this meaning?

8. Affirmative statements: Forming the simple present tense is easy. In the third person singular (that is, when the subject is a singular noun or the pronoun *he, she,* or *it*), add *-s* or *-es* to the end of the verb, as in sentence J. In all other cases, do not add anything.

The verb *have* is a special case. The third person singular is *has*.

> They *have* trouble with math.
> He *has* trouble with math.

9. Negative statements: To make the negative of the simple present tense, use a form of the auxiliary DO, either *do* or *does*. For the third person singular (singular noun, *he, she,* or *it* as the subject), use *does* and drop the *-s* or *-es* ending off the main verb, as in sentence J. Use *do* in all other cases.

Correct	*Incorrect*
She does not like it.	She does not likes it.
We do not get up very early.	We not get up very early.
He doesn't have an answer.	He doesn't has an answer.

10. Contractions: The DO auxiliary is often contracted with *not*, especially in conversation and informal writing:

| do + not | We *don't* want to leave now. |
| does + not | Our instructor *doesn't* assign homework on the weekends. |

SPELLING RULES FOR VERBS IN THE SIMPLE PRESENT TENSE

For the third person singular, add *-es* when the verb ends in *ch, sh, s, x, z,* and sometimes *o*. Otherwise, simply add *-s*.

watche*s*	fixe*s*	see*s*	find*s*
wishe*s*	buzze*s*	hear*s*	listen*s*
passe*s*	goe*s*	believe*s*	get*s*

If the verb ends in a consonant +*y*, change the *y* to *i* and add *-es*.

study	stud*ies*
carry	carr*ies*

If the verb ends in a vowel +*y*, simply add *-s*.

pay	pay*s*
destroy	destroy*s*

EXERCISE 2.1-H   CHECKING FORM (ORAL)

●・・・

verbs in the present tense

Assume that the meaning of each sentence is incorrect. Change it to a negative statement; then make an affirmative, truthful statement.

> **Example:** Four and four equals seven.
> *Four and four does not equal seven. It equals eight.*

1. The earth is flat.

2. A triangle has four sides.

3. This class has forty students.

4. English is easy to learn.

5. Turtles move very fast.

6. A refrigerator heats food.

7. This building has ten stories.

EXERCISE 2.1-I   EXPRESSING YOUR OWN IDEAS (ORAL)

●・・・

the simple present tense

Describe yourself in two ways. First, describe an activity of yours that is habitual. Next, describe yourself in terms of a present state or condition. After that, one of your classmates should report what you have said about yourself.

> **Examples:** (you) *I eat lunch in the cafeteria every day at noon. I like my English class, but I don't like the bus trip to campus.*
>
> (your classmate) *Maria eats lunch in the cafeteria every day at noon. She likes her English class, but she doesn't like the bus trip to campus.*

EXERCISE 2.1-J   FOCUSING ON THE VERB

●・・・

the simple present tense

Fill in each blank on page 30 with the correct simple present tense form of the verb in parentheses. Use the negative form if indicated.

1. I _____ (*think*, negative) that you should use the Ajax Company to draw plans for the new office complex. Many people _____ (*believe*) that their work _____ (BE) inferior.

2. George's story _____ (*have*, negative) much credibility with me because he frequently _____ (*stretch*) the truth.

3. My furnace _____ (*work*, negative) adequately when the temperature _____ (*get*) too cold outside. I _____ (*need*) to replace it with a more powerful one.

4. The political climate in this city _____ (*seem*) very uncertain now, so I _____ (*believe*, negative) that it _____ (BE) a good time for Melching to enter the race for mayor.

5. Our laboratory _____ (*use*) whatever equipment _____ (BE) available to us because the administration _____ (*give*, negative) us enough money to buy what we _____ (*need*).

6. The basic classification unit for plants _____ (BE) the species. Botanists _____ (*group*) related species into a larger unit: the genus. Some botantists _____ (*regard*, negative) the 80,000 species of fungi as plants. Instead, they _____ (*consider*) them as a separate kingdom.

EXERCISE 2.1-K   MAKING PHRASES INTO SENTENCES

the simple present tense

Make each group of words, phrases, and clauses into a complete affirmative or negative statement in the simple present tense, as indicated.

> **Examples:** his statements – BE – ridiculous (affirmative statement)
> *His statements are ridiculous.*
>
> she – want – help – with her calculus assignment (negative statement)
> *She doesn't want help with her calculus assignment.*

1. he – BE – in a good mood – this morning (negative statement)

   _____

2. the store clerks – clean – the shop – every morning (affirmative statement)

   _____

3. this morning's newspaper – predict – trouble in that part of the world (affirmative statement)

   _____

4. Sam – proofread – his papers – after he writes them (negative statement)

_____

5. your ideas – BE – very sound (negative statement)

_____

6. the bus to Northland Mall – run – every half hour – until midnight (affirmative statement)

_____

EXERCISE 2.1-L   STATING FACTS

the simple present tense

Write a sentence in the simple present tense that expresses a fact about each subject. Do not use the verb BE.

> **Example:** the sun
> _The sun radiates energy._

1. a dictionary

_____

2. libraries

_____

3. the human race

_____

4. war

_____

5. English teachers

_____

6. people in my country

_____

EXERCISE 2.1-M   RESPONDING TO INFORMATION

the simple present tense

Page 32 gives some information about the Principality of Monaco, a tiny country on the southern edge of France. Read the information carefully. Then write a paragraph that reports some of the information given to you. Use the simple present tense. You will have to choose appropriate verbs to construct your sentences.

Principality of Monaco
Population: 28,000
Urban: 100 percent
Ethnic groups: French, 58 percent; Monegasque, 19 percent; Italian, 17 percent
Languages: French (official), Monegasque (a blend of French and Italian), Italian, English
Religion: Roman Catholic, 95 percent
Government: constitutional monarchy
Suffrage: universal adult
Monetary unit: French franc
Area: 0.6 square mile (1.5 km²)
Other: popular tourist spot, beautiful seaside location, famous gambling casino, mild Mediterranean climate

EXERCISE 2.1-N   EXPRESSING YOUR OWN IDEAS

the simple present tense

In Exercise 2.1-M you wrote a paragraph describing the Principality of Monaco. Now write one or more paragraphs describing your native country. Report the same type of information that you wrote about Monaco. If you are not sure of some facts, refer to an almanac or an encyclopedia.

SECTION 2.2   Asking Questions in the Simple Present Tense

There are two main types of questions in English: yes-no questions and WH questions. First you will examine questions formed with the verb BE. Later you will practice questions formed with other verbs.

QUESTIONS WITH *BE*		
	Martha **is** a graduate student in political science.	
Yes-No Question:	**A.**	**Is** Martha a graduate student in political science? Yes, she is. (No, she isn't.)
WH Questions:	**B.**	**Who is** a graduate student in political science? Martha.
	C.	**What is** Martha? A graduate student in political science.

1. Yes-no questions: Yes-no questions are answered either *yes* or *no*. Examine sentence A. How is a yes-no question formed when the verb is BE?

Short answers are frequently used to answer yes-no questions. Notice that affirmative short answers do not use a contraction for the pronoun and verb unless they are followed by another word.

	Correct	*Incorrect*
Is Michael in the office?	Yes, he is.	Yes, he's.
	Yes, he's here.	
	No, he's not.	
	No, he isn't.	

Statements with *there* are transformed into yes-no questions in the same way. Notice that the short answer uses the word *there*.

Statement: There is a class in the evening.

Question: Is there a class in the evening?
Yes, there is. (No, there isn't.)

2. WH questions: WH questions ask for information. They begin with a question word such as *who, what, when, where,* or *why*. WH questions can be grouped into two categories: subject focus or predicate focus.

Subject focus questions ask for information about the subject. Examine the sample statement in the box. It can be divided into a subject and a predicate.

Subject: Martha

Predicate: is a graduate student in political science.

To ask about the subject of this statement, you must use a subject focus question. Simply replace the subject with the appropriate WH word, in this case, *who.*

Martha is a graduate student in political science.
Who is a graduate student in political science?

The verb in a subject focus question is always singular, even if the answer is expected to be plural.

What *is* on the floor above us?
The offices of the Department of Energy are on the next floor.

Predicate focus questions ask for information about the predicate. To form a predicate focus question, replace the predicate phrase with the question word, and move it to the beginning of the sentence. Move the verb BE in front of the subject, as on the top of page 34.

Martha is a graduate student in political science.
What is Martha?

3. WH question words: The question word *where* asks about place, *when* asks about time, and *why* asks about cause. Because this type of information is always given in the predicate, *where, when*, and *why* are always predicate focus questions.

The computer is *in the lab*.
Where is the computer?

George is in New York *this week*.
When is George in New York?

The students are upset *because the test was difficult.*
Why are the students upset?

EXERCISE 2.2-A   CHECKING FORM (ORAL)

yes-no questions with BE

Change each statement to a yes-no question.

1.   Your neighbor is an engineer.

2.   The windows are drafty.

3.   There is a problem with the lights.

4.   There are cups and saucers in the kitchen.

5.   Julie is upset about her history course.

6.   The politicians are anxious to debate.

EXERCISE 2.2-B   CHECKING FORM (ORAL)

WH questions with BE

Ask the question indicated by the WH word that is provided.

Example: Sherry is here. (who)
Who is here?

1.   The computer is in Henry's office. (where)

2.   Professor Thompson is a molecular engineer. (what)

3.   Riding a bicycle is easy. (what)

4. Mr. Mathews is worried because he hasn't heard from his son. (why)

5. The books that George needs are in the reference room. (where)

6. The children are tired because they were up late last night. (why)

EXERCISE 2.2-C   CHECKING FORM

WH questions with BE

Ask a WH question about the underlined word or phrase, as in the example. Also write the short answer.

> **Example:** Howard is a secretary.
> *What is he? A secretary.*

1. The students are angry.

   _____

2. The reports are on the director's desk.

   _____

3. The climate in this region is warm because of the water currents.

   _____

4. Dr. Samuels is an expert in the area of medical ethics.

   _____

5. The advice that you gave her is silly.

   _____

6. There are additional English classes on the weekends.

   _____

EXERCISE 2.2-D   MAKING PHRASES INTO SENTENCES

yes-no questions with BE

Form yes-no questions from the words, phrases, and clauses given. Use the simple present tense. Also provide a short answer, either affirmative or negative.

> **Example:** the children – BE – hard to control
> *Are the children hard to control? Yes, they are.*

1. all of the students – BE – here – today

   _____

   _____

2. you – BE – ready to go – now

_____

_____

3. the new weapons – that Congress has approved – BE – overpriced

_____

_____

4. Nelson's latest theory – about ion flow – BE – really very significant

_____

_____

5. the subject of poverty – BE – an appropriate topic – for our discussion

_____

_____

QUESTIONS WITH OTHER VERBS

Ornithologists study birds.

Yes-No Question:	**D.**	**Do** ornithologists study birds? Yes, they do. (No, they don't.)
WH Questions:	**E.**	**Who studies** birds? Ornithologists.
	F.	**What do** ornithologists **study**? Birds.

Most questions in the simple present tense of verbs other than BE require the use of the DO auxiliary, just as in the formation of negative statements.

4. Yes-no questions: To form yes-no questions in the simple present tense, use the auxiliary DO at the beginning of the sentence, as in sentence D. For a third person singular subject (singular noun, _he, she, it_), use _does_ and drop the present tense ending (·s) from the main verb. In all other cases, use _do._ Notice how this differs from yes-no questions with BE.

He *is* a student in the evenings.
Is he a student in the evenings? Yes, he is. (No, he isn't.)

He *studies* in the evenings.
Does he *study* in the evenings? Yes, he does. (No, he doesn't.)

Short answers to yes-no questions use the DO auxiliary. When the short answer is negative, the contraction *doesn't* or *don't* is usually used.

5. WH questions: WH questions with other verbs can also have either a subject focus or a predicate focus.

Subject focus questions begin with *who* or *what* and ask for information about the subject. Sentence E is an example. To form a subject focus question, simply replace the subject with the question word.

Ornithologists study birds.
Who studies birds? Ornithologists.

A bird has an extremely light skeleton.
What has an extremely light skeleton? A bird.

Notice that subject focus questions with *who* and *what* always use the third person singular verb form with the *-s* or *-es* ending, even if the expected answer is not in the third person singular.

Predicate focus questions ask for information about the predicate. To form a predicate focus question, use a form of the DO auxiliary, as in yes-no questions. If the main verb is in the third person singular, use *does* and drop the tense ending, *-s* or *-es*, from the main verb. Otherwise, use *do*. Sentence F is an example.

Ornithologists *study* birds.
What do ornithologists *study*?

A bird *has* an extremely light skeleton.
What does a bird *have*?

Darwin's finches *live* on the Galápagos Islands.
Where do Darwin's finches *live*?

6. *Who* versus *whom*:   When a predicate focus question asks about a person, the question word *whom* is considered more formal than *who*, although both are correct.

Subject Focus	*Predicate Focus*
Kathy tutors Greg and Sam.	Kathy tutors Greg and Sam.
Who tutors Greg and Sam?	*Whom* does Kathy tutor? OR
	Who does Kathy tutor?

7. Other WH question words: The question words *who, whom, what, when, where, why,* and *how* can all be used in predicate focus questions. *How* usually asks about an adverb or adverb phrase of manner (*easily; with difficulty; by car; on foot; by hand; by working hard*).

> Tim arrives late every day *because he has a job.*
> *Why* does he arrive late every day?

> Janet gets to school *by bus.*
> *How* does she get to school?

> Margaret plays the piano *beautifully.*
> *How* does she play the piano?

> You adjust the sound *by turning this knob.*
> *How* do you adjust the sound?

8. *What-do* questions: There is one other type of predicate focus question called the *what-do* question. It asks about the verb and the complement which follows it.

> Joe's roommate *works on his computer* in the evenings.
> *What does* Joe's roommate *do* in the evenings? Works on his computer.

In this type of question, the main verb is changed to *do*.

EXERCISE 2.2-E   CHECKING FORM (ORAL)

yes-no questions in the present tense

Change each statment to a yes-no question.

1.   The students come every morning.

2.   The sun rises in the east.

3.   The mail arrives in the afternoon.

4.   The history class meets in Bevis Hall.

5.   The instructor has a new car.

6.   There is a new textbook for this course.

EXERCISE 2.2-F   CHECKING FORM (ORAL)

WH questions in the present tense

For each sentence on page 39, ask the question indicated by the WH word that is provided.

Examples: Ms. Howard teaches the class. (who)
Who teaches the class?

The students understand differential equations. (what)
What do the students understand?

1. Robert uses Jane's book because he lost his own. (why)

2. The fumes from the chemical factory smell bad. (what)

3. They smell the fumes from the chemical factory. (what)

4. The erasers are on the chalk ledge. (where)

5. The teacher keeps the chalk on the chalk ledge. (where)

6. Professor Compton has the data that I need. (who)

EXERCISE 2.2-G　　EXPRESSING YOUR OWN IDEAS (ORAL)

yes-no questions in the present tense

Write a statement about one of your daily activities on a slip of paper. Do not write your name.

Example: *I take the North Street bus every day.*

Give your sentence to your instructor, who will distribute one to each student (not her or his own). Read the sentence you have received, and consider how to change it to a yes-no question. All students then should stand up and ask their questions of one another until they find the writer of the sentence they have been given.

Example: *Do you take the North Street bus every day?*
No, I don't. (Yes, I do.)

EXERCISE 2.2-H　　EXPRESSING YOUR OWN IDEAS (ORAL)

WH questions in the present tense

On a slip of paper, write a sentence about something that you do habitually or about a present state or condition that describes you. Put your name on the paper and give it to your instructor.

Examples: *I love classical music.*
I watch soap operas on television every day.

Your instructor will then read each sentence aloud, replacing a word or phrase with *someone, something, somewhere, sometime, for some reason, somehow,* or a similar expression—as in the examples on the next page.

Examples: *Carlos loves something.*
Tom watches something on television every day.

Now ask the question necessary to get the information that you need. The student who wrote the original sentence will give you the correct answer.

Examples: *Carlos, what do you love?*
Tom, what do you watch on television every day?

EXERCISE 2.2-I   CHECKING FORM

WH questions in the present tense

Write a WH question about the underlined word or phrase, as in the examples. Also write the short answer.

Examples: The new clerk at the store gives John advice about stereo components.
Who gives John advice about stereo components? The new clerk at the store.

They paint these figures by hand.
How do they paint these figures? By hand.

He goes to a movie every Friday.
What does he do every Friday? Goes to a movie.

1. The diagrams show the correct electrical connections.

    _____

    _____

2. Gary hopes for forgiveness because he never made this type of mistake before.

    _____

    _____

3. The police watch for speeders all along Route 71.

    _____

    _____

4. Ms. Fisher presents an agenda at the beginning of each meeting.

    _____

    _____

5. The concepts that we covered in the last class are important for the test.

    _____

    _____

EXERCISE 2.2-J   MAKING PHRASES INTO SENTENCES

statements and questions in the present tense

Use each group of words, phrases, and clauses to form the type of statement or question indicated in parentheses. If a WH question is specified, it should ask about the underlined words or phrase. Use the simple present tense.

Examples: Gloria – write – a letter – to her parents – every day
(affirmative statement)
Gloria writes a letter to her parents every day.

Howard – understand – the question (negative statement)
Howard doesn't understand the question.

the sun – rise – in the east (yes-no question)
Does the sun rise in the east?

Susan – go – to the library – every Saturday (WH question)
When does Susan go to the library?

1. Jonathan – get – to school – <u>by car</u> (WH question)

    _____

    _____

2. <u>Johnson and Clark</u> – want – information about the new procedure (WH question)

    _____

    _____

3. some doctors – want – nurses – to have more responsibility (negative statement)

    _____

    _____

4. the new plans – match – the style of the original structure (yes-no question)

    _____

    _____

5. the books that I reserved – BE – available – now (yes-no question)

    _____

    _____

6. <u>reading the classics</u> – give – him – great pleasure (WH question)

    _____

    _____

7. the conclusion – BE – incorrect – <u>because the equations are wrong</u> (WH question)

    _____

    _____

EXERCISE 2.2-K   RESPONDING TO INFORMATION

WH questions in the present tense

Read the following paragraph about monarch butterflies. Then create a test on the information by writing WH questions about it. Each question should correspond to the numbered sentence in the paragraph. Use the WH word provided.

(1) Monarch butterflies make a miraculous 2,000-mile journey every autumn. (2) These butterflies bear their young during the summer months in southern Canada and the northern United States. (3) They migrate south in the fall because they cannot survive the cold temperatures. (4) With no guide and no apparent method of navigation but with an inborn migratory instinct, they travel to the exact place where their ancestors wintered the year before. (5) The butterflies' winter quarters are in certain areas in the southern United States and throughout Mexico. (6) Millions of monarchs gather in each of these spots, which are usually no larger than ten acres. (7) In the spring, the insects fly north again for another summer of breeding.

Example: 1. what-do
What do monarch butterflies do every autumn?

2. when

_____

3. why

_____

4. how

_____

5. where

_____

6. how many

_____

7. when

_____

SECTION 2.3   Adverbs of Frequency

1. Use of adverbs of frequency: Adverbs of frequency tell how often something happens. These adverbs can be divided into two groups: affirmative and negative.

ADVERBS OF FREQUENCY

A. **How often** do the Thompsons go out?

B. They are **usually** home in the evening.

C. They **rarely** socialize.

Affirmative	*Negative*
always	occasionally
usually	seldom
frequently	hardly ever
often	scarcely ever
sometimes	rarely
generally	not ever
	never

2. *How often* questions: Questions with *how often* ask about the frequency of an activity, as in sentence A. Notice that these are predicate focus questions.

> How often does Phil call you? Scarcely ever.
> How often are you out of town? Frequently.

3. Affirmative statements: All adverbs of frequency can be placed in the middle of the sentence, next to the verb. The adverb of frequency follows the verb BE, as in sentence B. It comes before other verbs, as in sentence C.

> Fred *is always* late to class.
> We *rarely go* to a movie.

Some adverbs of frequency can also be placed at the beginning or at the end of the sentence, as well as in the middle. These adverbs of frequency include *sometimes, usually, frequently, often, generally,* and *occasionally.*

> *Sometimes* we go to a movie.   *Occasionally* Fred is late to class.
> We *sometimes* go to a movie.   Fred is *occasionally* late to class.
> We go to a movie *sometimes*.   Fred is late to class *occasionally*.

QUESTIONS WITH ADVERBS OF FREQUENCY   (*See page 44.*)

D. Are the Thompsons **usually** home in the evening?
Yes, they are.

E. Do they **ever** go out?
No, **rarely**.

---

4. Yes-no questions: When adverbs of frequency are used in yes-no questions, they are placed after the subject, as in sentence D on page 43.

> Do you *often* go to restaurants?
> > Yes, I do. (No, I don't.)

> Are you *always* so eager to go shopping?
> > Yes, I am. (No, I'm not.)

5. Questions with *ever*: When *ever* is used in a yes-no question, it is also placed immediately after the subject, as in sentence E. Answers to questions with *ever* usually include an adverb of frequency. Notice the two possible forms of short answers.

> Are you *ever* tired of studying English?
> > Yes, often.   No, never.
> > Yes, I often am.   No, I never am.

> Does this instructor *ever* give students time to ask questions?
> > Yes, usually.   No, hardly ever.
> > Yes, she usually does.   No, she hardly ever does.

NEGATIVE STATEMENTS WITH ADVERBS OF FREQUENCY

F. The Thompsons **generally** aren't out in the evening.

G. They **usually** don't socialize.

H. They don't **ever** go to parties.

I. They don't **always** stay home, but they **usually** do.

---

6. Negative statements: Affirmative adverbs of frequency can be used in negative statements. Most are placed in front of the negative auxiliary, as in sentences F and G. Two adverbs of frequency, *ever* and *always*, are placed after the negative auxiliary, as in sentences H and I. Negative adverbs of frequency are not used in negative sentences.

EXERCISE 2.3-A   CHECKING FORM (ORAL)

questions with *ever*

Each statement on page 45 contains an adverb of frequency. Listen carefully to each statement; then ask a question with *ever*, using the word or phrase provided in parentheses. Another student will answer your question.

> **Example:** Instructor: John usually takes the bus. (walk)
> > Student A: *Does he ever walk?*
> > Student B: *No, not often.*

1. John is frequently tired in the morning. (in the evening)

2. My friends rarely go to the lab. (to the library)

3. The English teachers are usually understanding. (unsympathetic)

4. The students in this class are always honest. (dishonest)

5. I generally watch the news on television. (read the newspaper)

6. Martha rarely studies on the weekends. (on weekdays)

7. Howard's answers are often good. (brilliant)

EXERCISE 2.3-B   CHECKING FORM (ORAL)

questions with *how often*

Your instructor will give you directions to ask one of your classmates a question with *how often*.

> **Examples:** Instructor: Ask (student X) about studying in the evening.
> You: *How often do you study in the evening?*
> Student X: *Rarely.*
>
> Instructor: Ask (X) about being on campus in the evenings.
> You: *How often are you on campus in the evenings?*
> Student X: *Frequently.*

1. Ask (X) about going to the library in the evening.

2. Ask (X) about writing home.

3. Ask (X) about being late to class.

4. Ask (X) about being homesick.

5. Ask (X) about riding the bus.

6. Ask (X) about watching television.

7. Ask (X) about going out with friends.

EXERCISE 2.3-C   RESTATING SENTENCES

adverbs of frequency

Each of the following statements gives you information about the frequency of an activity. Rewrite each sentence, using an adverb of frequency that you think is appropriate.

> **Example:** The students are late to class four days a week.
> *The students are usually late to class.*

1. My roommate goes to the library once or twice each term.

_____

2. It snows here at least once a week during the winter.

_____

3. His work is excellent all of the time.

_____

4. She hands in her assignments half of the time.

_____

5. The mayor and the council members argue at every meeting.

_____

6. This machine fails only once or twice every few years.

_____

EXERCISE 2.3-D MAKING PHRASES INTO SENTENCES

adverbs of frequency

Make each group of words, phrases, and clauses into a complete statement or a complete question in the simple present tense, as indicated. Use the adverb of frequency given.

> **Examples:** the information that he gives – BE – unreliable (negative statement with *ever*)
> *The information that he gives isn't ever reliable.*
>
> the students – understand – his explanations (question with *how often*)
> *How often do the students understand his explanations?*

1. the best answers – BE – very long (negative statement with *usually*)

_____

_____

2. the temperature in January – drop – below freezing (affirmative statement with *rarely*)
    The temperature in January rarely drop below freezing.

_____

3. the television networks – worry about – quality programming (question with *ever*)

_____

_____

4. the economic predictions – BE – correct (question with *how often*)

_____

_____

5. a poor grade – mean – a lazy student (negative statement with *always*)

_____

_____

6. this type of noise – indicate – a serious problem in the engine (affirmative statement with *generally*)

_____

_____

7. the faculty – meet – to discuss departmental matters (questions with *how often*)

_____

_____

3

The Simple Past Tense

The focus of Chapter 3 is the simple past tense. The formation and use of the past tense are reviewed, and several types of questions are introduced. In addition, this chapter examines two-word verbs and the expression *used to* for habitual activities in the past.

SECTION 3.1   The Simple Past Tense

THE PAST TENSE OF THE VERB *BE*

A. I / She / He / It **was** here a moment ago.

I / She / He / It **was not** in the next room.

B. You / We / They **were** upset this morning.

You / We / They **were not** very agreeable.

C. There **was** a problem last night.

There **was not** a problem before that.

D. There **were** a lot of people in class last night.

There **were not** many people in class the night before.

1. The use of the simple past tense: The simple past tense is used for events that were completed in the past. Expressions of past time, such as *yesterday, last night, last week, two weeks ago,* and *in 1988,* can be used with the simple past tense. Expressions of present time, such as *today, this morning,* and *this year,* can be used if that period of time is considered finished.

2. Affirmative and negative statements: The past tense of the verb BE has two forms: *was* and *were.* Use *not* after the verb to make it negative, as in the sample sentences in the right column of the box on page 49.

3. Contractions: In speech and informal writing, we often contract the past tense of BE and *not.*

> She *wasn't* in the next room.
> You *weren't* very agreeable.

4. *There* as subject: Remember that when *there* is the subject of the sentence, the verb BE must agree in number with the noun that follows, as in sentences C and D.

> A student *was* in the room a few minutes ago.
> Several students *were* here this morning.

> There *was* a student in the room a few minutes ago.
> There *were* several students here this morning.

THE PAST TENSE OF OTHER VERBS

E.	I **watched** a movie last night.	I **did not watch** the football game.
F.	You **studied** for only an hour yesterday.	You **did not study** the whole day.
G.	Janice **submitted** the report on Monday.	She **did not submit** it Tuesday.
H.	Michael **went** to the mall earlier today.	He **did not go** to the library.
I.	The package **came** in the morning.	It **did not come** in the afternoon.
J.	We **understood** the solution after class.	We **did not understand** it before that.
K.	Most of the students **wrote** lab reports.	They **did not write** term papers.

---

5. The past tense of regular verbs: The past tense form of regular verbs is formed by adding *-ed* to the verb, as in sentences E, F, and G. There is only one form, and it is used for all subjects. There are several spelling rules that you must use when forming the regular past tense. See the chart on page 52.

6. The past tense of irregular verbs: Many of the most frequently used verbs in English are irregular; that is, they have a special past tense form and do not use the *-ed* ending. Sentences I, J, and K demonstrate several irregular past tense forms (*go – went; come – came; understand – understood; write – wrote*). You probably know many of the irregular past tense forms already. A list of the irregular past tense forms is given in Appendix A at the end of the book.

7. Negative statements: To form the negative of the simple past tense of verbs, use the past form of the DO auxiliary, *did*, as in the sample sentences in the right column of the box. *Did* tells the listener or reader that you are expressing the past, so the main verb does not have the *-ed* ending. If the main verb is irregular, use the simple form (with no ending on the verb).

	Correct	*Incorrect*
I watched a movie.	I did not watch the game.	I did not watched the game.
I studied hard.	They did not study hard.	They not studied hard.
Cynthia came.	Sharon did not come.	Sharon did not came.
I understood the lecture.	Joe did not understand it.	Joe not understood it.

8. Contractions: *Did* is often contracted with *not*, especially in conversation and informal writing.

did + not   I *didn't* watch the game.

EXERCISE 3.1-A   CHECKING FORM (ORAL)
● ·

irregular past tense forms

Change each statement from the present to the past, and change the adverb of time to *yesterday*. The verbs are all irregular.

> **Example:** I come here every day.
> *I came here yesterday.*

1.   I drive to work every morning.

2.   I go to school every day.

3.   I run a mile every morning.

4.   I win the contest every year.

5.   I sing in the choir every Sunday.

6.   I read the newspaper every day.

7.   I swim a few laps every Saturday.

8.   I pay my rent every month.

9.   I fall on those narrow steps every once in a while.

10. I fight with my roommate every day.

11. I leave work early on Tuesdays.

12. I sleep late on Sundays.

SPELLING RULES FOR THE PAST TENSE OF REGULAR VERBS

There are several spelling rules you must use when forming the past tense with *-ed*. If the verb ends with the letter *e*, add only *-d*.

arrive – arrived
propose – proposed

If the verb ends in a consonant and *y*, change the *y* to *i* and add *-ed*.

hurry – hurried
reply – replied

However, if the verb ends in a vowel and *y*, simply add *-ed*.

play – played
enjoy – enjoyed

If the verb has one syllable and ends in consonant + vowel + consonant, double the final consonant before adding *-ed*. If the verb has more than one syllable, this rule also applies, but only if the final syllable is stressed.

One Syllable

stop – stopped
tap – tapped

More than One Syllable

refer – referred (stress on the final syllable)
omit – omitted (stress on the final syllable)
offer – offered (stress on the first syllable)
happen – happened (stress on the first syllable)

EXERCISE 3.1-B   CHECKING FORM (ORAL)

irregular past tense forms

Change each statement to the past tense, and change the adverb of time to the one given in parentheses. The verbs are all irregular.

> **Example:** He chooses the menu every day. (yesterday)
> *He chose the menu yesterday.*

1. He buys groceries every day. (this morning)

2. Jeannette speaks Spanish with her friends in the evening. (last night)

3. Michael bets money on the horses every Saturday. (last Saturday)

4. The students write essays on Mondays. (last Monday)

5. We sell our handicrafts at the flea market most weekends. (this past weekend)

6. Paul means no harm. (yesterday)

7. I have the flu today. (last month)

8. Lisa makes a mistake every day. (yesterday)

9. They take the bus in the morning. (this morning)

10. It costs a lot to take classes every term. (last term)

11. I bring a sandwich for lunch every day. (yesterday)

12. I know the answer to your question. (yesterday)

13. He puts his books beneath his desk at the beginning of each class. (just a moment ago)

EXERCISE 3.1-C   CHECKING FORM (ORAL)

irregular past tense forms

Change the verbs to the simple past tense, and change the adverb of time to the one given in parentheses. Omit the adverb of frequency. All the verbs are irregular.

> **Example:** We often meet new students. (this afternoon)
> *We met some new students this afternoon.*

1. I sometimes think about your problem. (this morning)

2. Professor Yoder frequently teaches this class. (last week)

3. We usually understand your concerns. (last weekend)

4.   David occasionally flies to New York. (last Saturday)

5.   I always shut the windows at night. (last night)

6.   My instructor often gives me extra time to finish. (yesterday)

7.   We usually find the answer quickly. (this morning)

8.   Donna sometimes leads the class. (last week)

9.   I sometimes hit the ball over the fence. (yesterday)

10. Ed occasionally loses his temper. (earlier today)

EXERCISE 3.1-D   EXPRESSING YOUR OWN IDEAS (ORAL)

the simple past tense

Answer the questions truthfully, using the simple past tense.

> **Example:** Where did you eat dinner last night?
> *I ate dinner in the cafeteria.*

1.   What did you have for breakfast this morning?

2.   Where did you live last year?

3.   When did you go to bed last night?

4.   Who did you speak to yesterday?

5.   Who was your best friend when you were a child?

6.   Why did you enroll in this class?

7.   How did you get to class this morning?

8.   When did you start studying English?

9.   When did you first come to this country?

10. What did you do last weekend?

EXERCISE 3.1-E   CHECKING FORM

affirmative and negative statements

Change the following sentences from the affirmative to the negative.

1.   Paul fell down when the soccer ball hit him.

   _____

2.   Mrs. Beck sold her house for as much money as she wanted.

   _____

3. The books for this course cost more than I expected.

_____

4. I slept well last night.

_____

Change the next group of sentences from the negative to the affirmative.

5. Bob and I didn't sing in the church choir last year.

_____

6. California didn't lead the nation in agricultural production in the 1970s.

_____

7. He didn't do his best work when he was under pressure.

_____

8. The photograph wasn't clear enough to be used.

_____

EXERCISE 3.1-F   FOCUSING ON THE VERB

the simple past tense

Fill in each blank with the correct form of the verb in the simple past tense.

1. Paul _____ (_play_, negative) very well in yesterday's baseball game. He _____ (_get_) two hits, but he _____ (_run_) poorly. His team _____ (_win_, negative) the game, and Paul _____ (_blame_) himself.

2. I _____ (_finish_, negative) the last laboratory assignment because I _____ (_understand_, negative) the directions very well. The lab instructor's explanations _____ (BE, negative) clear, and I _____ (_read_, negative) the written instructions.

3. Our math instructor _____ (BE, negative) here today, so Libby and I _____ (_go_) to the snack shop and _____ (_have_) a cup of coffee. We _____ (_talk_) about our plans for the summer break, but we _____ (_discuss_, negative) our class at all.

4. Although the play that I _____ (_see_) last night at the Beckman Theater _____ (BE, negative) especially good, the actors _____ (BE) enthusiastic and _____ (_work_) very hard. Most people in the audience _____ (_seem_) to like the performance, but the critics _____ (_appreciate_, negative) it.

5. The construction of the Washington Monument _____ (_involve_) almost a hundred years of planning and building. The original city plan for Washington _____ (_include_) a large statue of the first U.S.

president, but the government _____ (*have*, negative) enough
money to complete the project. The government _____ (*take*,
negative) up the project again until after Washington's death. Finally, in 1848,
construction _____ (*begin*) on the monument that stands today.
Workers _____ (*complete*) the monument in 1888.

EXERCISE 3.1-G MAKING PHRASES INTO SENTENCES

the simple present tense and the simple past tense

Make each group of words, phrases, and clauses into a complete statement
in the present tense or the past tense, as indicated.

> **Examples:** I – understand (negative) – the question that you asked (past
> tense)
> *I didn't understand the question that you asked.*
>
> the front door to the building – BE – open (present tense)
> *The front door to the building is open.*

1. my best answer – BE (negative) – good enough – for them (past tense)

   _____

   _____

2. the trip to Toronto – take – several hours – by car (past tense)

   _____

   _____

3. our project – BE (negative) – ready to hand in (present tense)

   _____

   _____

4. the students in that school – wear (negative) – uniforms (present tense)

   _____

   _____

5. the books that you asked about – BE – on the secretary's desk – yesterday (past
   tense)

   _____

   _____

6. the exam questions – cover (negative) – the chapters that I studied (past tense)

   _____

   _____

7. the first lecture – BE – on Friday afternoon (present tense)

_____

_____

EXERCISE 3.1-H   DISCRIMINATING TENSES

the simple present tense and the simple past tense

Fill in each blank with the correct form of either the simple present tense or the simple past tense, as appropriate.

1. Jonathan _____ (work) his hardest last term, but he still _____ (need) a lot of help in order to understand even the most basic math concepts. Math _____ (BE) an extremely abstract subject, and Jonathan _____ (have, negative) an easy time working with abstract notions.

2. When Harold _____ (start) with this company a few years ago, I _____ (think, negative) that he would become so successful so quickly. Now he _____ (BE) in charge of the operations division and _____ (supervise) more than fifty people.

3. I _____ (know) that learning a second language _____ (BE) difficult, but Elizabeth _____ (put, negative) forth much effort in her Spanish classes last year, so I _____ (have, negative) much sympathy for her now.

4. The weather forecasts on Channel 4 _____ (BE) usually wrong in the past, but their new meteorologist _____ (appear) to be better. She _____ (major) in meterology when she _____ (BE) in college, so she _____ (bring) a lot of knowledge and skills to her job.

EXERCISE 3.1-I   CORRECTING ERRORS

affirmative and negative statement in the past

Each sentence has one or more errors. Write the corrected sentence on the line provided.

> **Example:** Josh didn't kept the book for himself.
> _Josh didn't keep the book for himself._

1. The newspaper reporters did asked about the accident.

_____

_____

2. The students didn't understood the lectures that he gave.

_____

_____

3. We rarely was on time although we tried.

_____

_____

4. The prizes that they presented not seemed very valuable.

_____

_____

5. There weren't a correct answer to his question.

_____

_____

6. He winned a lot of money at the horse races.

_____

_____

EXERCISE 3.1-J   RESPONDING TO INFORMATION

the simple past tense

Read the information about the use of cosmetics through the ages. Then write sentences in the simple past tense, each one expressing some of the information that you were given. Choose appropriate verbs to state the ideas clearly. See the example on page 59.

3500 B.C.	Women in Egypt and Mesopotamia: use henna dye (on feet and hands) and eye shadow (for protection from evil)
750	Greek women: dye their hair black, use lead powder (to whiten skin)
150	Romans: use gold pigments (around the eyes), wood ash (on eyelids)
A.D. 10	Roman poet Ovid: writes the first book on cosmetics
200	Greek physician Galen: invents the first cold cream (mixture of water, beeswax, and olive oil)
1580	Queen Elizabeth of Great Britain: puts red dye on her hair and white makeup on her face, removes eyebrows, and does not allow mirrors in court
1700	In Europe and America, powder rooms become fashionable (to put powder on hair, wigs, faces).
1840	In Britain and America, heavy makeup for women goes out of style

> **Example:** *Around 3500 B.C., women in Egypt and Mesopotamia dyed their hands and feet with henna.*

EXERCISE 3.1-K   EXPRESSING YOUR OWN IDEAS

the simple past tense

Team up with two of your classmates (from different countries, if possible), and discuss how clothing fashions have changed in each of your countries during the past century. How did men dress in the past? How do they dress now? How did women dress? Did they wear makeup? How do they dress now? What type of makeup do they wear?

After you exchange information about fashions in your countries, write sentences in the past tense and in the present tense expressing the information that you have shared.

> **Example:** *Thirty years ago, American women didn't wear slacks. They always wore dresses or skirts. Now, many women wear slacks or jeans, even at their jobs or at school.*

SECTION 3.2   Asking Questions in the Simple Past Tense

QUESTIONS WITH *BE* (*See page 60*.)		
	Joan's brother **was** at Ohio State last year.	
Yes-No Question:	**A.**	**Was** Joan's brother at Ohio State last year? Yes, he was. (No, he wasn't.)
WH Questions:	**B.**	**Who was** at Ohio State last year? Joan's brother.
	C.	**Where was** Joan's brother last year? At Ohio State.
Tag Questions:	**D.**	Her brother **was** at Ohio State last year, **wasn't he**? Yes, he was. (No, he wasn't.)
	E.	Her brother **wasn't** at Ohio State last year, **was he**? Yes, he was. (No, he wasn't.)

1. Yes-no questions: Form yes-no questions with past tense BE in the same way as for the simple present tense, as in sentence A on page 59. Simply move the verb to the beginning of the sentence.

Statement: The final exam was difficult.

Question: Was the final exam difficult?
Yes, it was. (No, it wasn't.)

2. WH questions: Form WH questions with past tense BE in the same way as for the simple present tense, as in sentences B and C.

The Republican candidate was in Dayton last night.

Subject Focus: Who was in Dayton last night?

Predicate Focus: Where was the Republican candidate last night?

3. Tag questions: Tag questions (sentences D and E) begin with a statement and then add a question tag, which consists of the verb BE and the pronoun form of the subject. If the statement is affirmative, the tag is negative. If the statement is negative, the tag is affirmative.

(Affirmative statement)   *(Negative Tag)*

Your friends *were* here this afternoon, *weren't* they?

(Negative Statement)   *(Affirmative Tag)*

Your friends *weren't* here this afternoon, *were* they?

If the statement contains a negative adverb of frequency, such as *never* or *seldom*, the statement is negative, and the question tag must be affirmative.

(Negative Statement)   *(Affirmative Tag)*

Your friends *were never* here this afternoon, *were* they?

Tag questions are answered with short answers, just like yes-no questions. But the meaning of a tag question is somewhat different. Tag questions are used, usually in conversation, when the speaker already has a belief. In sentence D, for example, the speaker already believes that Joan's brother was at Ohio State last year. The speaker asks the tag question simply to confirm this belief, to see if it is correct. In this case, the statement is affirmative, and the question tag is negative.

Joan's brother was at Ohio State last year, wasn't he?

However, if the speaker suspects that Joan's brother was not at Ohio State and wants to check if this belief is correct, the statement will be negative and the question tag affirmative.

Joan's brother wasn't at Ohio State last year, was he?

By contrast, when speakers ask yes-no questions, they have not already formed a belief. They are asking for an answer, not confirming their assumptions.

Was Joan's brother at Ohio State last year?

Tag questions are formed with the present tense of BE in the same way. If you think the train is late but want to confirm this belief with someone else (because your watch is broken), you might ask:

The train is late, isn't it?

EXERCISE 3.2-A   CHECKING FORM (ORAL)

yes-no questions with BE in the simple past tense

Listen to the present tense statements about your classmates. Ask a yes-no question in the past tense.

> **Example:** (Student X) is often busy in the afternoons. Ask about yesterday afternoon.
> *Were you busy yesterday afternoon?*
> *Yes, I was. (No, I wasn't.)*

1. (X) is often late to class. Ask about this morning.

2. (X) is usually on time to class. Ask about yesterday.

3. (X) is often tired in the morning. Ask about yesterday morning.

4. (X) is often in the library in the evenings. Ask about last evening.

5. (X) is usually a serious student. Ask about last term.

EXERCISE 3.2-B   CHECKING FORM (ORAL)

WH questions with BE in the simple past tense

Ask the question indicated by the WH word that is provided.

> **Example:** The festival was in May. (when)
> *When was the festival?*

1. Professor Thompson was the guest speaker at yesterday's lecture. (who)

2. The lecture was in the main auditorium. (where)

3. Lon's answers were incorrect because he used the wrong formula. (why)

4. The most recent TOEFL was in the middle of March. (when)

5. Some new lab equipment was in the box. (what)

EXERCISE 3.2-C   CHECKING FORM (ORAL)

tag questions with BE in the present tense and the past tense

If you had the belief indicated in each sentence, what tag question might you ask?

> **Examples:** You think that English is easy.
> *English is easy, isn't it?*
>
> You don't think that George was happy last year.
> *George wasn't happy last year, was he?*

1. You don't think that Tom is late.

2. You think that Mary is a senior.

3. You don't think that John's answer was wrong.

4. You think that the grammar test was yesterday.

5. You think that Mr. Johnson was the chemistry instructor last year.

QUESTIONS WITH OTHER VERBS (*See page 63.*)		
		Joan's brother **drove** the old car for several years.
Yes-No Question:	F.	**Did** her brother **drive** the old car for several years? Yes, he did. (No, he didn't.)
WH Questions:	G.	**Who drove** the old car for several years? Joan's brother.
	H.	**Whose brother drove** the old car for several years? Joan's.
	I.	**Which car did** her brother **drive** for several years? The old one.
	J.	**How long did** her brother **drive** the old car? For several years.
Tag Questions:	K.	Joan's brother **drove** the old car, **didn't he**? Yes, he did. (No, he didn't.)
	L.	Joan's brother **didn't drive** the old car, **did he**? Yes, he did. (No, he didn't.)

4. Yes-no questions: Form yes-no questions in the past tense in the same way as those in the simple present tense, but use the past tense of the DO auxiliary—*did* instead of *do* or *does*. Do not use the past tense form of the main verb. See sentence F on page 62.

	Correct	*Incorrect*
He worked hard.	Did he work hard?	Did he worked hard?
He knew the answer.	Did he know the answer?	Did he knew the answer?

5. Short answers: To form short answers to yes-no questions, repeat the auxiliary *did*. When the short answer is negative, the contraction *didn't* is usually used.

Did you go to class this morning? No, I didn't.

6. Subject focus WH questions: To form a WH question with a subject focus, no auxiliary is used. Replace the subject with the question word, as in sentence G. Do not change the main verb.

Joan's brother drove the old car for several years.
Who drove the old car for several years? Joan's brother.

Faulty electric wiring caused the fire.
What caused the fire? Faulty electric wiring.

7. Predicate focus WH questions: To form a WH question with a predicate focus, use the past tense form of the DO auxiliary—*did*. The main verb should be in the simple form (*did* tells the listener that the tense is past).

	Correct	*Incorrect*
Mary started *at noon.*	When did she start?	When did she started?
They bought *groceries.*	What did they buy?	What did they bought?

8. Tag questions: To form tag questions with the simple past tense or the simple present tense, you must use the DO auxiliary, as in sentences K and L.

(Affirmative Statement)   *(Negative Tag)*

Your sister *comes* here often, *doesn't* she?

(Negative Statement)   *(Affirmative Tag)*

The equipment *didn't work* properly, *did* it?

9. *Whose*:   The WH question word *whose* shows a possessive relationship, as in sentence H. This particular sentence has a subject focus. Questions with *whose* can also have a predicate focus.

The professor liked *our project.*
Whose project did the professor like? Ours. (Our project.)

Notice that there are two possible answers: *Ours* or *Our project*. When the possessive pronoun is used as an adjective in front of a noun, it has one form. When the possessive pronoun functions alone, as a noun, it has another form.

Possessive Adjective	*Possessive Pronoun*
It is *my* idea.	It is *mine*.
It is *your* idea.	It is *yours*.
It is *his* idea.	It is *his*.
It is *her* idea.	It is *hers*.
It is *our* idea.	It is *ours*.
It is *their* idea.	It is *theirs*.

10. *How long*: The WH question expression *how long* refers to length of time rather than specific time, as in sentence J on page 62. A question with *how long* is answered with an adverb of time that indicates a period of time, often an expression beginning with *for*.

How long did you work? For eight hours.
When did you finish? At midnight.

11. *Which*: Use the WH question word *which* when the information that you are asking about is a choice that is known to both you and the listener. In sentence I, the speaker wants to know *which* car Joan's brother drove (perhaps the old one or the new one). Questions with *which* can have either a subject focus or a predicate focus.

Subject Focus: The young child fought hard.

Which child fought hard? The young child. (The young one.)

Predicate Focus: They bought *the expensive model*.

Which model did they buy? The expensive model. (The expensive one.)

EXERCISE 3.2-D   CHECKING FORM (ORAL)

yes-no questions in the simple past tense

Listen to your instructor's statements about your classmates. Ask your classmate a yes-no question in order to confirm or disprove your instructor's statement. Your classmate should reply with a short answer.

Example: I think that Sharon went downtown yesterday.
Sharon, did you go downtown yesterday?
Yes, I did. (No, I didn't.)

1. I think that (X) drove to school today.

2. I think that (X) spoke to her/his parents last night.

3. I think that (X) wrote a letter home yesterday.

4. I think that (X) was busy last weekend.

5. I think that (X) made himself/herself a big breakfast this morning.

EXERCISE 3.2-E   CHECKING FORM (ORAL)

WH questions in the simple past tense

Ask the question indicated by the WH word that is provided.

> **Example:** Jonathan brought the food. (who)
> *Who brought the food?*

1. Denise visited the laboratory earlier today. (who)

2. A supersonic aircraft made that loud booming sound. (what)

3. Kathy found the answer by looking in an almanac. (how)

4. Keith sold his old math books last week. (when)

5. George's friend came along. (whose)

6. Everyone left the room because it was too cold. (why)

EXERCISE 3.2-F   CHECKING FORM (ORAL)

tag questions in the present tense and in the past tense

If you had the belief indicated in each item below, what tag question might you ask?

> **Example:** You think that the guests enjoyed the meal.
> *The guests enjoyed the meal, didn't they?*

1. You think that most farmers had a bad year last year.

2. You don't think that this exercise is easy.

3. You don't think that John finished his work.

4. You don't think that I bought any groceries.

5. You don't think that the sun rises in the west.

6. You think that Susan kept her promise.

EXERCISE 3.2-G   FORMING QUESTIONS

yes-no questions in the present tense and in the past tense

Create yes-no questions in the present tense and in the past tense that will help you obtain the information indicated.

> **Example:** You want to know if John made the soccer team.
> *Did John make the soccer team?*

1. You want to know if Sharon liked the movie at the Roxy Theater.

    _____

2. You want to know if Barbara enjoyed the food in France.

    _____

3. You want to know if studying every night ruined Martha's social life.

    _____

4. You want to know if Gary seems upset with his classes.

    _____

5. You want to know if your package arrived yesterday.

    _____

EXERCISE 3.2-H   ASKING QUESTIONS

tag questions in the present tense and in the past tense

Add a question tag to each statement.

1. The best advice is free, _____
2. The farmers had bad luck with the weather this year, _____
3. We don't need more help, _____
4. The delivery men put the supplies in the wrong place, _____
5. You read the textbook before you came to class, _____

EXERCISE 3.2-I   ASKING QUESTIONS

WH questions in the simple past tense

Write a WH question about the underlined word or phrase, as in the example on page 67. Also write the short answer.

Examples: Janice and Sue studied for three hours last night.
How long did they study last night? For three hours.

Ed bought the red car.
Which car did he buy? The red one.

1. The Wittings spent the day at the zoo last Saturday.

_____

2. The history exam was the most difficult one.

_____

3. They didn't like Professor Johnson's lecture.

_____

4. Harry's friends came before the meeting was finished.

_____

5. The consultants completed their reports three months ago.

_____

6. A movie that John saw last year caused him to change his career.

_____

7. She made an error because John gave her the wrong data.

_____

8. The mayor's argument convinced the city council.

_____

EXERCISE 3.2-J   MAKING PHRASES INTO SENTENCES

questions in the present tense and in the past tense

Form the type of sentence indicated. If a WH question is specified, form it so that it asks about the underlined words. If you create a question, provide the answer.

Examples: he – write – the report – yesterday (yes-no question, past tense)
Did he write the report yesterday? Yes, he did.

the company – make – this equipment – by hand (WH question, present tense)
How does the company make this equipment? By hand.

1. Professor Glenn's lecture – BE – the best one – in the series (WH question, past tense)

_____

_____

2. Harold – take – the news – <u>with a lot of screaming and crying</u> (WH question, past tense)

_____

_____

3. Ms. Stratton – enjoy – her job – <u>because it is stimulating</u> (WH question, present tense)

_____

_____

4. this theater – show – always – art films (negative statement, past tense)

_____

_____

5. Sara – _call_ – <u>the police</u> – when she saw the accident (WH question, past tense)

_____

_____

6. <u>the second</u> report – stimulate – a lot of discussion (WH question, past tense)

_____

_____

7. the lab – BE – available – <u>for four hours</u> – every day (WH question, present tense)

_____

_____

EXERCISE 3.2-K   CORRECTING ERRORS

questions in the past tense

There is at least one error in each sentence. Find all mistakes, and write the corrected sentence on the line.

1. Whose book you did borrow yesterday?

_____

2. The Garners aren't lawyers, aren't they?

_____

3. Which student did fail the course?

_____

4. Did the temperature change affected plant life in the area?

_____

5. What do the Thompsons did last summer?

_____

EXERCISE 3.2-L   EXPRESSING YOUR OWN IDEAS
● ·

WH questions in the present tense and in the past tense

In this activity you will interview one of your classmates. First, write five interview questions about your classmate's past, using the simple past tense. You might want to consider topics such as these:

> Date of arrival in the United States
> Reason for choosing this school
> Activity or profession before coming to the United States
> Previous study of English
> Hobbies and interests in home country

Next, write five more interview questions, this time about your classmate's life in the present, using the simple present tense. You might want to consider the following topics:

> Present residence
> Study habits
> Leisure activities
> Positive aspects of present situation
> Negative aspects of present situation

After you have written your questions, team up with your classmate and interview each other.

EXERCISE 3.2-M   RESPONDING TO INFORMATION
● ·

WH questions in the past tense

Read the paragraph about the author Robert Louis Stevenson. Then write questions about the information. Each question should correspond to the numbered sentence in the paragraph. Use the WH word provided on page 70.

> (1) Robert Louis Stevenson wrote his macabre novel The Strange Case of Dr. Jekyll and Mr. Hyde in the winter of 1885. (2) The idea for the book came to him during a nightmare. (3) Stevenson began the novel the next morning. (4) He wrote nonstop for three days and nights. (5) When he finished, he read his manuscript to his wife, Fanny. (6) They had a violent argument because she disliked the story. (7) Stevenson then threw the manuscript on the fire and burned it, but he rewrote the 30,000-word story the next week. (8) Stevenson finally published the novel in 1886.
>
> **Example: 1.**   when
> > *When did Stevenson write the The Strange Case of Dr. Jekyll and Mr. Hyde?*

2. when

_____

3. when

_____

4. how long

_____

5. what-do

_____

6. why

_____

7. when

_____

8. when

_____

SECTION 3.3   Habitual Action in the Past

. . . .

HABITUAL ACTION IN THE PAST
A. The Youngs **used to live** in the city. (They no longer do.)
B. They **used to enjoy** all the noise and activity. (They don't anymore.)
C. Mr. Young **didn't use to mind** the traffic jams. (Now he does.)
D. Mrs. Young **didn't use to be** afraid of the high crime rate. (Now she is.)

1. _Used to_ for the habitual past: The expression _used to_ indicates that an activity was habitual in the past or that a state existed in the past. _Used to_ also implies there has been a change, that the activity or state no longer exits. _Used to_ is followed by the simple verb (with no tense ending).

2. Affirmative statements: The affirmative statement A tells us that the Youngs lived in the city in the past, and it implies that they no longer live there. Sometimes a clause is added to emphasize that the activity or state is no longer true.

George used to be afraid of flying, *but now he isn't.* (afraid of flying)
I used to wake up early every day, *but now I don't.* (wake up early every day)

3. Negative statements: Negative statements indicate that an activity or state was not true in the past and imply that the activity or state exists at the present time. Sentence C tells us that Mr. Young didn't mind the city traffic jams in the past, but it implies that he minds them now. Sometimes a second clause is added to make clear that the activity or state does exist at present.

George didn't use to fly very often, *but now he does.* (fly often)
I didn't use to get up late, *but now I do.* (get up late)

When making a negative statement with *used to* + Verb, treat the word *used* as a regular verb, adding the past form of the DO auxiliary, *did*, and omitting the *-d* ending from *used*.

John *used* to smoke.
John *didn't use* to smoke.

EXERCISE 3.3-A   CHECKING FORM (ORAL)

● ·

used to in affirmative statements

Each pair of sentences tells of a change in habitual activity. Rephrase the meaning, using *used to* in the affirmative.

Example: Before she had a job, Mrs. Taylor read the newspaper every morning. Now, she rarely has time to read it.
Mrs. Taylor used to read the newspaper every morning, but she doesn't anymore.

1. Sara watched a lot of television when she was young. She doesn't even own a television set now.

2. John was afraid of his own shadow when he was a child. As an adult, he's very bold.

3. The Thompsons traveled frequently when they were newly married. They rarely travel now.

4. Maureen was good with money when she was younger. Now she spends every dime.

5. Professor Wycoff got to class late every day at the beginning of the term. Now he always comes on time.

6. I hated American food when I first arrived. Now I like it.

EXERCISE 3.3-B   CHECKING FORM (ORAL)

used to in negative statements

Each pair of sentences tells of a change in habitual activity or state. Rephrase the meaning, using *used to* in the negative.

> **Example:** Herb drove recklessly when he was younger. Now he's a careful driver.
> *Herb didn't use to be a careful driver, but now he is.*

1. Jane didn't treat people with consideration when she was a teenager. Now she treats people kindly.

2. Sam didn't worry about his grades when he was younger. Now he studies very hard. *Sam didn't use to worry about his grades when he was younger but now*

3. Lisa didn't enjoy college her first year. Now she likes it.

4. When he had his old job, Mr. Ross didn't take work home. Now he brings work home every night.

5. Susan didn't argue with people when she was younger. Now she argues with everyone.

6. I didn't earn much money when I first started to work. Now I have a good salary.

EXERCISE 3.3-C   RESTATING IDEAS

used to for the habitual past

Read each pair of sentences. Then restate the information using *used to*.

> **Example:** John was in poor physical condition until recently. He exercises regularly now.
> *John used to be in poor physical condition, but now he exercises regularly.*

1. The housing costs in this area were very high until recently. They are reasonable now.

   _____

   _____

2. Cancer was usually a terminal illness in the past. Doctors cure some forms of it now.

   _____

   _____

3. Crime wasn't a problem in rural areas in the past. People who live in those areas have to be careful now.

_____

_____

4. People went to a lot of movies in the past. They watch television and rent videotapes now.

_____

_____

5. People traveled by train in the past. They usually fly now.

_____

_____

EXERCISE 3.3-D   EXPRESSING YOUR OWN IDEAS
● ·

used to for the habitual past

Write three sentences that describe past situations in your country that are no longer true. Use _used to_ in affirmative statements.

> **Example:** _The cities in my country used to be small, but now they are major population centers._

1. _____

2. _____

3. _____

Now write three sentences that describe present situations in your country that were not true in the past. Use _used to_ + Verb in negative statements.

> **Example:** _The schools in my country didn't use to use our native language, but now they do._

4. _____

5. _____

6. _____

SECTION 3.4   Two-Word Verbs
· ·

1. Two-word verbs: Each of sentences A through G on page 74 has a two-word verb. These are formed with a verb and a preposition or an adverb (often called a particle). Their meaning is usually different from the mean-

●
TWO-WORD VERBS		
Separable Verbs:	**A.**	They **thought over** *the situation* for several days.
	B.	They **thought** *the situation* **over** for several days.
	C.	They **thought** *it* **over** for several days.
Nonseparable Verbs:	**D.**	They **asked for** *the reference books* at the library.
	E.	They **asked for** *them* at the library.
	F.	They **caught on** (to the idea) quickly.
	G.	They **caught on** (to it) quickly.

ing of the two words alone, and they commonly have a one-word synonym. Two-word verbs are frequently used in conversation and informal writing.

| They *thought over* the situation. | = | They *considered* the situation. |
| They *asked for* the books. | = | They *requested* the books. |

Some very common two-word verbs are listed in the chart on page 75. More can be found in Appendix B.

2. Separable two-word verbs: Some two-word verbs are separable. The object of the verb can be placed either between the two parts of the verb or after the second part.

| John *thought over* the problem. | He *thought* the problem *over*. |
| We *called off* our trip. | We *called* our trip *off*. |

However, if the object is a pronoun, it must be placed between the two parts of the two-word verb.

Correct	*Incorrect*
John *thought* it *over*.	John *thought over* it.
We *called* it *off*.	We *called off* it.

If the object of a separable two-word verb is more than two or three words long, the verb is usually not separated.

| *Awkward* | *Better* |
| They *thought* the situation that you mentioned *over* for several days. | They *thought over* the situation that you mentioned for several days. |

3. Nonseparable two-word verbs: Other two-word verbs are nonseparable. The objects of these verbs cannot be placed between the two parts of the verb.

Correct	*Incorrect*
They *asked for* the books.	They *asked* the books *for*.
He just *got over* the flu.	He just *got* the flu *over*.

Some nonseparable two-word verbs are intransitive and have no object. However, they may sometimes be followed by a prepositional phrase, as in sentences F and G.

COMMON TWO–WORDS VERBS

Separable

> call off — to cancel (something)
> call up — to telephone (someone)
> fill out — to complete (something, usually a form)
> leave out — to omit
> look up — to find information in a reference book or directory
> pick out — to choose (something or someone)
> put off — to delay or postpone (something)
> put on — to dress in clothes
> talk over (with someone) — to discuss (something) (with someone)
> try out — to test (something or someone)
> wake up — to stop sleeping, or to cause (someone) to stop sleeping

Nonseparable

> ask for — to request
> call on — to visit (someone), or to ask (someone) to speak
> carry on (with) — to continue (with) (something)
> come across — to find (something) by chance
> get in(to)/get out of — to enter/to leave (a room, a building, a car, or a taxi)
> get on/get off — to enter/to leave (a means of transportation, such as a train, a plane, a boat, or a bicycle)
> get over — to recover from (something, often a loss or an illness)
> look into — to investigate
> look up to — to admire (someone)
> run into — to meet (someone) by chance
> run out of — to exhaust the supply of (something)

EXERCISE 3.4-A   CHECKING FORM (ORAL)

nonseparable two-word verbs

Answer each question on page 76 with a complete statement with *I*. Change the object to a pronoun in your answer.

Example: Who asked for John?
I asked for him.

1. Who looked into the problem?

2. Who ran out of gasoline?

3. Who called on Jane last night?

4. Who came across the definition?

5. Who caught on to the new procedures first?

6. Who ran into John yesterday?

7. Who got into the car first?

EXERCISE 3.4-B CHECKING FORM (ORAL)

separable two-word verbs

Answer each question with a complete sentence with *yesterday*. Change the object to a pronoun in your answer.

Example: When did you think over the problem?
I thought it over yesterday.

1. When did you look up the definition?

2. When did you fill out the forms?

3. When did you call up Mary?

4. When did you pick out your topic?

5. When did you call off the trip?

6. When did you try out the new computer?

EXERCISE 3.4-C UNSCRAMBLING SENTENCES

separable and nonseparable two-word verbs

Unscramble each group of words, phrases, and clauses to make an affirmative or negative statement. If the verb is separable, place the object between the two parts of the verb.

Example: think – very – we – over – the possibilities – carefully – not – did
We didn't think the possibilities over very carefully.

1. the train – got – I – when I reached Fifth Avenue – off

     _____

     _____

2. the forms – you – out – not – did – fill – correctly

     _____

     _____

3. the children – because the weather had turned cold – on – put – their heavy coats

     _____

     _____

4. not – most students – the concept of derivations – do – to – on – catch – easily

     _____

     _____

5. talked – his problems – Howard – with his parents – over

     _____

     _____

6. from my friends – did – I – special help – for – ask – not

     _____

     _____

EXERCISE 3.4-D   ANSWERING QUESTIONS

two-word verbs

Answer each question truthfully. Use the two-word verb in your answer.

1. Do you ever put anything off? What types of things?

     _____

2. What kind of information do you look up in a thesaurus?

     _____

3. Who do you look up to most?

     _____

4. Whom do you usually talk your problems over with?

     _____

5. Does your instructor call on you often?

     _____

4 Gerunds and Infinitives

This chapter examines different uses of gerunds and infinitives. In the first two sections, you will practice using them as verbal complements. The third section reviews the use of gerunds and infinitives as subjects. The last section deals with various expressions of purpose.

SECTION 4.1   **Verbal Complements**

SECTION 4.2   **Verbal Complements with Second Subjects**

SECTION 4.3   **Gerunds and Infinitives as Subjects**

SECTION 4.4   **Expressions of Purpose**

SECTION 4.1   Verbal Complements

INFINITIVES AS COMPLEMENTS
A.   David *would like* **some relaxation** this weekend.
B.   He *would like* **to rest** for a day or two.
C.   He *doesn't want* **to work**.
D.   He *intends* **not to get out** of bed.

1. Complements: In the basic sentence patterns we have examined so far, the complement following a transitive verb has been an object: a noun, a pronoun, or a noun phrase. In sentence A, the noun phrase *some relaxation* functions as the object of the verb.

2. Infinitive complements: It is possible to use infinitives (*to* followed by the simple form of the verb) as objects after certain verbs. In sentence B, the infinitive *to rest* serves as the object of the verb *would like*. The subject of the sentence, *he*, acts as the subject of both verbs, *would like* and *to rest*.

Complement

Sandra would like	*a good Italian meal* tonight. (noun phrase object)
She wants	*to eat* at the new Italian restaurant. (infinitive complement)
She refuses	*to go* anywhere else. (infinitive complement)

3. Negative statements: Sentences with infinitive complements can be made negative in two ways. The more common way is to make the first verb, or main verb, negative, as in sentence C.

David *doesn't want* to work.
He *doesn't intend* to do anything this weekend.

It is also possible to leave the first verb affirmative but make the infinitive negative, as in sentence D. To make the infinitive negative, simply place *not* in front of it.

David intends *not to get out* of bed.
He plans *not to exert* himself.

Notice that where you place the negative can sometimes result in a difference in meaning.

They *didn't promise* to go with us. (They made no promise at all.)
They promised *not to go* with us. (They made a promise, which was to stay, not go.)

VERBS FOLLOWED BY INFINITIVE COMPLEMENTS

Main Verb + *to* + Verb

Example:　David would like to rest for a day or two.

appear	get	pretend
ask	happen	promise
beg	hope	refuse
choose	intend	seem
dare	learn	wait
decide	need	want
deserve	offer	wish
expect	plan	would like
fail	prepare	

EXERCISE 4.1-A   CHECKING FORM (ORAL)

● ·

infinitive complements

Create a short sentence with an infinitive complement, using the verbs and the adverb of time or manner given.

> **Example:** plan – study – tonight
> *He plans to study tonight.*

1. refuse – study – all the time
   He refused to study all the time.
2. intend – call – tonight
   I intend to call tonight.
3. want – finish – quickly
   I want to finish quickly.
4. promise – clean up – tomorrow
   I promise to clean up tomorrow.
5. hope – go – next week
   I hope to go the zoo next week.

6. expect – write – soon
   I expect to write a essay soon.
7. need – pass – this term
   I need to pass the exam this term.
8. ask – speak – every day
   I ask to speak the speech every day.
9. deserve – win – this time
   I deserve to win the game this time.
10. would like – succeed – tomorrow
    I would like to succeed the exam

GERUNDS AS COMPLEMENTS

E.   Margaret *enjoys* choir practice every week. (noun phrase object)

F.   She *enjoys* **singing** with other people.

G.   She *doesn't enjoy* **singing** alone.

H.   She *appreciates* **not hearing** her own voice very clearly.

---

4. Gerund complements: It is also possible to use gerunds (the -*ing* form of the verb, or *Ving*) as complements after some verbs. In sentence F, *singing* acts as the object of the verb *enjoy*. Again, the subject of the sentence, *she*, functions as the subject of both verbs, *enjoy* and *singing*.

	Complement
Sandra likes	*good Italian food.* (noun phrase object)
She enjoys	*eating* at the new Italian restaurant. (gerund complement)
She dislikes	*going* anywhere else. (gerund complement)

5. Negative statements: Sentences with gerund complements can also be made negative in two ways. The more common way is to make the first verb, or main verb, negative, as in sentence G.

> Margaret *doesn't enjoy singing* alone.
> She *doesn't appreciate hearing* her own voice.

It is also possible to leave the first verb affirmative but make the gerund negative, as in sentence H. To make the gerund negative, simply place *not* in front of it.

> She *appreciates not hearing* her own voice.
> She *enjoys not worrying* about how she sounds.

VERBS FOLLOWED BY GERUND COMPLEMENTS

Main Verb + *Ving*

Example: Margaret finished singing.

admit	enjoy	postpone
appreciate	finish	practice
avoid	imagine	recommend
consider	involve	report
delay	mind	resent
dislike		

tardanza (delay)

In addition, certain Verb + Noun expressions are commonly followed by gerund objects:

have trouble	He *has trouble understanding* the equations.
have a problem	They *have a problem completing* their work on time.
have difficulty	I *have difficulty expressing* myself.
spend time	She *didn't spend much time preparing* for the test.

EXERCISE 4.1-B   CHECKING FORM (ORAL)

gerund complements

Create a short sentence with a gerund complement, using the words given. Use the past tense.

> **Example:** consider – ask – him – yesterday
> *We considered asking him yesterday.*

1.   enjoy – see – you – yesterday

2.   postpone – drive – to Vancouver – last week

3.   spend time – study – the problem

4.   admit – borrow – her car – this morning

5. dislike – cook – our own meals

6. avoid – talk – to them – last week

7. finish – work – on the project

8. have trouble – write – the paper – last term

9. practice – use – verbal objects

SPELLING RULES FOR *Ving* **FORMS**

To create a gerund, add *-ing* to the end of the verb. If the verb ends in a consonant and the letter *e*, drop the *e* before adding *-ing*.

hope	hoping
smile	smiling

If the verb ends in *y*, simply add *-ing*. Make no other changes.

pay	paying
study	studying

If the verb has one syllable and ends in consonant + vowel + consonant, double the final consonant before adding *-ing*. If the verb has more than one syllable, this rule also applies, but only if the final syllable is stressed.

One Syllable

stop	stopping
tap	tapping

More Than One Syllable

refer	referring (stress on the final syllable)
omit	omitting (stress on the final syllable)
offer	offering (stress on the first syllable)
happen	happening (stress on the first syllable)

EXERCISE 4.1-C   CHECKING FORM (ORAL)

infinitive complements and gerund complements

Using the words provided on page 84, create a short sentence in the past tense that uses either an infinitive complement or a gerund complement.

> **Example:** choose – go
> *They chose to go.*

1.	promise – write	7.	spend time – talk
2.	delay – come	8.	happen – come
3.	resent – work	9.	ask – drive
4.	want – join	10.	have difficulty – understand
5.	need – try	11.	deserve – pass
6.	learn – swim	12.	wait – leave

VERBS FOLLOWED BY EITHER INFINITIVES OR GERUNDS

I.   We *started* **to work** on the next chapter last night.

J.   We *started* **working** on the next chapter last night.

---

6. Infinitive complements or gerund complements with no change in meaning: Certain verbs can be followed by either an infinitive complement or a gerund complement with no difference in meaning. Examine sentences I and J. Both forms, *started to work* and *started working*, are correct and have the same meaning.

> I *like to attend* the concerts in the old music hall.
> I *like attending* the concerts in the old music hall.

Verbs which can be followed by either an infinitive complement or a gerund complement are listed in the chart on page 85.

7. Infinitive complements or gerund complements with differences in meaning: A few other verbs can have either an infinitive object or a gerund object but differ in meaning depending on the pattern.

> We *stopped* to ask directions. (We stopped some other activity so that we could ask directions.)
> We *stopped* asking directions. (We were asking directions earlier, but we stopped doing so.)

> He *forgot* to write his name. (He didn't write it.)
> He *forgot* writing his name. (He wrote his name, but then forgot that he had done so.)

> She *remembers* to call her parents every week. (First she remembers that she should call them, and then she calls.)
> She *remembers* calling her parents last week. (She called her parents last week. Now she remembers that she called them.)

8. *What-do* questions: There are two ways to ask a *what-do* question with an infinitive object or a gerund object. Look at these sentences:

> *Statement:* He *refused to leave*.
> *Question:* What did he *do*? Refused to leave.
>   What did he *refuse to do*? Leave.

> *Statement:* She *finished reading* the newspaper.
> *Question:* What did she *do*? Finished reading the newspaper.
>   What did she *finish doing*? Reading the newspaper.

Can you explain the difference in meaning in each pair of questions? How are the questions formed differently?

9. Reducing the infinitive complement: It is possible to reduce the infinitive complement when answering a question. Look at this short dialogue:

> A: Did you write the essay yet?
> B: No, but I *plan to write* it this evening. OR
>   No, but I *plan to* this evening.

The second answer omits the verb portion of the infinitive but retains the word *to*. Because it is clear that the speakers are discussing the activity of writing, it is not necessary to repeat that verb.

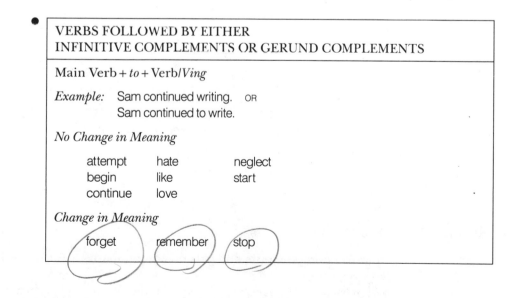

VERBS FOLLOWED BY EITHER
INFINITIVE COMPLEMENTS OR GERUND COMPLEMENTS

Main Verb + *to* + Verb/*Ving*

Example: Sam continued writing.   OR
   Sam continued to write.

No Change in Meaning

attempt	hate	neglect
begin	like	start
continue	love	

Change in Meaning

forget	remember	stop

EXERCISE 4.1-D   EXPRESSING YOUR OWN IDEAS (ORAL)

verbal complements

Answer each question using an infinitive or a gerund complement.

1. Did you start to do anything this morning? What?
2. Is there anything you hate doing? What?
3. Is there anything you forgot to do yesterday? What?
4. Is there anything you avoided doing last week? What?
5. Is there anything you sometimes refuse to do? What?

EXERCISE 4.1-E   RESPONDING TO QUESTIONS

two-word verbs and reduced infinitive complements

Answer each question with a full negative response, changing the object to its pronoun form. Then add a clause using the verb in parentheses.

> **Example:** Did you call off your meeting today? (*plan*)
> *No, I didn't call it off today, but I plan to tomorrow.*

1. Did John call on his friends today? (*want*)

   _____

2. Did Janet pick out the articles today? (*need*)

   _____

3. Did you talk over the problem with John today? (*intend*)

   _____

4. Did the Weavers try out the new computer today? (*hope*)

   _____

5. Did Paul look up the addresses today? (*promise*)

   _____

EXERCISE 4.1-F   DISCRIMINATING FORM

infinitive complements and gerund complements

Fill in each blank space with the correct form of the verb, either a gerund or an infinitive.

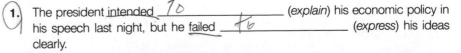

1. The president intended _to_____ (*explain*) his economic policy in his speech last night, but he failed _to_____ (*express*) his ideas clearly.

(handwritten top margin: forgot -ing always.)

2. We considered _____ _ing_ *(p85)* _____ (*wait*) until next year to move but de-
    cided _____ *To* _____ (*begin*) _looking_ *to look* _____ (*look*) for a new
    apartment now.

3. Our instructor planned _____ *To* _____ (*make*) an assignment yesterday,
    but she forgot _____ *To* _____ (*give*) it to us.

4. If you delay _____ *ing* _____ (*ask*) for permission, the committee may
    decide _____ *not to grant* _____ (*grant*, negative) your request.

5. Many of the students stopped _____ *~~to~~ ing* _____ (*attend*) the class toward
    the end of the term because they wanted _____ *To* _____ (*start*)
    _____ *ing* _____ (*study*) for the final examination.

6. Did you remember _____ *To* _____ (*spend time*) _____ *relaxing* _____ (*relax*) as
    the doctor told you?

EXERCISE 4.1-G   MAKING PHRASES INTO SENTENCES

verbal complements in statements and questions

Form a sentence as indicated from the words, phrases, and clauses provided.
Each sentence will have a verbal complement, either an infinitive or a ger-
und. If a WH question is specified, form it so that it asks about the underlined words or phrases.

> **Examples:** the treasurer – neglect – explain – the mistake (statement, past
> tense)
> *The treasurer neglected to explain the mistake.*
>
> Professor Johnson – plan – grade – the papers – tomorrow (WH
> question, present tense)
> *What does Professor Johnson plan to do tomorrow?*

1. Robert – want (negative) – come – to the meeting – yesterday (statement, past
    tense)

    _____

    _____

2. you – forget – call – the babysitter – this morning (yes-no question, past tense)

    _____

    _____

3. the police – report – see – someone strange – by the back of the building – last
    night (statement, past tense)

    _____

    _____

4. the teachers – enjoy – <u>talk about</u> – <u>their students</u> – when they get together (WH question, present tense)

_____

_____

5. Sean – avoid – talk – to everyone – <u>because he is so shy</u> (WH question, present tense)

_____

_____

6. <u>the last chapter in the book</u> – seem – BE – the most insightful (WH question, present tense)

_____

_____

EXERCISE 4.1-H   EXPRESSING YOUR OWN IDEAS

verbal complements

Complete each sentence with your own ideas. Use an infinitive or a gerund as the complement of the main verb.

1. My government plans _to change the money_____

2. I am not prepared _to do the Homework_____

3. Americans seem _to be on time_____

4. I often fail _to do the homework_____

5. Our teacher appreciates _studying with us_____

6. The students in this class expect _to get good jobs._____

SECTION 4.2   Verbal Complements with Second Subjects

INFINITIVE COMPLEMENTS WITH OPTIONAL SECOND SUBJECTS
A. Robert *asked* **to leave** the meeting early because he was exhausted.
B. He *asked **us** to take* notes for him.

1. Verbal complements without second subjects: In Section 4.1 you saw that the object of certain verbs can be in the form of a verbal complement, either an infinitive or a gerund. When this is the case, the subject of the sentence acts as the subject of both verbs. In sentence A, for example, *Robert* functions as the subject of both *asked* and *to leave*.

> I expect to go this evening. (I expect that I will go.)
> Jane asked to talk to Jim. (Jane asked that she be allowed to talk to Jim.)

2. Infinitive complements with optional second subjects: It is sometimes possible to add a second subject between the main verb and the infinitive or the gerund that follows. With some main verbs that take infinitive complements, a second subject is optional. Examine sentence B. The pronoun *us* has been placed between the main verb *asked* and the infinitive *to take*. *Us* acts as the object of the main verb, so the object form of the pronoun is used. *Us* also functions as the subject of the infinitive—the notes are taken by *us*, not by Robert.

> I expect *you* to go this evening. (I expect that *you* will go.)
> Jane asked *Margaret* to talk to Jim. (Jane asked that *Margaret* talk to Jim.)

VERBS FOLLOWED BY INFINITIVE COMPLEMENTS WITH OPTIONAL SECOND SUBJECTS

Main Verb + (Second Subject) + *to* + Verb

Example: John would like to ask a question.
          John would like me to ask a question.

ask	expect	prepare
beg	get	want
choose	need	would like
dare		

The verb *get* changes meaning depending on whether there is a second subject or not.

> I got to talk with them before they left. (I was permitted to talk with them; I had a chance to talk with them.)

> I got my friend to talk with them before they left. (I convinced or persuaded my friend to talk with them.)

EXERCISE 4.2-A   CHECKING FORM (ORAL)

infinitive complements with optional second subjects

For each group of words and phrases on page 90, create a short sentence with an infinitive complement and a second subject. Use the name of one of your classmates for the second subject.

Example: expect – help me – this evening
I expect Laura to help me this evening.

1. want – come with us – last night

2. get – study with me – yesterday

3. need – loan me some money – this weekend

4. choose – play on our soccer team – last term

5. beg – drive me home – yesterday

INFINITIVE COMPLEMENTS WITH REQUIRED SECOND SUBJECTS

C.   The workers *convinced* **the management** **to shorten** the workday.

D.   My doctor *advised* **me** **to take** it easy.

---

3. Infinitive complements with required second subjects: Some verbs must have a second subject if there is an infinitive complement, as in sentences C and D. In sentence C, the second subject (*the management*) is required with the main verb *convince* and the infinitive complement. In sentence D, the second subject (*me*) is required with the main verb *advise*.

Correct

They convinced *us* to attend.
Susan advised *Ann* to be more polite.

Incorrect

They convinced to attend.
Susan advised to be more polite. `

4. Negative statements: The infinitive complement is made negative by placing *not* directly in front of it, after the second subject.

We advised Jonathan *not* to go.
Your report convinced me *not* to change suppliers.

VERBS FOLLOWED BY INFINITIVE COMPLEMENTS WITH REQUIRED SECOND SUBJECTS

Main Verb + Second Subject + *to* + Verb

Example: Howard convinced us to rearrange our schedules.

advise	force	persuade
allow	hire	remind
challenge	instruct	require
command	invite	teach
convince	order	tell
encourage	pay	urge
forbid	permit	warn

EXERCISE 4.2-B   CHECKING FORM (ORAL)

infinitive complements with required second subjects

Use each group of words and phrases to create a short sentence in the past tense with an infinitive complement and a second subject. Use the name of one of your classmates for the second subject.

> **Example:** advice – apply for a scholarship
> *I advised Rob to apply for a scholarship.*

1. challenge – play me at table tennis

2. encourage – ask for some help

3. invite – join us for dinner

4. tell – leave me alone

5. urge – spend more time on his project

6. pay – wash my car

7. remind – arrive early

8. persuade – take this course

9. allow – copy my notes

10. teach – speak some phrases in my language

**GERUND AND SIMPLE VERB COMPLEMENTS
WITH SECOND SUBJECTS**

E.   We *heard* **the choir** sing.

F.   We *heard* **the choir** singing.

---

5. Verbs of perception with required second subjects: Another group of verbs must have a second subject when they are followed by a gerund or by the simple form of the verb (without *to*). These verbs describe perception or observation. Examine sentences E and F. The second subject is *the choir*, and either the simple verb (*sing*) or the gerund form (*singing*) can follow.

When the simple form (Verb) is used, the sentence means that the entire activity was observed. When the gerund form (*Ving*) is used, the speaker observed only part of the activity.

**VERBS FOLLOWED BY GERUND OR SIMPLE VERB COMPLEMENTS
WITH REQUIRED SECOND SUBJECTS**

Main Verb + Second Subject + Verb/*Ving*

Example: John felt the car go out of control.
              John felt the car going out of control.

feel	look at	overhear
hear	notice	see
listen to	observe	watch

EXERCISE 4.2-C   CHECKING FORM (ORAL)

verbs of perception with second subjects

Use each group of words and phrases to create a short sentence in the past tense with a gerund complement or a simple verb complement and a second subject. Use the name of one of your classmates for the second subject.

> **Example:** hear – give you directions this morning
> *I heard Fred give you directions this morning.*   OR
> *I heard Fred giving you directions this morning.*

1.   watch – do the lab experiment yesterday

2.   notice – avoid the teacher's questions this morning

3.   overhear – whisper to you a few minutes ago

4. observe – get off the bus earlier today

5. see – speak to you yesterday

6. listen to – complain to our instructor this morning

7. hear – give the teacher an excuse a few minutes ago

SIMPLE VERB COMPLEMENTS
WITH REQUIRED SECOND SUBJECTS

G. The police *made **the crowd of people** move* away from the building.

H. They *had **them** stand* on the other side of the street.

I. They *didn't let **them** get* near the burning building.

---

6. Simple verb complements with required second subjects: There is a small group of verbs that can be followed by a second subject and the simple form of another verb, but never a gerund. Look at sentences G, H, and I. In sentence G, the main verb, *made*, has a second subject, *the crowd of people*, before the simple verb complement *move*. Only three verbs fall into this category: *have*, *let*, and *make*.

使役動詞

7. Causatives: *Have* and *make* take on special meaning when they are used in this pattern. Both mean something similar to *cause* and therefore are sometimes called causatives.

Have is used in this pattern when a person asks someone else to do something, hires someone else to do something, or has the authority, position, or money to ask someone else to perform a task.

> I *had* my friend pick up the equipment for me. (I asked her to do something for me.)

Make is used for causation when force (or the threat of force) is implied on the part of the subject.

> The sergeant *made* his men march another ten miles.

8. The verb *help*:   *Help* is unique because it can be followed by either an infinitive or a simple verb complement. Use of a second subject is optional.

> They *helped carry* the equipment.
> They *helped to carry* the equipment.
> They *helped* their friends *carry* the equipment.
> They *helped* their friends *to carry* the equipment.

9. **What-do questions:**   *What-do* questions can be asked using the various patterns with verbal complements and second subjects.

> She wants her friends to help her with the project.
> *What does* she *want* her friends *to do*? Help her with the project.
>
> He saw some students cheating on the exam.
> *What did* he *see* some students *doing*? Cheating on the exam.

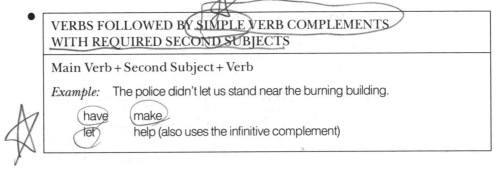

VERBS FOLLOWED BY SIMPLE VERB COMPLEMENTS WITH REQUIRED SECOND SUBJECTS

Main Verb + Second Subject + Verb

Example: The police didn't let us stand near the burning building.

have   make
let   help (also uses the infinitive complement)

EXERCISE 4.2-D   CHECKING FORM (ORAL)

simple verb complements with second subjects

Use each group of words and phrases to create a short sentence in the past tense with a simple verb complement and a second subject. Use the name of one of your classmates for the second subject.

> **Example:** make – open the door for me this morning
> *I made Jonathan open the door for me this morning.*

1. make – carry my books for me yesterday

2. let – borrow my grammar book this morning

3. help – study for the grammar test last night

4. have – open the window just a minute ago

5. make – promise to call me last week

EXERCISE 4.2-E   ANSWERING QUESTIONS (ORAL)

verbal complements with second subjects

Answer the following questions about your classmates in full statements.

> **Examples:** Do you advise anyone here to work harder?
> *Yes, I advise Dan to work harder.*
>
> Do you see anyone here writing?
> *Yes, I see Sue writing.*

1. Do you notice anyone looking out the window?

2. Do you overhear anyone whispering?

3. Who do you expect not to be here tomorrow?

4. Who do you want to answer the next question?

5. Does the instructor ever have anyone erase the chalkboard?

6. Does the instructor ever remind anyone here not to be late to class?

7. Do you ever notice anyone fall asleep in class?

EXERCISE 4.2-F   ANSWERING QUESTIONS (ORAL)

verbal complements with second subjects

Answer the following questions about your classmates.

Example: What do you expect Janice to do today?
I expect her to pay me back the money that she owes me.

1. What did you persuade (X) not to do yesterday?

2. What did you see (X) doing this morning?

3. What do you notice (X) doing everyday?

4. What did you make (X) do last week?

5. What do you want (X) not to do tonight?

6. What did you tell (X) to do yesterday?

7. What do you hear (X) doing every day?

8. What did you have (X) do this morning?

EXERCISE 4.2-G   DISCRIMINATING FORM

4/8 Quiz

verbal complements

Fill in each blank with the correct form of the verbal complement.

1. The Ajax Company had all its employees _undergo_ (undergo) a security clearance because a few of them had been observed _reading_ (read) documents that needed _to be_ (BE) kept secret. The company also instructed its workers _not to talk_ (talk, negative) about their jobs outside of the factory. The employees _resented being_ (BE) treated in this manner and decided _to_ (fight) the new rules.

2. This winter promises ___to be___ (BE) severe, so the students who come from warmer climates need ___to___ (buy) heavy winter coats. We should also warn them ___not to___ (stay, negative) outside too long when it is both cold and windy.

3. If you hear the car ___making___ (make) that strange noise again, please tell the mechanic ___to___ (repair) it. I have asked him ___to___ (fix) it before, but he never seems ___to___ (discover) what the problem is.

4. I got my friends ___to___ (help) me ___to___ (move) the heaviest furniture last week. I should remember ___to___ (thank) them again for their help.

5. When we overheard the children ___ing___ (complain) about us, we told ourselves ___not to be___ (BE, negative) upset. The situation convinced us ___to be___ (BE) more understanding in the future and ___to be___ (BE) more considerate of their feelings.

EXERCISE 4.2-H   MAKING PHRASES INTO SENTENCES

verbal complements

Make a complete statement from each set of words, phrases, and clauses. *Add a second subject if necessary.* Use the tense indicated.

> **Example:** my neighbor – permit – borrow – his tools (past tense)
> *My neighbor permitted me to borrow his tools.*

1. Dr. Weaver's mistakes – force – redo – the entire project (past tense)

   _____

   _____

2. we – notice – talk – after everyone left (past tense)

   _____

   _____

3. Dave and Mary – invite (negative) – join them – because they didn't have room in their car (past tense)

   _____

   _____

4. several journalists – report – see – the new administrators – talk – with their advisers (past tense)

   _____

   _____

5. this assignment – challenge – think – deeply about the issues (past tense)

_____

_____

6. the newscasters – delay – report – the story – for several reasons (past tense)

_____

_____

7. no one – expect – develop – a cure – in the near future (present tense)

_____

_____

EXERCISE 4.2-I   COMPLETING SENTENCES

verbal complements

Complete each sentence with your own ideas. Use a verbal complement. _You may need to add a second subject to some sentences._

1. Our teachers encourage _____

2. The rules forbid _____

3. I noticed _____

4. Very hot weather forces _____

5. The students get _____

6. The store clerk saw _____

7. John's failing grade convinced _____

8. The president's adviser chose _____

9. My instructor has _____

10. My friend's parents let _____

EXERCISE 4.2-J   REPORTING INFORMATION

verbal complements

Ask your instructor to give you advice about studying English. Write down the suggestions your instructor gives you; then report each of them, using the verbs provided as main verbs. Write your sentences on p. 98.

Examples: Teacher: You should study every day.
(advise) _Our instructor advises us to study every day._

Teacher: You shouldn't watch television or listen to the radio while you study.

(want) *Our instructor doesn't want us to watch television or listen to the radio while we study.*

1. would like

_____

2. advise

_____

3. try to persuade

_____

4. urge

_____

5. remind

_____

6. tell

_____

7. expect

_____

SUMMARY CHART OF VERB COMPLEMENT PATTERNS

Group 1:   Main Verb + *to* + Verb
I decided to leave early.

Group 2:   Main Verb + *Ving*
I enjoy studying English.

Group 3:   Main Verb + *to* + Verb/*Ving*
I started to write my report.
I started writing my report.

Group 4:   Main Verb (+ Second Subject) + *to* + Verb
I asked to go.
I asked Ann to go.

Group 5:   Main Verb + Second Subject + *to* + Verb
I persuaded Howard to join us.

Group 6:   Main Verb + Second Subject + Verb/*Ving*
I watched the plane leave.
I watched the plane leaving.

Group 7:   Main Verb + Second Subject + Verb
I made the children quiet down.

SECTION 4.3   Gerunds and Infinitives as Subjects

. . . .

VERB FORMS AS SUBJECTS

A. **Yesterday's lesson** was *difficult*.

B. **Understanding yesterday's lesson** was *difficult*.

C. **To understand yesterday's lesson** was *difficult*.

D. *It* was *difficult* **to understand yesterday's lesson**.

---

1. Gerunds and infinitives as subjects: In the sentences we have examined so far, the subject has always been a noun, a pronoun, or a noun phrase, as in sentence A, where *yesterday's lesson* is the subject.

It is also possible to use gerunds and infinitives as the subjects of sentences, as in sentences B and C, where *understanding yesterday's lesson* and *to understand yesterday's lesson* serve as subjects.

Notice that both gerund subjects and infinitive subjects are treated in the third person singular, so the main verb of each example sentence is *was*, not *were*.

> Asking for some help *isn't* the end of the world.
> Reading the articles *was* extremely time-consuming.

2. *It* as the subject: Sentences with infinitive subjects are grammatically correct but unusual. When an infinitive subject is followed by a linking verb and an adjective, it is more common to begin the sentence with the word *it* and delay the infinitive phrase to the end, as in sentence D, *It was difficult to understand the lesson*. Adjectives which are often used in this pattern include the following:

amusing	easy	hard
boring	economical	important
challenging	embarrassing	impossible
common	essential	necessary
confusing	exciting	possible
convenient	exhausting	satisfying
dangerous	fascinating	traditional
difficult	frightening	typical
disappointing	good	usual

Here are some more examples of such sentences:

> *It* was *exciting* to watch such a good performance.
> *It* is *essential* to understand this sentence pattern.
> *It* isn't *necessary* to complete the work today.

SENTENCES WITH *FOR* PHRASES
E.   **English** was *easy for me*.
F.   **Learning English** was *easy for me*.
G.   **To learn English** was *easy for me*.
H.   **It** was *easy for me* **to learn English**.

3. Adding a *for* phrase: A phrase with *for* can be added to these sentences, as in examples E through H. In each of these sentences, *for me* indicates to whom the subject applies. Notice that the phrase with *for* follows the adjective in all the sentences.

> Understanding yesterday's lesson was *difficult for me*.
> It was *difficult for me* to understand yesterday's lesson.
> Skiing is *exciting for John*.
> It is *exciting for John* to ski.

4. The verbs *take* and *cost*:   *Take* and *cost* can also be used in sentences with *it* and a delayed infinitive subject.

> It *takes* several hours *to assemble* the equipment.
> It *cost* a lot of money *to run* last year's campaign.

A *for* phrase can be placed after the object, or an indirect object can be placed directly after the verb.

> It takes several hours *for us* to assemble the equipment.
> It takes *us* several hours to assemble the equipment.

EXERCISE 4.3-A   CHECKING FORM (ORAL)

gerunds as subjects

Change each statement to the form with a gerund subject.

> **Example:** It's important to study hard.
> *Studying hard is important.*

1.   It was amusing to watch that movie.

2.   It is exciting to water-ski.

3.   It is economical to take the bus.

4.   It was hard for them to pass that course.

5. It is dangerous to climb mountains.

6. It is convenient for me to live close to school.

7. It is unusual for Joe to make that kind of mistake.

EXERCISE 4.3-B   CHECKING FORM (ORAL)

it as the subject

Change each statement to the form with *it* and a delayed infinitive subject.

> **Example:** Reading the newspaper every day is important.
> *It is important to read the newspaper every day.*

1. Getting anywhere on time is impossible for George.

2. Having a large family dinner is traditional on Thanksgiving Day.

3. Exercising hard is good for your heart.

4. Driving to campus is easy for her.

5. Not falling behind in your school work is essential.

6. Working on this assignment is challenging for me.

7. Thinking about the possibility of war is frightening.

EXERCISE 4.3-C   EXPRESSING YOUR OWN IDEAS (ORAL)

gerunds as subjects

Answer each question, using a gerund as the subject.

> **Example:** Name something that is necessary for you.
> *Learning English quickly is necessary for me.*

1. Name something that is dangerous.

2. Name something that is good for you.

3. Name something that is impossible for you.

4. Name something that you think is essential.

5. Name something that you think is frightening.

6. Name something that is difficult for you.

7. Name something that is easy for you.

EXERCISE 4.3-D   EXPRESSING YOUR OWN IDEAS (ORAL)

it as the subject

Answer each question, using *it* and a delayed infinitive subject.

> **Example:** What is easy for you to do?
> *It is easy for me to cook a good meal.*

1. What is hard for you to do?

2. What is unusual for you to do?

3. What is essential for you to do?

4. What is dangerous for you to do?

5. What is impossible for you to do?

6. What is inconvenient for you to do?

7. What is fun for you to do?

EXERCISE 4.3-E   CHECKING FORM

gerunds as subjects and *it* as the subject

Change each statement to the form with a gerund subject.

> **Example:** It's fascinating to visit new places.
> *Visiting new places is fascinating.*

1. It was almost impossible for the new mayor to control the city council.

   _____

2. It is essential for anyone who is interested in this topic to read this new book.

   _____

3. It was exciting to see the production process in action.

   _____

4. It is exhausting to keep up with all the work that is required.

   _____

Change statements 5–8 to the form with *it* and a delayed infinitive subject.

> **Example:** Understanding the subtle points of the argument is necessary.
> *It is necessary to understand the subtle points of the argument.*

5. Duplicating the experiment exactly is almost impossible.

_____

_____

6. Not appearing too eager is very difficult for me.

_____

_____

7. Refusing to accept other viewpoints is common for him.

_____

_____

8. Fitting together all the pieces of a complex puzzle is very satisfying.

_____

_____

EXERCISE 4.3-F　RESTATING SENTENCES

it **as the subject**

Write a sentence that describes each situation, as in the example.

> **Example:** George learns languages quickly. He says that it's easy.
> *It's easy for George to learn languages quickly.*

1. Martha goes grocery shopping only once a month. It's economical.

_____

_____

2. Parents are concerned about their children. It's typical.

It's typical for parents to be concerned about their children

_____

3. The new employees learned their jobs very quickly. It was essential.

_____

_____

4. The farmers didn't use any insecticides. It was unnecessary.

It was unnecessary for farmers to use any insecticides

_____

5. Nations can achieve peace among themselves. It's possible.

_____

_____

EXERCISE 4.3-G   RESPONDING TO INFORMATION

. . . .

it as the subject

Read the paragraphs carefully. Then create sentences which restate information from the sentences indicated. Make your sentences with *it* and a delayed infinitive subject, as in the example. Use the adjective which is given.

(1) According to some recent research, it appears that certain trees can communicate with one another. (2) Dr. Gordon Orians and Dr. David Rhoades, both of the University of Washington, carried out their study in 1982. (3) They knew that trees often defend themselves against attacks by insects. (4) In order to discover how trees can do this, the researchers had to place swarms of caterpillars and webworms on the branches of willow trees and alder trees. (5) They found the answer to their question without difficulty. (6) Soon after the insects began their attack, the trees started to produce chemicals that are both bad-tasting and harmful to the insects.

(7) Even more interesting, however, was the fact that nearby trees, which had not been attacked by the caterpillars and webworms, also produced these chemicals. (8) This discovery suggested that the trees passed information to one another. (9) Orians and Rhoades had difficulty explaining this phenomenon. (10) The trees could not have communicated the information directly because they were too far apart.

(11) Some scientists now believe that the ability for plants to communicate is not unusual. (12) They suspect that plants under attack by insects may release airborne chemicals, known as pheromones, that warn neighboring plants.

Example: (sentence 1) *possible*
   It is possible for certain trees to communicate with one another.

1.   (sentence 3) *common*

   _____

   _____

2.   (sentence 4) *necessary*

   _____

   _____

3.   (sentence 5) *easy,* or *not difficult*

   _____

   _____

4.   (sentence 9) *hard,* or *difficult*

   _____

   _____

5. (sentence 10) *impossible*

It was impossible for th tree to communicated
the information directly because They were too far apart.

6. (sentence 11) *usual*

It is usual for plant to communicate.

7. (sentence 12) *possible*

SECTION 4.4   Expressions of Purpose

. . . .

EXPRESSIONS OF PURPOSE

   Why do you go to the grocery early in the morning?

A. I go there early in the morning **so that I can find fresh produce**.

B. I go there early in the morning **in order to find fresh produce**.

C. I go there early in the morning **to find fresh produce**.

D. I go there early in the morning **for fresh produce**.

---

1. Questions of purpose with *why*:   A question with *why* can be answered with an expression of purpose. In Chapter 1 you saw that a dependent clause beginning with *so that* can express purpose, as in sentence A. Remember that a clause has its own subject and its own verb.

2. Infinitive expressions of purpose: It is also possible to express purpose with an infinitive phrase, as in sentences B and C. The full phrase begins with the words *in order to* followed by the simple verb form. However, it is common to reduce the phrase by omitting *in order*.

> Howard told a lie *in order to protect* himself.
> Howard told a lie *to protect* himself.

3. Prepositional phrases of purpose: Purpose can also be expressed with a prepositional phrase with *for* followed by a noun, as in sentence D.

> Martha called me *for some information*. (in order to get some information)
> I paid a lot of money *for this course*. (in order to take this course)

EXERCISE 4.4-A   CHECKING FORM (ORAL)

prepositional phrases of purpose

In each sentence, change the infinitive expression of purpose to a prepositional phrase with *for*.

> **Example:** They bought supplies in order to do their project.
> *They bought supplies for their project.*

1. We phoned Mr. Samuels in order to get his opinion.

2. Ms. Stratton exercises regularly in order to remain in good health.

3. Lisa went to the pharmacy in order to buy her medicine.

4. We visited New York in order to see some Broadway plays.

5. I listened to the radio in order to get some news about the election.

6. We crossed our fingers in order to have good luck.

EXERCISE 4.4-B   CHECKING FORM (ORAL)

infinitive phrases of purpose

Change the prepositional phrase of purpose to an infinitive phrase with *in order*.

> **Example:** Sandra bought the magazine for the article about bicycling.
> *Sandra bought the magazine in order to read the article about bicycling.*

1. I wrote to that company for its catalog.

2. Margaret drove to the bank for some money.

3. Ken went to the mall for some new clothes.

4. All the students walked to the cafeteria for lunch.

5. Some of the students watch television every night for their English.

6. We went to the party for a good time.

EXERCISE 4.4-C   DISCRIMINATING FORM

for **versus** *to* **in expressions of purpose**

Fill in each blank with either *for* or *to*.

1. We put on heavy coats _____ keep warm.

2. My friends went to an amusement park _____ some excitement.

3. Paul uses a computer _____ his work.

4. The sirens sounded _____ warn the residents.

5. The newspaper printed this article _____ inform its readers about health hazards.

6. The magazine received several awards _____ its coverage of the tragedy.

EXERCISE 4.4-D   COMPLETING SENTENCES

expressions of purpose

Complete each statement with an expression of purpose. Use either *for* + Noun or *in order to* + Verb.

1. My instructor called _____

2. We drove to New York _____

3. You should see a doctor _____

4. I am studying English _____

5. David took his wallet out of his pocket _____

6. Martha looked in the telephone directory _____

7. Michael looked at his watch _____

5 The Present Progressive Tense and the Past Progressive Tense

This chapter examines the present progressive tense and the past progressive tense and then reviews the use of adverbial clauses and phrases of time.

SECTION 5.1   The Present Progressive and the Past Progressive

SECTION 5.2   Adverbial Clauses of Time

SECTION 5.3   More Adverbial Expressions of Time

SECTION 5.1   The Present Progressive and the Past Progressive

---

THE PRESENT PROGRESSIVE TENSE
A. The technicians **are working** on the fifth floor of our building this week.
B. Right now, they **are assembling** the new equipment.
C. They **are not installing** it yet.
D. Their foreman **is** usually **complaining** about the job whenever I see him.

1. Progressive tenses: The progressive tenses show that an activity has duration, that it takes place over a period of time. The verb phrase is made progressive by using BE as an auxiliary and the present participle (*Ving*) form of the main verb.

2. The present progressive tense: Sentences A through D are in the present progressive tense. Notice that the present form of BE is used, followed by the present participle. The auxiliary BE must agree with the subject of the sentence in person and number.

3. Negative statements: To make the present progressive tense negative, make the auxiliary BE negative by adding *not* after it, as in sentence C. Do not add the DO auxiliary.

Correct	*Incorrect*
John isn't talking now.	John doesn't talking now.

4. Uses of the present progressive: The present progressive tense is used in three different situations.

Activity at the moment of speaking: Actions which are in progress at the moment of speaking are usually expressed in the present progressive. This use of the present progressive shows that the activity started in the past, is in progress at the time of speaking, and will probably continue and be completed in the future. Sentence B uses this meaning of the present progressive.

> Jessica is working in the library now.
> We are reading about the progressive at the moment.

Common adverbs of time which are used with the present progressive at the moment of speaking include *now, this minute, right now,* and *at the moment.*

Temporary state: The present progressive can indicate an activity occurring in the general present time (not necessarily at the moment of speaking) *which is considered to be temporary.* Sentence A expresses this meaning. The technicians are working on the fifth floor this week, but not necessarily at this moment. And this activity is considered temporary; after this week, the technicians will probably be working somewhere else in the building.

> Dena is teaching in New York this year. (temporary, for this year only)
> Dena teaches in New York. (a permanent situation)

Common adverbs of time which are used with the present progressive to express a temporary state include *this year, this week, this month, today,* and *this morning.*

Habitual activity: Sometimes the present progressive expresses habitual activity, especially if the speaker shows disapproval. An adverb of frequency is generally used for this meaning. Note that the adverb is placed between the BE auxiliary and the main verb.

> Those students are always asking ridiculous questions.
> Pat is usually talking on the phone whenever I need to see him.

EXERCISE 5.1-A   CHECKING FORM (ORAL)

statements in the present progressive

Change each statement to the present progressive tense. Add the time adverb *now*.

> **Example:** Jason goes to work every day.
> *He is going to work now.*

1. We sit in class every day.

2. Roy doesn't read the newspaper every day.

3. They study English grammar every day.

4. Jane fixes breakfast every day.

5. Joe and Sam eat lunch in a restaurant every day.

6. Tim pretends to know the answer every day.

EXERCISE 5.1-B   EXPRESSING YOUR OWN IDEAS (ORAL)

the present progressive

Answer each question with a full statement, using the present progressive tense.

1. Where are you living now?

2. Are you playing any sports this year? Which ones?

3. Who are you talking to now?

4. Why are you studying English this term?

5. Are you making new friends in this class? Who are they?

6. Where are you sitting now?

THE PAST PROGRESSIVE TENSE

E.   Ms. Anker **was reading** the newspaper when we arrived at noon yesterday.

F.   She **was not preparing** for our meeting.

---

5. The past progressive tense: Sentences E and F use the past progressive tense. The past form of BE is used as an auxiliary, followed by the present participle form of the verb (*Ving*).

6. Negative statements: To make the past progressive tense negative, make the auxiliary BE negative by adding *not* after it, as in sentence F. Do not add the DO auxiliary.

Correct	*Incorrect*
Sara wasn't working very hard.	Sara didn't working very hard.

7. Uses of the past progressive: The past progressive tense is used in two different situations.

Activity occurring at a point in the past: The past progressive is used most commonly to show that an activity was in progress at some particular point in time in the past. The activity started before that time, was in progress at that time, and possibly continued and was completed after that time. Examine sentence E. It states that Ms. Anker began to read the newspaper before we arrived at noon yesterday and that she continued to read it at the time of our arrival.

> We were studying at noon yesterday.
> Don was working for the telephone company when I met him.

Time adverbials that are often used with this meaning of the past progressive include adverb clauses of time with *when* and adverbs of specific past time (*at noon, yesterday, in 1988*).

Past duration: The past progressive is also used to emphasize the duration (length of time) of a past activity. Adverb expressions of time with *for* are common with this usage.

> Maggie was living in a hotel for months.
> Terry was working on his graduate degree for seven years.

8. Stative verbs: Some verbs are generally not used in progressive tenses because they indicate a continuing state of knowledge, perception, or condition rather than an activity. These are called stative verbs. Some of the most common stative verbs are the following:

believe	love	remember
belong	mean	see
hate	need	seem
have (= possess)	owe	think (= believe)
hear	own	understand
know	possess	want
like	prefer	

EXERCISE 5.1-C   CHECKING FORM (ORAL)

statements in the past progressive

Disagree with each statement, using the past progressive tense. Add an adverb clause of time with *when I saw.*

> **Example:** I don't think that Kathy walked downtown yesterday.
> *You're wrong. She was walking downtown when I saw her.*

1. I don't think that Fred and Ethel talked to each other yesterday.

2. I think that Ricky worked hard yesterday.

3. I don't think that Joan spoke to anyone yesterday.

4. I think that Lucy enjoyed the performance yesterday.

5. I don't think that the teachers disagreed with each other yesterday.

EXERCISE 5.1-D   EXPRESSING YOUR OWN IDEAS

the past progressive

Answer each question with a full statement, using the past progressive tense.

1. What were you doing last night around 8:00 P.M.?

2. Who were you talking with earlier today?

3. Where were you going when I saw you before class?

4. Where were you living last year?

5. What were you doing before class today?

QUESTIONS IN PROGRESSIVE TENSES

	The technicians are assembling the new equipment now.
Yes-No Question:	**G.** **Are** the technicians **assembling** the new equipment now? Yes, they are. (No, they aren't.)
WH Questions:	**H.** **Who is assembling** the new equipment now? The technicians.
	I. **What are** the technicians **assembling** now? The new equipment.
	J. **What are** the technicians **doing** now? Assembling the new equipment.
	Ms. Anker was reading the newspaper at noon.
Yes-No Question:	**K.** **Was** she **reading** the newspaper at noon? Yes, she was. (No, she wasn't.)
WH Questions:	**L.** **Who was reading** the newspaper at noon? Ms. Anker.
	M. **What was** Ms. Anker **reading** at noon? The newspaper.
	N. **What was** Ms. Anker **doing** at noon? Reading the newspaper.

---

9. Yes-no questions: To form yes-no questions with progressive tenses, move the BE auxiliary to the beginning of the sentence, as in sentences G and K. Do not add the DO auxiliary.

Correct	*Incorrect*
Were you studying all last night?	Did you studying all last night?

10. WH questions: Subject focus WH questions are made by placing the WH word in the subject position, as in sentences H and L.

Predicate focus WH questions are formed by placing the WH word at the beginning of the sentence and moving the BE auxiliary in front of the subject, as in sentences I and M.

Correct	*Incorrect*
What was she reading?	What she was reading?

11. *What-do* **questions:** *What-do* questions are formed with the present participle form of DO—*doing*, as in sentences J and N.

> *What are* you *doing*?
> I'm assembling the new equipment.

12. **Tag questions:** Tag questions in progressive tenses are formed using the BE auxiliary in the question tag after the statement.

> The technicians are assembling the equipment now, *aren't* they?
> Ms. Anker wasn't reading the newspaper, *was* she?

EXERCISE 5.1-E   CHECKING FORM (ORAL)

WH questions in the progressive

Ask the question indicated by the WH word that is provided.

> **Example:** Howard was studying for his exam last night. (when)
> *When was he studying for his exam?*

1. Jack is changing his mind. (who)

2. The Porters were driving to Cincinnati yesterday. (where)

3. Fred was traveling to New York by car. (how)

4. Diane is writing the report now because she won't have time later. (why)

5. John and Susan were walking to Ives Hall earlier today. (where)

6. The furnace is making all that noise. (what)

7. Ted is reading Brian's notes. (whose)

8. Sam was using the new typewriter yesterday. (which)

EXERCISE 5.1-F   FORMING QUESTIONS AND NEGATIVES

the present progressive and the past progressive

Change each statement on page 116 to the negative form or to a question form, as indicated. If the instructions specify a WH question, form the question so that the underlined words will provide the answer.

> **Examples:** They are coming now. (yes-no question)
> *Are they coming now?*
>
> She was reading the newspaper. (WH question)
> *What was she reading?*

1. Bob and Eric were trying to understand <u>Johnson's</u> article for their assignment. (WH question)

   _____

2. They are researching their project <u>by reading all the old manuscripts</u>. (WH question)

   _____

3. They are finding a lot of information on their topic. (negative statement)

   _____

4. Some other students are investigating the same topic. (yes-no question)

   _____

5. <u>The librarian</u> is helping them find materials in the archives. (WH question)

   _____

6. They were <u>looking for information</u> incorrectly. (WH question)

   _____

7. Their instructor is giving them <u>three more weeks</u> to complete their project. (WH question)

   _____

EXERCISE 5.1-G   DISCRIMINATING TENSES

simple and progressive tenses in the present and in the past

Fill in each blank with an appropriate form of the verb in parentheses. Use the simple present, the simple past, the present progressive, or the past progressive. In some cases there may be more than one possibility.

Feb. 3.
past → past progressive
present → present "

1. The film that we _____ (*watch*) now _____ (*show*) the destruction that a major earthquake _____ (*cause*).

2. It _____ (BE, negative) essential for you to come to the meeting today, but I _____ (*expect*) you to come to yesterday's meeting. Everyone _____ (*wonder*) what was wrong when you _____ (*arrive*, negative).

3. Monica _____ (*try*) to call Mr. Samuels before class last Monday, but no one _____ (*answer*) the phone. Perhaps he _____ (*walk*) to class at that time. He _____ (*like*, negative) to be late, so he sometimes _____ (*leave*) for class earlier than necessary.

4. We _____ (*plan*, negative) to go out tonight. It _____ (*snow*) now, and the temperature _____ (*drop*) fast. We _____ (*think*, negative) that you should go out, either.

5. The actors _____ (*prepare*) for the performance when we arrived at six last night. They _____ (*say*, negative) anything to us, but we _____ (*knew*) that they _____ (BE) behind schedule. I _____ (*hope*) that they _____ (*have*, negative) the same problem now. It _____ (*get*) late, and the audience will arrive soon.

6. The new administration _____ (*increase*) taxes substantially last year, but it _____ (*propose*, negative) any new increase at the present time. Most voters _____ (*oppose*) the idea of higher taxes whenever the subject is mentioned, so with a new election coming soon, the administration _____ (*want*, negative) to cause any controversy.

EXERCISE 5.1-H   COMPLETING SENTENCES

the present progressive and the past progressive

Using your own ideas, complete each sentence in the present progressive tense.

1. I _____ at this moment.

2. The students in this class _____ right now.

3. I think my parents _____ this minute.

4. The world economic situation _____ now.

5. The superpowers _____ lately.

Using your own ideas, complete each sentence in the past progressive tense.

6. Some of my friends _____ last night.

7. Our English instructor _____ all week.

8. I _____ last September.

9. _____ when we arrived.

10. _____ for several years.

EXERCISE 5.1-I   RESPONDING TO INFORMATION

the present progressive

Each sentence on page 118 gives you information about a future activity. What do you think is probably happening *now*?

Example: John has a test tomorrow.
He is probably studying for the test now.

1. The Porters leave for the airport in half an hour.

   _____

2. Mary and Janet will eat dinner in just a few minutes.

   _____

3. The theater troupe gives its first performance of a new play tonight.

   _____

4. The president makes his State of the Union address next week.

   _____

5. Susan needs to hand in her term paper tomorrow.

   _____

SECTION 5.2 Adverbial Clauses of Time

· ·

ADVERBIAL CLAUSES OF TIME
A. Bob and Janet were arguing **when I saw them yesterday**.
B. They stopped **as soon as they saw me coming**.
C. But they probably continued **after I left**.

1. Adverbial clauses of time: Sentences A, B, and C contain adverbial clauses of time. Remember that adverbial clauses are dependent clauses, so they must be attached to a main, or independent, clause.

Main Clause	*Adverbial Clause*
Bob and Janet were arguing	when I saw them yesterday.
They stopped	as soon as they saw me coming.
But they probably continued	after I left.

2. Forming adverbial clauses of time: Adverbial clauses of time begin with an adverbial subordinator, a word such as *when, while, as soon as, before,* or *after*. The adverbial subordinator indicates the time relationship between the two clauses. The adverbial subordinator must be followed by a subject and a predicate. What are the adverbial subordinators in sentences A, B, and C?

3. The placement of adverbial clauses of time: In sentences A, B, and C, the adverbial clauses have been placed after the main clause. When this is the case, no punctuation is needed except, of course, the period at the end of the sentence. Adverbial clauses can also be placed at the beginning of the sentence. When this is the case, a comma usually follows the adverbial clause.

When I saw Bob and Janet yesterday, they were arguing.
As soon as they saw me coming, they stopped.
But after I left, they probably continued.

EXERCISE 5.2-A   CHECKING FORM (ORAL)

moving adverbial clauses of time

Move the adverbial clause of time to the beginning of the sentence.

Example: We left as soon as the movie was over.
As soon as the movie was over, we left.

1. The students began to talk after class was over.

2. Donald paid his bills before he left for vacation.

3. Mr. Jennings gave us the information as soon as he found it.

4. Debbie was living in California when she got married.

5. Barbara and Diane looked away when they saw me.

6. We usually order fish when we go to this restaurant.

CO–OCCURRING ACTIVITIES OF DIFFERENT DURATION
(*Page 120*)

D.   The class was discussing a film **when** I arrived.

E.   I arrived { **while** / **when** } the class was discussing a film.

F.   Jeannette is usually working **when** I call.

G.   I usually call { **while** / **when** } Jeannette is working.

4. Co-occurring activities of different duration: The subordinators *when* and *while* can be used to show that a shorter activity takes place during another, longer activity. The longer activity begins earlier and is in progress when the shorter activity begins. A progressive tense is used for the longer activity, and a simple tense is used for the shorter activity. *When* can be used before either the shorter activity or the longer activity. *While* can be used only before the longer activity. (See the box on page 119.)

Situation: The class discussed a film from 9:00 to 9:45. I arrived at 9:30.
The class was discussing a film *when I arrived.*
I arrived *while the class was discussing a film.*
I arrived *when the class was discussing a film.*

EXERCISE 5.2-B   CHECKING FORM (ORAL)

when versus while

Restate each sentence, using *while* instead of *when*, as in the example.

Example: When I heard your voice, I was working in the equipment room.
I heard your voice while I was working in the equipment room.

1.   When the electricity went out, we were making dinner.

2.   When the fire alarm sounded, students were changing classes.

3.   When Philip called, I was doing my grammar assignment.

4.   When it started to rain last night, we were waiting for a taxi.

5.   When I wrote these letters, I was listening to Professor Sander's lecture.

EXERCISE 5.2-C   COMBINING SENTENCES (ORAL)

co-occurring activities of different duration

Read each situation; then create a sentence with *when* or *while* that will relate the two events. More than one solution may be possible.

Examples: The thunderstorm started at 2:00.
The children played outside from 1:30 to 2:10.
When the thunderstorm started, the children were playing outside.
The thunderstorm started while the children were playing outside.

1.   Janet and I studied in the library from 7:00 to 11:00 last night.
At 9:00 we saw Professor Hansen.

2. Harry takes a break between 10:00 and 10:30 every day.
I try to call him at 10:15.

3. Students work on their term papers during the last three weeks of the term.
Professor Swanson meets with students individually during that time.

4. The tornado struck at 5:00.
Many people drove home between 4:00 and 6:00.

5. We heard the good news on July 15.
We took a vacation in California during the month of July.

CO–OCCURRING ACTIVITIES OF SIMILAR DURATION
H.   We ate dinner **while** we watched the news.
I.   We were eating dinner **while** we were watching the news.
J.   We often eat dinner **while** we watch the news.
K.   We often eat dinner **when** we watch the news.

5. Co-occurring activities of similar duration: *When* and *while* can also be used to show that two activities of the same duration happen at the same time. One activity is not longer than the other. *While* shows this time relationship if the tenses of both clauses are the same (both are simple past, past progressive, or simple present), as in sentences H, I, and J. *When* can be used if both clauses are in the simple present tense, as in sentence K.

Situation: We ate dinner from 6:00 to 7:00. We watched the news from 6:00 to 7:00.
We *ate* dinner while we *watched* the news.
We *were eating* dinner while we *were watching* the news.

Situation: We eat dinner every day from 6:00 to 7:00. We watch the news every day from 6:00 to 7:00.
We often *eat* dinner while we *watch* the news.
We often *eat* dinner when we *watch* the news.

EXERCISE 5.2-D   COMBINING SENTENCES (ORAL)

co-occurring activities of similar duration

Read each situation on page 122; then create a sentence with *when* or *while* that will relate the two events. More than one solution may be possible.

Examples: Sam shopped for supplies from noon to 2:00.

John packed for their camping trip from noon to 2:00.

While Sam was shopping for supplies, John was packing for their trip.

While Sam shopped for supplies, John packed for their trip.

Sam was shopping for supplies while John was packing for their trip.

Sam shopped for supplies while John packed for their trip.

1. Michael and I cleaned the lab equipment from 9:00 to 11:00.
Anita and Liz wrote the lab report from 9:00 to 11:00.

2. Mr. Cooper watches television from 7:00 to 9:00 every evening.
His children do their homework from 7:00 to 9:00.

3. Mrs. Newman taught three classes yesterday morning.
Her colleagues attended a conference yesterday morning.

4. Jonathan daydreams from 10:00 to 11:00 every day.
He listens to his physics lecture from 10:00 to 11:00 every day.

5. My brother served in the army from 1985 to 1987.
I attended college from 1985 to 1987.

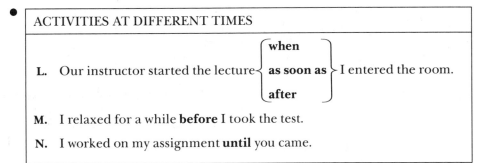

ACTIVITIES AT DIFFERENT TIMES

L. Our instructor started the lecture ⎰ **when** / **as soon as** / **after** ⎱ I entered the room.

M. I relaxed for a while **before** I took the test.

N. I worked on my assignment **until** you came.

---

6. Activities at different times: The subordinators *when, as soon as, after, before,* and *until* can be used to show that two activities happen at different times.

Before: The subordinator *before* is followed by a later event, as in sentence M.

  Situation: I relaxed from noon to 2:00. I took my test at 2:10.
I relaxed for a while *before I took my test.*
I was relaxing for a while *before I took my test.*

After: The subordinator *after* is followed by an earlier event, as in sentence L.

> *Situation:* I entered the room at 9:00. My instructor started the lecture
> at 9:10.
> My instructor started the lecture *after I entered the room.*

As soon as: The subordinator *as soon as* has the same meaning as *immediately after*.

> *Situation:* I entered the room at 9:10. My instructor started the lecture
> at 9:11.
> My instructor started the lecture *as soon as I entered the room.*

When: The subordinator *when* can be used to show that two activities happen at different times, but *only if* the verbs in both clauses are in the simple present tense or the simple past tense, as in sentence L. In this case, *when* has a meaning similar to *as soon as* or *immediately after*.

> *Situation:* I entered the room at 9:10. My instructor started the lecture
> at 9:11.
> My instructor started the lecture *when I entered the room.*
> My instructor started the lecture *as soon as I entered the room.*
> My instructor started the lecture *immediately after I entered the
> room.*

> *Situation:* John gets home at 10:00. He immediately turns on the lights.
> John turns on the lights *when he gets home.*
> John turns on the lights *as soon as he gets home.*
> John turns on the lights *immediately after he gets home.*

Notice the difference in the meaning of *when*, depending on the tenses used.

> Eric was cooking dinner when I got home. (He started cooking before I got
> home.)
> Eric cooked dinner when I got home. (He started cooking after I got home.)

Until: The subordinator *until* is used if an earlier activity continues up to the time that another activity begins, as in sentence N. The earlier activity then stops.

> *Situation:* I worked on my assignment from 5:00 to 8:00. You came to see
> me at 8:00.
> I was working on my assignment *until you came.*

7. Asking questions with adverbial clauses of time: When a complex sentence with an adverbial clause of time is made into a question, the main clause is transformed into the question. The adverb clause remains unchanged.

> Howard relaxed for a while before he took the test.
> Did he relax for a while before he took the test?
> What did he do before he took the test?

EXERCISE 5.2-E   COMBINING SENTENCES (ORAL)

activities at different times

Read each situation; then create a sentence with *before*, *after*, *as soon as*, *until*, *while*, or *when* that will relate the two events. More than one solution may be possible.

1.   I get home from work at 6:00 P.M. every day.
     I usually start dinner right away.

2.   Michael phoned at 3:00.
     I tried to take a nap from 2:00 to 5:00.

3.   Janet finishes her assignments after supper every evening.
     Then she goes out with her friends.

4.   I study from 4:00 to 6:30 every evening.
     The news comes on television at 6:30, so I stop studying.

5.   The Jacksons vacationed by the ocean during August.
     Their neighbors looked after the Jackson's house during August.

6.   We arrived in Cincinnati at 7:30.
     At 7:35 we checked into our hotel.

EXERCISE 5.2-F   ANSWERING QUESTIONS (ORAL)

adverbial clauses of time

Answer each question, using an adverbial clause of time with *when*, *while*, *before*, *after*, or *as soon as*. You might want to modify the adverbial subordinator to an expression such as *right after*, *a little before*, or *shortly after*.

> **Example:** Did you see your friends yesterday? When?
> *I saw them while/when I was walking to class.*
> *I saw them a little before class started.*

1.   Did you have a cup of coffee yesterday? When?

2.   When do you usually eat breakfast?

3.   When do you study English every day?

4.   When did you last write to your family?

5.   When was the last time that you were upset?

6.   Did you call your friends last night? When?

7.   When did you come to this school?

8.   When are you sometimes tired?

EXERCISE 5.2-G   EXPRESSING YOUR OWN IDEAS (ORAL)

adverbial clauses with *until*

Answer each question with a sentence containing an adverbial clause using *until*.

> **Example:** How long did you study last night?
> *I studied until you called me.*

1.   How long did you watch television yesterday?

2.   How long did you wait at the bus stop?

3.   How long did you stay at the library?

4.   How long do you work on your assignments in the evening?

5.   How long did you sit in the restaurant yesterday?

6.   How long do you study on weekends?

EXERCISE 5.2-H   EXPRESSING YOUR OWN IDEAS (ORAL)

adverbial clauses of time

Answer each question with a complete sentence. Place the adverbial clause at the beginning of your answer.

> **Example:** What were you doing when your friend called yesterday?
> *When my friend called, I was watching television.*

1.   What do you do when a friend stops by unexpectedly?

2.   What did you do after class finished yesterday?

3.   What were you doing when the electricity went out last night?

4.   What do you usually do before you have a test?

5.   What do you do until class begins?

6.   What do you do as soon as classes are over on Friday?

7.   What were you doing while you were eating breakfast this morning?

EXERCISE 5.2-I   DISCRIMINATING SUBORDINATORS

adverbial subordinators of time

Fill in each blank on page 126 with an appropriate adverbial subordinator of time. There may be more than one possibility in some cases.

1. The instructor announced the exam _____ class ended on Friday. _____ the students heard about it, they started to protest.

2. _____ you spoke to me earlier, I was thinking about all the work that I have to do next week. I would like to complete some of my assignments _____ we go to the movie so that I won't be worrying the whole time.

3. We were arguing about finding a good topic _____ you made your suggestion. _____ you leave this afternoon, let's discuss it further.

4. _____ the city condemned these buildings, the residents in adjoining neighborhoods began to complain. They won't be happy _____ the city is willing to listen to their ideas.

5. Howard was shocked _____ he heard the bad news. _____ he realized how bad the situation was, he called some friends to get their reactions. Then he fixed himself something to eat _____ he listened to the radio for further information.

6. The audience applauded enthusiastically _____ the curtain was drawn. _____ the actors came out to take another bow, the audience cheered even more loudly.

7. We tried to assemble Jane's new bicycle _____ it was delivered, but _____ we were working on it, we realized that several necessary pieces were missing.

EXERCISE 5.2-J   MAKING PHRASES INTO SENTENCES

adverbial clauses of time

Make complete sentences from the words and phrases given. Each sentence should have an adverbial clause of time. Add an appropriate adverbial subordinator where you see an X, and choose verb tenses that will make your sentence meaningful. More than one adverbial subordinator may be possible.

> **Example:** I – plan – study – tonight // X – I – know – all the material – perfectly
> *I plan to study tonight until I know all the material perfectly.*

1. they – BE – ready – go – yesterday // X – their car – break down

_____

_____

2. we – want (negative) – leave – tonight / / X – the party – BE – over

_____

_____

3. the new governor – raise – taxes / / X – he – take – office – last month

_____

_____

4. we – continue – swim – yesterday / / X – it – get – dark

_____

_____

5. Martha – hear – her friend – laugh / / X – she – leave – the room – this morning

_____

_____

6. Gary – tell – us – stop – fight / / X – he – see – us – argue – last night

_____

_____

7. I hope – drive – to New York / / X – I – finish – my last exam – this afternoon

_____

_____

EXERCISE 5.2-K   COMPLETING SENTENCES

adverbial clauses of time

Complete each sentence with your own ideas.

1. Before I begin to write a paper, _____

_____

2. As soon as I heard the bad news, _____

_____

3. I called my friends when _____

_____

4. In the evenings, I usually study until _____

_____

5. People seem to get angry when _____

_____

EXERCISE 5.2-L   EXPRESSING YOUR OWN IDEAS

adverbial clauses of time

Team up with a classmate for this exercise. Both you and your classmate should consider what you normally do on a typical Wednesday. Write a schedule of activities for your classmate. Here is an example:

7:00	Wake up; get dressed
7:30–8:00	Eat breakfast; read the newspaper
8:00–9:00	Commute to school
9:00–11:00	Attend English classes
11:00–3:00	Work as a cashier in the cafeteria
1:00	Grab a sandwich for lunch
3:00–4:30	Attend English classes
5:00–6:00	Commute home on the bus; try to do assignments on the bus

Based on the schedule that you have created for your classmate, write sentences that express time relationships about different activities. Each sentence should contain an adverbial clause of time. Try to vary the adverbial time subordinators (*when, while, before, after, until, as soon as*).

> *Chris gets dressed before he eats breakfast.*
> *He usually reads the newspaper while he eats.*
> *After he commutes to school, he attends English classes for two hours.*
> *He often grabs a sandwich for lunch while he is working as a cashier in the cafeteria between 11:00 and 3:00.*

EXERCISE 5.2-M   RESPONDING TO INFORMATION

adverbial clauses of time

Examine the list of facts about the rise and fall of ancient Egypt. Construct sentences which express time relationships between various events. Each sentence should contain an adverbial clause of time. Try to vary the adverbial time subordinators (*when, while, before, after, until, as soon as*). The first three sentences have been started for you (see page 129).

c. 3100 B.C.	Menes unifies Upper Egypt and Lower Egypt; the Egyptians invent hieroglyphic writing
c. 2650	Imhotep builds the Step Pyramid at Sakkare
c. 2560	Workers begin construction of the Giza pyramids and the Sphinx
2181	End of the Old Kingdom; papyrus already in use
1786	Invasions from the east; the Middle Kingdom collapses
1567	The Egyptians repulse invaders and establish the New Kingdom

c. 1450	The Egyptian Empire extends from the Sudan to Syria
1200–1100	The Libyans invade Egypt; the pharaohs' powers decline
c. 940	Libyan kings reunite Egypt
525	The Persian Empire absorbs Egypt
404	Egypt restores its independence
332	Alexander the Great conquers Egypt
285	Ptolemy II comes to the throne; he quickly begins to make Alexandria the center of Greek culture
c. 50	Cleopatra secures the throne
c. 30	Cleopatra commits suicide; Egypt becomes a province of the Roman Empire

Example: *Imhotep built the Step Pyramid 450 years after Menes unified Upper Egypt and Lower Egypt.*

1. Workers began construction of the Giza pyramids and the Sphinx one hundred years after _____

   _____

2. Papyrus was already in use in Egypt when _____

   _____

3. Approximately 200 years before the Egyptians established the New Kingdom, ___

   _____

4. _____

   _____

5. _____

   _____

6. _____

   _____

7. _____

   _____

8. _____

   _____

SECTION 5.3   More Adverbial Expressions of Time

1. Reduced adverbial phrases: It is possible to reduce an adverbial clause of time to a phrase. Omit the subject and use the present participle (*Ving*) form of the verb, as in sentences A through D in the box on page 130.

REDUCED ADVERBIAL PHRASES

A.   We finally got a table in our favorite restaurant *after* **waiting for an hour**.

B.   You need to proofread your paper *before* **giving it to the instructor**.

C.   I like to study *while* **listening to the radio**.

D.   He always points out places of interest *when* **giving a tour of the city**.

E.   She lived in London *prior to* **coming to the United States**.

The full form of sentence A is: "We finally got a table at our favorite restaurant *after we waited for an hour*." The full form of sentence B is: "You need to proofread your paper *before you give it to the instructor*."

In order to reduce an adverb clause to a phrase, the subject of both clauses must be the same. Look what happens when the subjects are not the same.

Full Form:

The waiter led us to a table *after we waited for an hour*. (We waited for an hour.)

Reduced Form:

The waiter led us to a table *after waiting for an hour*. (The waiter waited for an hour.)

Adverbial clauses with the subordinators *after, before, while,* and *when* can be reduced to phrases in this manner. In addition, a phrase with the present participle form of the verb (*Ving*) can follow *prior to*, as in sentence E. *Prior to* means *before*. It cannot act as an adverbial subordinator and be followed by a complete clause.

Correct	*Incorrect*
He lived here prior to moving.	He lived here prior to he moved.

2. Prepositional phrases of time: The subordinators *after, before,* and *until* can function as prepositions of time, as in sentences F, G, and H on page 131. They are followed by a noun or a noun phrase, with no verb form. *During, for,* and *prior to* can also function in a similar manner.

During must be followed by a period of time.

> I want to go to Mexico during the summer break.
> Anthony became ill during the night.

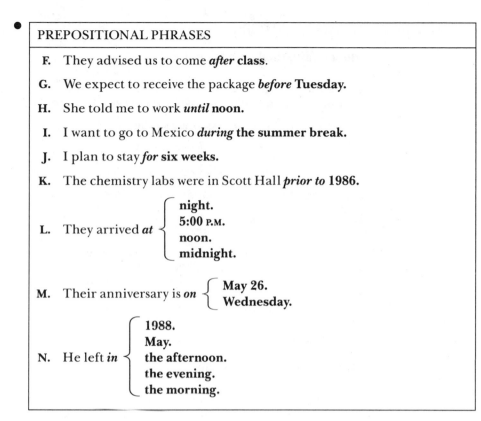

PREPOSITIONAL PHRASES

F. They advised us to come *after* **class.**

G. We expect to receive the package *before* **Tuesday.**

H. She told me to work *until* **noon.**

I. I want to go to Mexico *during* **the summer break.**

J. I plan to stay *for* **six weeks.**

K. The chemistry labs were in Scott Hall *prior to* **1986.**

L. They arrived *at* {
 night.
 5:00 P.M.
 noon.
 midnight.

M. Their anniversary is *on* {
 May 26.
 Wednesday.

N. He left *in* {
 1988.
 May.
 the afternoon.
 the evening.
 the morning.

For is followed by a length of time (usually measured in units, such as days, hours, or years).

> I plan to stay for six weeks.
> Amanda studied for several hours last night.

Prior to is followed by a point in time.

> The chemistry labs were in Scott Hall prior to 1986.
> No books purchased prior to September 15 can be returned.

The prepositions *at*, *on*, and *in* are frequently used to indicate time.

At is generally followed by a specific point in time, such as *5:00 P.M.*, or by the expressions *noon*, *night*, and *midnight*, as in sentence L.

On can be followed by a day of the week or by a specific date (month and day), as in sentence M.

In is followed by a year, a month (without a day), and expressions like *the afternoon* and *the evening*, as in sentence N.

EXERCISE 5.3-A   CHECKING FORM (ORAL)

reduced adverbial phrases of time

Reduce the adverbial clause of time to a phrase by omitting the subject and changing the verb to the present participle form.

> **Example:** We left after we finished the exam.
> *We left after finishing the exam.*

1. He gave me the book before he went on his trip.

2. She relaxed after she completed the assignment.

3. We usually listen to music while we study.
We usually listen to music while studying.

4. He uses a word processor when he writes a paper.
He uses a word processor when writing a paper.

5. They often go out to eat after they teach their last class.
They often go out to eat after teaching their last class.

6. I get very nervous before I take a test.
I get very nervous before taking a test.

EXERCISE 5.3-B   CHECKING FORM (ORAL)

prepositional phrases of time

Beginning with the first sentence in each column, change the sentence by substituting the phrase given. You will have to change the preposition of time also.

> **Examples:** 1. They received the message on June 3.
>   2. September
>   *They received the message in September.*
>   3. 7:00 A.M.
>   *They received the message at 7:00 A.M.*

1. We heard the news at night.	10. I read the report.
2. the afternoon	11. 1987
3. February 1	12. Friday
4. Tuesday	13. night
5. January	14. several hours
6. noon	15. our lunch hour
7. our vacation	16. October 30
8. 8:00 P.M.	17. a few minutes
9. class	18. the morning

EXERCISE 5.3-C   REDUCING CLAUSES

adverbial phrases of time

Reduce the adverbial clause of time in each sentence by omitting the subject and changing the verb to the present participle. Do not reduce a clause if its meaning would change.

> **Example:** After we drove for an hour, we finally decided that we were lost.
> *After driving for an hour, we finally decided that we were lost.*

1.   When you do this type of exercise, you need to look at the subject carefully.

   _____

   _____

2.   They gave me the answers before I left class.

   _____

   _____

3.   The city developed a lot of new housing before it ran out of money.

   _____

   _____

4.   While we were writing the specifications for the new lab, our consultant gave us some important information.

   _____

   _____

5.   After the hurricane destroyed several coastal towns, it turned east toward the mainland.

   _____

   _____

6.   Ryan continued spending money even after his parents warned him not to.

   _____

   _____

EXERCISE 5.3-D   DISCRIMINATING PREPOSITIONS

prepositions in time expressions

Fill in each blank with an appropriate preposition or adverbial subordinator.

1.   We worked _____ the test was over _____ 3:00 P.M.

2. Ed planned to stay _____ one month, but now it looks like he will have to leave _____ May.

3. I enjoy watching the news on television _____ eating dinner, especially _____ the weekend.

4. Last night, we watched a movie _____ midnight, but then we decided it was time to go to bed.

5. Howard's birthday is _____ April 7, which is _____ the most beautiful part of spring.

6. We need to talk _____ a few minutes _____ you leave this afternoon.

7. _____ 1987, we always vacationed at the ocean _____ the summer. Now we go to the mountains.

EXERCISE 5.3-E   CORRECTING ERRORS

expressions of time

Each sentence has one or more errors. Find the mistakes and correct them.

1. Prior to he came last night, we were studying.

_____

2. The children were playing while I arrived.

_____

3. My boss gave me the report as soon as having it.

_____

4. Professor Roper taught during two months at the winter.

_____

5. Kathy relaxed in an hour before she took the test.

_____

6. Sam and George got out of the car when overheating.

_____

7. We asked the instructor for an explanation while the class.

_____

6 Future Time

This chapter examines several ways to express future time in English, first with *will* and the expression BE *going to* and then with the present progressive tense and the simple present tense. Clauses of future time are discussed in the third section. The placement of direct objects and indirect objects is the focus of the final section of this chapter.

SECTION 6.1   Future Time with *Will* and BE *Going To*

SECTION 6.2   Future Time with Other Verb Constructions

SECTION 6.3   Clauses of Time in the Future

SECTION 6.4   Direct Objects and Indirect Objects

SECTION 6.1   Future Time with *Will* and BE *Going To*

FUTURE TIME WITH *WILL* (*See page 136.*)		
Statements:	**A.**	Professor Jameson **will introduce** a new topic in class tomorrow.
	B.	She **will not spend** any more time on this topic.
Questions:	**C.**	**Will** she **introduce** a new topic in class tomorrow? Yes, she will. (No, she will not.)
	D.	**Who will introduce** a new topic in class tomorrow? Professor Jameson.
	E.	**What will** Professor Jameson **introduce** in class tomorrow? A new topic.
	F.	**What will** Professor Jameson **do** in class tomorrow? Introduce a new topic.

1. Future time with *will*:   Future time can be expressed with *will*, as in sentences A and B on page 135. *Will* is followed by the simple form of the verb. Do not add the third person singular ending *-s* or *-es* to the main verb. Do not place the word *to* between *will* and the main verb.

Correct	*Incorrect*
Beth will bring the book tonight.	Beth will brings the book tonight.
	Beth will to bring the book tonight.

2. Negative statements: To make a statement with *will* negative, simply place *not* between *will* and the simple verb, as in sentence B. *Will not* is often contracted to *won't*.

> She *will not spend* any more time on this topic. (She *won't* spend any more time on it.)
> Beth *will not bring* the book tonight. (She *won't* bring it.)

3. Yes-no questions: To ask a yes-no question, move *will* to the beginning of the sentence, as in sentence C. *Will* acts as the auxiliary of the main verb, so the DO auxiliary is not used.

Correct	*Incorrect*
Will she introduce a new topic?	Does she will introduce a new topic?

Short answers to yes-no questions use *will*.

> Will Beth bring the book tonight?
>   Yes, she *will*.
>   No, she *will not*. (No, she *won't*.)

4. WH questions: To make a subject focus WH question, substitute the WH question word for the subject, as in sentence D.

> *Professor Jameson* will introduce a new topic tomorrow.
>   *Who* will introduce a new topic tomorrow?

To make a predicate focus WH question, place the WH word at the beginning of the sentence, and move *will* before the subject, as in sentence E.

> Bob will meet us *in front of Gordy Hall* this evening.
> *Where* will Bob meet us this evening?

How are *what-do* questions formed with *will*? Study sentence F, and then state the rule.

5. Tag questions: To make a tag question, use *will* in the question tag.

> The store will be open until nine o'clock tonight, *won't it?*
> Emily won't pass the course, *will she?*

6. Contractions: Contractions with *will* are common, especially in conversation.

I will	=	I'll	will not	=	won't
you will	=	you'll			
he will	=	he'll			
she will	=	she'll			
we will	=	we'll			
they will	=	they'll			

In conversation, it is also common to use a spoken contraction with subjects other than pronouns, although this is considered too informal for most writing.

Mary will help. = Mary'll help.

Shall is occasionally used in American English to emphasize the speaker's determination to do something.

We shall succeed. (Nothing will get in our way!)

EXERCISE 6.1-A   CHECKING FORM (ORAL)

future time with *will*

Change each statement to the future with *will*. Use the adverb of time *tomorrow*.

Example: He goes there every day.
He will go there tomorrow.

1. She walks to school every day.

2. They ride the bus every day.

3. He doesn't come to class every day.

4. We don't complete the assignments every day.

5. I fix my own breakfast every day.

6. They read the newspaper every day.

FUTURE TIME WITH *BE GOING TO*		
Statements:	**G.**	Ryan's classmates **are going to meet** at the library tonight.
	H.	They **are not going to meet** in Mount Hall.
Questions:	**I.**	**Are** they **going to meet** at the library tonight? Yes, they are. (No, they aren't.)
	J.	**Who is going to meet** at the library tonight? Ryan's classmates.
	K.	**Where are** Ryan's classmates **going to meet** tonight? At the library.
	L.	**What are** Ryan's classmates **going to do** tonight? Meet at the library.

7. Future time with BE *going to***:**   The expression BE *going to* also expresses future events. It is followed by the simple form of the verb, as in sentence G.

8. Negatives and questions: BE acts as the auxiliary in sentences with BE *going to*. How are negative sentences made? (See sentence H.) How are yes-no questions formed? (See sentence I.) How are WH questions constructed? (See sentences J, K, and L.) How should a tag question be formed?

9. Using BE *going to***:**   Be *going to* is frequently used in conversation, less frequently in formal writing. In speech, the words *going to* are sometimes reduced so that they sound more like "gonna." When writing, be careful to use the full form, *going to.*

10. *Go* + **Verb:**   The verb *go* is often followed by a gerund (*Ving*) to express certain activities. Do not confuse this use with BE *going to* for future meaning.

> We go camping every weekend in the summer.

EXERCISE 6.1-B   CHECKING FORM (ORAL)

BE *going to* **to indicate the future**

Change each statement to the future with BE *going to*. Use the adverb of time *next week*.

> **Example:** We often study together.
> *We are going to study together next week.*

1. We often call him.

2. They often remind him to come.

3. She doesn't usually drive there by herself.

4. I don't often attend the meetings.

5. We frequently let him come with us.

6. He often has us do his work for him.

THE FUTURE PROGRESSIVE
M.   The actors **will be rehearsing** at 8:00 this evening.
N.   They **will not be giving** a real performance.

---

11. The future progressive: The future with *will* can be made progressive, as in sentence M. The modal *will* is followed by *be* and the main verb in its present participle (*Ving*) form. The future progressive emphasizes continuing action or duration at a point of time in the future.

> I'*ll be studing* in the library at 3:00 tomorrow.
> We'*ll be vacationing* in Europe in June.

Notice that the future progressive tense has two auxiliaries in front of the main verb, *will* and *be*. The first auxiliary is used in making negatives and questions. Try making different types of questions from sentence M.

EXERCISE 6.1-C   CHECKING FORM (ORAL)

the future progressive

Change each statement to the future progressive. Use *at midnight* as the adverb of time. Add the adverb *still* to show that there will be no change in activity from now until midnight.

> **Example:** He is working now.
> *He will still be working at midnight.*

1. They are meeting now.

2. He is talking with his friends now.

3. We are repairing the equipment now.

4. She is practicing now.

5. I'm studying now.

6. They are rehearsing the play now.

7. We are checking the machinery now.

EXERCISE 6.1-D   ASKING QUESTIONS (ORAL)

future time

Ask the question necessary to get more information, as in the example.

> **Example:** George is going to help. (who)
> *Who is going to help?*

1. Jason will pay the bill. (who)

2. They are going to go to Cleveland tonight. (where)

3. Roberta will finish the job with Bob's help. (how)

4. Janet is going to clean up after the party. (who)

5. Jack will be coming here at 8:00 P.M. (when)

6. Sandy and Jim will talk about their research project tomorrow. (what)

7. You are going to read John's notes. (whose)

8. Bev will be trying again tomorrow. (when)

EXERCISE 6.1-E   EXPRESSING YOUR OWN IDEAS (ORAL)

future time

Answer each question, using the same tense as in the question.

1. What will you be doing at 8:00 tonight?

2. Will you continue studying English next term?

3. Where are you going to go after class?

4. What will you do this weekend?

5. Where are you going to go on your next vacation?

6. When are you going to invite me to dinner?

7. Who will answer the next question?

EXERCISE 6.1-F   FOCUSING ON THE VERB

future time

Fill in each blank with the correct form of the verb in parentheses. Use *will*, BE *going to*, or the future progressive, as indicated.

1. Tonight, we _____ (*see*, BE *going to*, negative) a movie as we had planned to earlier. Instead, we _____ (*visit, will*) some friends of ours who just moved back to town. We _____ (*return*, future progressive) home about 11:00 P.M.

2. The architects _____ (*finish, will*, negative) the plans for the new building until next year, but construction _____ (*begin*, BE *going to*) immediately thereafter. A year and a half from now, the steel framework _____ (*rise*, future progressive). We _____ (*move, will*) our offices into the new building as soon as it's completed.

3. I _____ (*work*, future progressive) when you arrive this afternoon, so please go in and make yourself comfortable. I _____ (*get, will*) home at about 6:00 P.M. A few other friends _____ (*join*, future progressive) us for dinner.

4. The school _____ (*try*, BE *going to*) to raise money to build a new library because the present one _____ (BE, *will*, negative) large enough in a few years. The administration _____ (*use*, BE *going to*) the old building when the new one is finished.

5. The university press _____ (*publish*, future progressive) Wilson's book at this time next year. I know that it's a novel set in the future, but he _____ (*tell, will*, negative) me anything more about it.

EXERCISE 6.1-G   FORMING NEGATIVES AND QUESTIONS

future time

Change each statement on page 142 to the negative or a question form, as specified. If a WH question is indicated, form it so that the underlined words answer the question.

> **Examples:** They are going to sell their old car. (WH question)
> *What are they going to sell?*

We will leave early tonight. (negative statement)
We won't leave early tonight.

1. The students in the other class will be making their presentations tomorrow. (WH question)

   _____

2. The new governor is going to cut expenditures by reducing welfare benefits. (WH question)

   _____

3. The students in the history class are going to go on a field trip. (WH question)

   _____

4. The new economic policy will be successful. (yes-no question)

   _____

5. The officers will be interviewing candidates for the job next week. (WH question)

   _____

6. Technology will solve all of our problems in the future. (negative statement)

   _____

7. Most of the students will come tonight. (tag question)

   _____

8. The new visiting professor is going to stay here for only a year. (WH question)

   _____

EXERCISE 6.1-H   MAKING PHRASES INTO SENTENCES

past, present, and future time

Make a complete statement from each group of words, phrases, and clauses. You may have to add a second subject. Use the verb tense indicated in parentheses. Then change the statement to the negative or question form, according to the instructions.

> **Example:** the students – want – leave – immediately (simple past tense)
> *The students wanted to leave immediately.*
> Change to a question with *who*.
> *Who wanted to leave immediately?*

1. they – expect – go – with us – yesterday (past progressive tense)

   _____

   Change to a question with *when*.

   _____

2. the reporters – need – get – the entire story – from you (simple present tense)

_____

Change to a negative statement.

_____

3. engineers – examine – the water line – later today (future progressive tense)

_____

Change to a _what-do_ question.

_____

4. Jonathan – want – read – the second article (simple past tense)

_____

Change to a question with _which_.

_____

5. the voters – dislike – hear – such radical ideas (future with _will_)

_____

Change to a tag question.

_____

6. the customers – see – the manager – about their complaints (future with BE _going to_)

_____

Change to a question with _who_. (predicate focus)

_____

7. they – encourage – attend – the meeting (simple past tense)

_____

Change to a yes-no question.

_____

EXERCISE 6.1-I   EXPRESSING YOUR OWN IDEAS

future time

A hundred years from now, cities will be very different from the ones we know today. What do you think the cities of the future will be like? Write sentences which make predictions about cities a century from now. Use the future (with _will_ or BE _going to_) or the future progressive.

> **Example:** Prediction about housing
> _In the city of the future, people will live underground in order to conserve energy._

1. Prediction about transportation

_____

_____

2. Prediction about food

_____

_____

3. Prediction about education

_____

_____

4. Prediction about health care

_____

_____

5. Prediction about climate control

_____

_____

6. Prediction about work or employment

_____

_____

SECTION 6.2   Future Time with Other Verb Constructions

Two other verb constructions are commonly used to indicate future activity. Read sentences A and B. Do you see that each expresses a future event?

FUTURE TIME
A.   We **are leaving** for Chicago tomorrow morning.
B.   Our plane **departs** at 7:00 A.M.

1. The present progressive for future time: The present progressive tense can be used to describe future activity, as in sentence A. An adverb of future time, such as _tomorrow morning_, is usually added. The present progressive is used when future events are _fixed_ or _certain_. It is often used with verbs of motion:

arrive	fly	sail
come	go	start
depart	head	stay
drive	leave	

Notice how the present progressive indicates future time in this sentence:

Emily and Sara are staying until Saturday.

2. The simple present for future time: The simple present tense can also be used to describe fixed future activity, as in sentence B. Again, an adverb of future time is generally added, and the future activity is considered certain or definite. Like the present progressive tense, the simple present tense is frequently used for future time with verbs of motion.

The boat sails at dawn tomorrow.
I fly to Chicago next week.

In addition, the verbs *plan*, *want*, and *intend* are generally used in the present tense, although they may refer to future situations.

We *plan* to leave tomorrow morning. (not *will plan*)
Nancy *wants* to visit Paris next summer. (not *will want*)
I *intend* to write my report sometime next week. (not *will intend*)

EXERCISE 6.2-A   CHECKING FORM (ORAL)

the present progressive for future time

Change each statement from the future with *will* to the future with the present progressive tense.

Example: I will go tonight.
I am going tonight.

1.   We'll meet John at 2:00.

2.   Jane and Alice won't start their classes until Monday.

3.   I'll arrive at 8:45 this evening.

4.   Amy will come home next Tuesday.

5.   We won't depart until noon.

6.   The ship will sail for Bermuda in one hour.

EXERCISE 6.2-B   CHECKING FORM (ORAL)

the simple present for future time

Answer each question on page 146 with the simple present tense. Use the adverb of time that is provided.

Example: Do you know when the plane is going to leave? (at 4:00 P.M.)
Yes, it leaves at 4:00 P.M.

1. Do you know when the train is going to arrive? (at noon)

2. Do you know when the meeting is going to start? (at 2:00 this afternoon)

3. Do you know when Sam is going to leave? (next Tuesday)

4. Do you know when the store is going to open? (in a few minutes)

5. Do you know when the mail is going to come? (around 4:00 P.M.)

6. Do you know when tomorrow's game is going to start? (at 1:00)

EXERCISE 6.2-C   ANSWERING QUESTIONS (ORAL)

future time

Answer each question, using the same verb construction as in the question.

1. What are you doing tonight?

2. When do you have your next exam?

3. When will you finish studying English?

4. When are you handing in your assignment?

5. Where are you going to go this weekend?

6. How are you getting home after class?

EXERCISE 6.2-D   FOCUSING ON THE VERB

future activity

Fill in each blank with the correct form of the verb given in parentheses. Use the verb construction that is indicated.

1. At 4:00 today the research team _____ (*announce*, present progressive) a major new project which they _____ (*conduct*, future progressive) over the next five years. The federal government _____ (*fund*, will) most of the project. The researchers _____ (*try*, BE *going to*) to obtain the rest of the money they need from private industry. They _____ (*meet*, simple present) with industrial leaders next Thursday.

2. When we have a better understanding of the relationship between culture and poverty in our society, we _____ (*begin*,

will) to address the problem more intelligently. More and more social scientists _____ (*study*, future progressive) this topic over the next few years. We _____ (*need*, simple present) to start making significant progress, so we must have stronger support from government agencies.

3. I _____ (*leave*, present progressive) for San Francisco in a few hours. My plane _____ (*depart*, simple present) at 4:30, so I _____ (*drive*, *will*) to the airport at 3:00. I _____ (*plan*, simple present) to check in at the ticket counter early because I have to pay for my ticket. The plane _____ (*arrive*, simple present) in San Francisco at about 6:00, and by 8:00 I _____ (*enjoy*, future progressive) big-city nightlife.

EXERCISE 6.2-E   RESPONDING TO INFORMATION

future activity

Imagine that you are going on a trip to New York City. Here is a partial itinerary that you have prepared. On page 148 write one or two sentences for each day on the itinerary, expressing future time with *will*, BE *going to*, the simple present, the present progressive, or the future progressive. You may be able to combine several ideas into one sentence. You will have to add specific information as indicated where you see parentheses.

December 10:	Depart from (name of your airport) at (time) Arrive at John F. Kennedy Airport at 8:00 P.M. Taxi to the Roosevelt Hotel Rest, prepare for next day
December 11:	Boat trip around Manhattan in morning Need to meet (person) at the Museum of Natural History at (time) Tour the museum until (time) Dinner at a restaurant with (person) and (person)
December 12:	Times Square, theater district, Empire State Building in morning Central Park in afternoon Broadway show in evening
December 13:	Museum of Modern Art in morning Visit old friend for lunch at Plaza restaurant Taxi to JFK at (time) Plane leaves at (time), arrive in (name of city) at (time)

1. December 10:

_____

_____

_____

2. December 11:

_____

_____

_____

3. December 12:

_____

_____

_____

4. December 13:

_____

_____

_____

EXERCISE 6.2-F   EXPRESSING YOUR OWN IDEAS

future activity

Work with one or two of your classmates to plan a four-day trip that you would like to take to another city. Create a day-by-day itinerary, as in Exercise 6.2-E. Then write a paragraph that describes your trip, using appropriate verb constructions to express future time (*will*, BE *going to*, the simple present, the present progressive, or the future progressive).

Itinerary

Day 1   _____

_____

_____

Day 2   _____

_____

_____

Day 3 _____

_____

_____

Day 4 _____

_____

_____

SECTION 6.3   Clauses of Time in the Future

· ·

ADVERBIAL CLAUSES FOR FUTURE ACTIVITY

A. The students will be setting up a lab assignment **when you observe them tomorrow.**

B. Please don't disturb them **while they are working.**

C. They will start the next unit **after they complete this experiment next week.**

D. They are to hand in their lab reports **as soon as they finish them.**

E. I am going to grade their reports **before they begin the next lab assignment.**

---

1. Adverbial clauses of future time: Adverbial clauses of time never use *will* or BE *going to* for future time, even when the activity in the clause is clearly in the future. Instead, the simple present or the present progressive is used, as in sentences A through E.

Most commonly, the simple present tense is used in a clause of future time. Examine sentence A. The adverbial clause *when you observe them tomorrow* clearly expresses future activity, but the simple present tense is used.

The present progressive tense can be used in a clause of future time to indicate duration of the activity. Look at sentence B. There are two future events. The present progressive has been used in the adverbial clause to show that working is the longer activity.

2. Future tense forms in the main clause: The main clause can be expressed in any of the future tense forms which we have examined so far. In sentence A, the main clause uses the future tense, *will be setting up*. What tenses or verb constructions are used in the main clauses of the other sample sentences?

EXERCISE 6.3-A   CHECKING FORM (ORAL)

adverbial clauses in future time

Expand the reduced adverbial time phrase in each sentence to a full adverbial clause, as in the example.

> **Example:** He will call us before leaving next month.
> *He will call us before he leaves next month.*

1. Pat will talk to us after working out the details this evening.

2. Sue will have to ask for permission before going.

3. We will discuss the matter while driving home.

4. They won't laugh when observing you.

5. Martha is going to ask you some questions before beginning to write.

6. We will notify you after considering your request.

EXERCISE 6.3-B   ANSWERING QUESTIONS (ORAL)

adverbial clauses in the future

Answer each question with a full sentence, using a future adverbial clause of time with *before, after, as soon as, until, when,* or *while.*

1. When are you going to leave today?

2. When will you study tonight?

3. How long are you going to study English?

4. When are you going to relax this term?

5. When will we have the next exam?

6. How long are you going to stay in (city)?

EXERCISE 6.3-C   DISCRIMINATING TENSES

choosing tenses for future time

Fill in each blank with an appropriate form of the verb in parentheses. More than one tense may be acceptable in some cases.

1. While the other students _____ (*work*) on
   their papers tomorrow, I _____ (*discuss*)
   my topic with the instructor.

2. I _____ (*take*) some aspirin and
   _____ (*go*) to bed as soon as I
   _____ (*get*) home tonight.

3. The university _____ (*begin*) construction on the new
   chemistry laboratory after _____ (*raise*) enough money
   for the project sometime next year.

4. Before _____ (*commit*) himself to the new
   job, Howard _____ (*think about*) how
   much time he has to spare for the additional responsibilities.

5. A construction crew _____ (*work*) in the
   building when you _____ (*come*) tomorrow, so you may have to use the side door.

6. We _____ (*interrupt*, negative) while you
   _____ (*present*) your plans later this afternoon.

EXERCISE 6.3-D RESTATING

clauses and phrases in future time

Combine each pair of sentences into one complex sentence with an adverbial clause of time. Choose an appropriate subordinator: *before, after, as soon
as, until, when,* or *while*. In some cases you may be able to reduce the
adverbial time clause to a phrase with the *-ing* form of the verb. There may
be more than one way to combine the sentences.

> **Example:** He is going to call me tonight.
> Then I will have the necessary information.
> *After he calls me tonight, I will have the necessary information.*

1. Ethel is going to go shopping. At the same time, we will be watching the movie.

   _____

   _____

2. Janet and Susan will keep working. Then their time will be up (and they will stop
   working).

   _____

   _____

3. Our instructor will grade the essays. Then he will immediately hand them back to us.

_____

_____

4. You will return next week. At that time, I will reimburse you for the plane ticket.

_____

_____

5. I will try to convince Margaret to take the job. Then she is going to leave for Austin.

_____

_____

6. The repairman will fix this telephone. At the same time, he will be installing the new equipment.

_____

_____

7. Dan is going to find a good topic. Then he will immediately begin writing his paper.

_____

_____

EXERCISE 6.3-E   RESPONDING TO INFORMATION

clauses and phrases in future time

Look back at the itinerary information in Exercise 6.2-E. For each day on the itinerary, write one complex sentence that reports some of the information. Your sentences should contain future adverbial clauses of time.

> **Example:** December 10:
> *As soon as I arrive at Kennedy Airport, I'll take a taxi to the Roosevelt Hotel.*

1. December 10:

_____

_____

2. December 11:

_____

_____

3. December 12:

_____

_____

4. December 13:

_____

_____

EXERCISE 6.3-F   DISCRIMINATING TENSES

past, present, and future time

Fill in each blank with an appropriate verb form. There may be more than one possibility in some cases.

1. Some friends _____ (*give*) us this painting as a gift while they _____ (*visit*) us last
summer. I _____ (*put*) it on a wall in this room because I
_____ (*like*) _____ (*look at*) it
while I _____ (*relax*) in the evenings.

2. After _____ (*see*) the poor results on our
mid-term exams, our instructor _____ (*decide*)
_____ (*let*) us _____ (*have*) an-
other chance. There _____ (BE) a repeat test for anyone
who _____ (*want*) _____ (*take*)
one next Thursday before we _____ (*have*) our regular
lecture.

3. As soon as the present tenants _____
(*find*) new housing within the next few months, the city
_____ (*tear down*) several blocks of
apartments in order _____ (*clear*) space
for the new government office complex. Many people
_____ (*fight*) against the plan when they
first _____ (*hear*) about it last year, but it
_____ (*appear*) now that there
_____ (BE) no way to fight city hall.

4. Crime in this town _____ (BE) very low in
the past, but now it _____ (*increase*) at
an alarming rate. Last month, while _____ (*walk*) home
from a corner grocery store, several elderly women
_____ (BE) seriously hurt by muggers. Incidents such as

that one _____ (become) more and more common these days, and many residents _____ (BE) worried about their safety.

SECTION 6.4   Direct Objects and Indirect Objects

DIRECT OBJECTS AND INDIRECT OBJECTS
A.   Mr. Donaldson showed **his client** *the new plans*.
B.   He showed *the new plans* **to his client**.
C.   He showed *them* **to his client**.
D.   He showed *them* **to him**.
E.   We are going to buy **Susan** *these flowers*.
F.   We are going to buy *these flowers* **for Susan**.
G.   We are going to buy *them* **for Susan**.
H.   We are going to buy *them* **for her**.

1. Direct objects: Recall from Chapter 1 that a transitive verb has an object. The *direct object* of the verb is the person or thing which the subject directly acts on.

Subject	Verb	Direct Object
Mr. Donaldson	showed	the new plans.
We	are going to buy	these flowers.

2. Indirect objects: A verb is sometimes followed by a second object, called the *indirect object*. The indirect object is the person or thing which in some way receives the direct object. Notice that the indirect object follows a preposition, usually *to* or *for*.

Subject	Verb	Direct Object	Indirect Object
Mr. Donaldson	showed	the new plans	*to* his client.
We	are going to buy	these flowers	*for* Susan.

3. Placement of objects after the verb: In sentences B through D and F through H, the indirect objects are placed after the direct objects, and the preposition *to* or *for* is added. The choice of *to* or *for* depends on the main verb. We will call this arrangement pattern 1.

Pattern 1

Subject + Verb + Direct Object + *to* or *for* + Indirect Object

Howard wrote a letter *to* his parents last week.
Mary got some records *for* her brother.

After certain verbs, it is possible to reverse the order of the direct and indirect objects. In this case, the preposition is *not* used. We will call this arrangement pattern 2.

Pattern 2

Subject + Verb + Indirect Object + Direct Object

Howard wrote his parents a letter last week.
Mary got her brother some records.

Many verbs use only pattern 1. Some verbs can use either pattern 1 or pattern 2. See the charts on pages 156 and 157.

4. Pronouns as objects: When the direct object is a pronoun, it must come before the indirect object (pattern 1), as in sentences C, D, G, and H.

Correct	*Incorrect*
He showed them to his client.	He showed his client them.
He showed them to him.	He showed him them.

5. Long objects: If either the direct object or the indirect object is fairly long, it is better to place it second if possible.

Awkward	*Better*
I gave the book *that I found in the shop around the corner* to her.	I gave her *the book that I found in the shop around the corner.*

6. Asking questions with indirect objects: When a WH question asks about the direct object, *to* or *for* for the indirect object is optional *if the verb can use either pattern 1 or pattern 2.* If the verb uses only pattern 1, *to* or *for* is necessary in the question.

Verbs Which Use Either Pattern 1 or Pattern 2

Statement: He gave the instructor *the book.*   OR
          He gave *the book to* the instructor.

Question: *What* did he give the instructor?   OR
          What did he give *to* the instructor?

Verbs Which Use Only Pattern 1

Statement: He delivered *the book to* his instructor.

Question: *What* did he deliver *to* his instructor?

When the WH question asks about the indirect object, it is better to use the preposition *to* or *for*. The preposition can be left at the end of the sentence, or it can be moved to the front with the question word.

> *Statement:*   He gave *the instructor* the book.
> *Question:*   *To whom* did he give the book?   OR
>   *Who(m)* did he give the book *to*?

When the preposition is placed at the beginning of the sentence, *whom* must be used rather than *who*.

7. ***For*** **meaning** *on behalf of*:   A phrase with *for* can indicate that an action is performed on behalf of someone else. Such a *for* phrase does not involve an indirect object.

> Howard gave Janice a message *for me*. (He gave it to Janice on my behalf, because I was unable or unwilling to do it myself.)
> Will you make the children lunch *for me*? (Will you do it instead of me?)

VERBS FOLLOWED ONLY BY PATTERN 1

Pattern 1:   Subject + Verb + Direct Object + *to/for* + Indirect Object
            The doctor prescribed some medicine for me.

admit (to)	deliver (to)	pronounce (for)
announce (to)	describe (to)	propose (to)
answer (for)	drive (for)	prove (to)
arrange (for)	entrust (to)	recommend (to)
begin (for)	explain (to)	report (to)
cash (for)	finish (for)	return (to)
clarify (for)	fix [= repair] (for)	say (to)
close (for)	indicate (to)	start (for)
communicate (to)	introduce (to)	suggest (to)
declare (to)	mention (to)	translate (for)
dedicate (to)	prescribe (for)	

Correct: Amy started the car for David.
Incorrect: Amy started David the car.

EXERCISE 6.4-A   CHECKING FORM (ORAL)

object, from pattern 1 to pattern 2

All of the following statements use pattern 1. Change each statement to pattern 2.

VERBS FOLLOWED BY EITHER PATTERN 1 OR PATTERN 2

Pattern 1:   Subject + Verb + Direct Object + *to/for* + Indirect Object
               I lent my textbook to Sara.

Pattern 2:   Subject + Verb + Indirect Object + Direct Object
               I lent Sara my textbook.

bake (for)	loan (to)	sell (to)
build (for)	mail (to)	send (to)
buy (for)	offer (to)	sew (for)
cook (for)	order (to)	show (to)
draw (for)	owe (to)	sing (to)
find (for)	pass (to)	take (to)
get (for)	pay (to)	teach (to)
fix [= prepare] (for)	pour (for)	tell (to)
give (to)	read (to)	throw (to)
hand (to)	rent (to)	write (to)
lend (to)		

Pattern 1:   He mailed the letter to his sponsor.   I got a present for Sue.
Pattern 2:   He mailed his sponsor the letter.   I got Sue a present.
Pattern 2:   He mailed him his letter.   I got her a present.

Example: He gave the book to Jane.
          He gave Jane the book.

1. Jonathan handed the package to me.

2. John is going to fix a big dinner for us.

3. We will mail the letter to Emily tomorrow.

4. Ron offered his help to George.

5. I want to find a present for my roommate.

6. Bobby drew a picture for his parents.

7. I am going to read John's letter to you.

8. Mr. Fineman rented the apartment to us.

EXERCISE 6.4-B   CHECKING FORM (ORAL)

objects, pattern 1 with *to*

Add the indirect object *him* to each statement on page 158, using pattern 1 with *to*. These verbs cannot be used with pattern 2.

Example: I admitted my mistake.
I admitted my mistake to him.

1. We announced the news.

2. I tried to communicate my concerns.

3. Ms. Cassidy will dedicate her book.

4. George and Martha are going to deliver the package.

5. I am describing my ideas.

6. We explained our new plan.

7. The engineers will indicate some changes.

8. I will introduce my friends.

9. Beth is going to mention some names.

10. We proposed a different topic.

11. They will attempt to prove their theory.

12. I am going to recommend a plan of action.

13. The police will be reporting the incident.

14. Someone needs to suggest the idea.

EXERCISE 6.4-C   CHECKING FORM (ORAL)

objects, pattern 1 with *for*

Add the indirect object *us* to each statement, using pattern 1 with *for*. These verbs cannot use pattern 2.

Example: He answered the question.
He answered the question for us.

1. They will arrange a schedule.

2. Mr. Rogers began the story.

3. Mary will translate the poem.

4. Sandra cashed a check.

5. You need to clarify your meaning.

6. I want someone to close the door.

7. Samuels will be driving the car.

8. They always finish the job.

9. The mechanic fixed the car.

10. The doctor won't prescribe any medicine.

11. You need to pronouce this word.

12. Hank is going to start the engine.

EXERCISE 6.4-D   CHECKING FORM (ORAL)

objects, pattern 1 with *to* or *for*

Add the indirect object *me* to each statement, using pattern 1 with either *to* or *for*.

Examples: They passed the food.
They passed the food to me.

He began the tape.
He began the tape for me.

1. Beth drew a picture.

2. The boys read a book.

3. Jason wrote a letter.

4. You need to describe the problem.

5. Dr. Owens is going to answer the question.

6. Bob owes a lot of money.

7. Greg and Sam are getting some new supplies.

8. Margaret sold the books.

9. You didn't introduce your friends.

10. Professor Sedwick is going to return my project.

11. They will be ordering the equipment.

12. Brian tried to explain the problem.

13. Kathy closed the window.

14. The students are going to read the article.

EXERCISE 6.4-E   DISCRIMINATING PREPOSITIONS

prepositions with objects

Read the sentences carefully. Fill in each blank with *to* or *for*, or leave it empty, as appropriate.

1. Before you go, please clarify _____ this paragraph _____ me.

2. _____ whom are you getting _____ all those supplies _____ ?

3. I paid _____ the store manager _____ all the money that I owed.

4. Mrs. Simpson is going to entrust _____ this valuable painting _____ you.

5. How are you going to tell _____ them _____ the truth about what happened?

6. When did Johnson arrange _____ the registration materials _____ you?

7. The Dickersons promised to save _____ all their old magazines _____ me.

8. When you give _____ Howard _____ the broken clock, he will repair _____ it _____ you.

9. It's necessary for you to report _____ the crime _____ the police.

10.   The media criticized the mayor because he found _____ his old friends _____ jobs.

EXERCISE 6.4-F   UNSCRAMBLING SENTENCES

direct objects and indirect objects

Unscramble the words, phrases, and clauses in order to create a meaningful sentence. You may have to add the preposition *to* or *for* for indirect objects that follow pattern 1.

> **Example:** checks – the same teller – yesterday – cashed – both of us
> *The same teller cashed checks for both of us yesterday.*

1.   us – tomorrow – is going to explain – our math instructor – derivations

Our math instructor is going to explain derivations to us tomorrow.

_____

2.   I – during yesterday's meeting – recommended – my advisers – an entirely new program

During yesterday's meeting, I recommended an entirely new program to my advisers.

_____

3.   freshman students – the English department – beginning next year – will offer – several new courses

_____

_____

4.   their colleagues – need to prove – the researchers – the validity of their results

_____

_____

5.   her – are going to take – several of the students – this evening – that pile of books

_____

_____

6.   last week – some questions – the senator – at the press conference – refused to answer – us

_____

_____

7.   me – when I begin my project – will lend – the school officials – the equipment that I need

_____

_____

7

The Perfect Tenses

In this chapter you will review and practice the perfect tenses in the time frames of the past, the present, and the future. The perfect tenses view an activity as occurring before a moment of reference. The present perfect tense expresses a time before the present moment. The past perfect tense expresses a time before a past moment. And the future perfect tense expresses a time before a future moment.

SECTION 7.1   The Present Perfect Tense

SECTION 7.2   The Present Perfect Progressive Tense

SECTION 7.3   The Past Perfect Tense and the Past Perfect Progressive Tense

SECTION 7.4   The Future Perfect Tense

SECTION 7.1   The Present Perfect Tense

THE PRESENT PERFECT		
Statements:	**A.**	The governor **has agreed** to debate Mr. Stevens.
	B.	But his advisers **have not decided** on a date or a location.
Questions:	**C.**	**Has** the governor **agreed** to debate Mr. Stevens? Yes, he has. (No, he hasn't.)
	D.	**Who has agreed** to debate Mr. Stevens? The governor.
	E.	**Whom has** the governor **agreed** to debate? Mr. Stevens.

1. The present perfect tense: Sentences A through E are in the present perfect tense. The present perfect is used to express activity in the past which in some way is relevant in the present time.

2. Affirmative statements: The present perfect tense is formed with the auxiliary HAVE and the past participle (*Ven*) of the main verb. The HAVE auxiliary is in the present tense (*has* or *have*) and must agree with the subject of the sentence in both person and number. The past participle of most verbs is identical to the past tense.

	HAVE	*Past Participle (Ven)*	
Sara	has	looked	at the book already.
The Johnsons	have	lived	here for years.
The governor	has	agreed	to debate Mr. Stevens.

3. Irregular past participles: Verbs which have irregular past tense forms also use irregular forms for the past participle. Look at the following sentences.

> We have *seen* that movie already.
> Greg has *given* money to charity for years.

You will find a list of irregular past participles in Appendix A, along with the past tense forms of the irregular verbs. It is important that you learn these irregular past participle forms.

4. Negative statements: Negative statements are formed by placing *not* after the HAVE auxiliary, as in sentence B. HAVE is often contracted with *not* (*hasn't* or *haven't*).

> His advisers *haven't* decided on a date or a location.
> Kathy *hasn't* spoken with Tim for over a month.

5. Yes-no questions: To form a yes-no question, simply move the HAVE auxiliary to the beginning of the sentence, as in sample sentence C. Use the HAVE auxiliary in the short answer.

> *Has* the governor *agreed* to debate Mr. Stevens? Yes, he *has*.
> *Has* Kathy *spoken* with Tim this month? No, she *hasn't*.

Ever used in yes-no questions in the present perfect means *at any time in the past* (up to the present). *Ever* is placed between the subject and main verb.

> Have you *ever* been to New York?
> Has John *ever* spoken to you about his classes?

Do not use the DO auxiliary with present perfect tense questions. DO is used with the simple present tense and the simple past tense only.

John has spoken to Mr. Thompson.	*Has* he spoken to Mr. Thompson?
John speaks to Mr. Thompson often.	*Does* he speak to Mr. Thompson often?

John spoke to Mr. Thompson yesterday.   *Did* he speak to Mr. Thompson yesterday?

6. WH questions: WH questions are formed in the usual way. To make a subject focus question, simply place the WH word at the beginning of the sentence, as in sample sentence D.

The governor has agreed to debate Mr. Stevens.
Who has agreed to debate Mr. Stevens? The governor.

To form a predicate focus question, place the WH word at the beginning of the sentence, and move the HAVE auxiliary in front of the subject. Do not add the DO auxiliary.

The governor *has agreed* to debate Mr. Stevens.
Who(m) has the governor *agreed* to debate? Mr. Stevens.

7. Tag questions: To form a tag question with the present perfect, use the HAVE auxiliary in the question tag.

The governor *has* agreed to debate Mr. Stevens, *hasn't* he?
His advisers *haven't* decided on a date and a location, *have* they?

8. Contractions: The HAVE auxiliary is frequently contracted with either the subject or *not*:

I have	=	I've	has not	=	hasn't
you have	=	you've	have not	=	haven't
he has	=	he's			
she has	=	she's			
it has	=	it's			
we have	=	we've			
they have	=	they've			

9. *Have* as a main verb versus the HAVE auxiliary: Remember that *has* or *have* can function as an auxiliary (in the present perfect tense) or as a main verb (in the simple present tense). Negative statements and questions are formed differently.

Have *as a Main Verb*

Jonathan *has* a new job.
He *doesn't have* his old job anymore.
Does he *have* a new job?

HAVE *as an Auxiliary*

Jonathan *has found* a new job.
He *hasn't worked* for over a year.
Has he *found* a new job?

EXERCISE 7.1-A CHECKING FORM (ORAL)

the present perfect tense

Respond to each negative statement about the past, using an affirmative statement in the present perfect tense. Use the adverb of time given in parentheses.

> **Example:** George didn't go out with us last month. (this month)
> *But he's gone out with us this month.*

1. John didn't attend classes last week. (this week)

2. Mary didn't pay her bills last week. (this week)

3. Harold didn't sleep well last week. (this week)

4. Janet didn't do her assignments last term. (this term)

5. Cheryl didn't visit us last month. (this month)

6. Tim didn't buy his books yesterday. (today)

7. Emily didn't speak to me yesterday. (today)

8. Michael and Tom didn't get in trouble last week. (this week)

EXERCISE 7.1-B CHECKING FORM (ORAL)

questions with *ever* in the present perfect

Using each verb phrase given, ask your classmate a yes-no question with *ever* in the present perfect. Then your classmate should answer your question.

> **Example:** forget someone's name
> *Have you ever forgotten someone's name?*
> *Yes, I have. I've forgotten people's names many times.*

1. fly in a plane

2. ride on a train

3. drive a motorcycle

4. travel around the world

5. see the Taj Mahal

6. visit Paris

7. go camping

8. get to class late

EXERCISE 7.1-C   CHECKING FORM (ORAL)

WH questions in the present perfect

For each sentence, ask the question indicated by the WH word.

1.   Howard has taken the book. (who)

2.   The Melchings have moved to Detroit. (where)

3.   Jimmy has broken my expensive vase. (what)

4.   Helen has succeeded by working hard. (how)

5.   Sam has been very quiet today because he was afraid of offending you. (why)

6.   The Davidsons have bought the old Tilling house. (which)

7.   The committee has chosen Mr. Bryant's proposal. (whose)

USING THE PRESENT PERFECT
F. We **have lived** in Los Angeles for two months.
G. My roommate **has** already **visited** the Hollywood studios a number of times.
H. He **has visited** several other tourist attractions this week.

10. The use of the present perfect tense: The present perfect is used to indicate activity in the past which is somehow connected to the present time. There are three major uses of the present perfect tense.

Past activity continuing to the present time: The present perfect can report an activity or a state that began in the past and continues up to and even into the present time. This use of the present perfect tense generally includes a time adverbial such as *since, for, up to now,* or *so far.*

> *Situation:*   We moved to Los Angeles two months ago, in April. We still live there.
> We *have lived* in Los Angeles for two months.
> We *have lived* in Los Angeles since April.
> We *haven't made* many friends so far.

Since is followed by a point in time. The point in time can be represented by a phrase or by a complete clause.

> *Situation:*   We came to this country in 1988. We started to study here at that time. We still study here.

We have studied here *since 1988.*
We have studied here *since we came to this country.*

Notice that the full clause with *since* uses the simple past tense, not the present perfect. *Since* is used only when the verb of the main clause is in a perfect tense; it cannot be used with the simple past tense, which indicates that an activity was completed in the past.

Correct	*Incorrect*
She has needed new glasses since last summer. (She continues to need them now.)	She needed new glasses since last summer.

For is followed by a period of time. The period of time must be expressed by a phrase, not by a clause.

They have studied here *for three months.*

For can be used with different tenses. Examine the differences in meaning among the following statements.

They *study* for two hours every evening.
They *are studying* for a few minutes before the exam.
They *studied* for eight hours last week. (an eight-hour period last week)
They *have studied* for eight hours so far. (from eight hours ago until now)

Time adverbials with *since* and *for* answer the question *how long.*

How long have you lived in Cleveland?
For three years.
Since 1985.

Past activity which might be repeated in the present or the future: The present perfect tense may be used for an activity or a state that happened in the past and might be repeated in the future, as in sentence G on page 165.

My roommate *has* already *visited* the Hollywood studios a number of times.
I*'ve* frequently *eaten* in that restaurant.
They*'ve rebuilt* that engine a number of times.
I *haven't eaten* breakfast this morning. (It is still morning, so I can still eat breakfast.)

In all these examples, there is the possibility that the activity will occur again in the future. When adverbs of frequency are used, as in the second example, they are placed between the HAVE auxiliary and the main verb (*have frequently eaten*). If it is impossible for the activity to be repeated in the future, the simple past tense is used.

The late Mr. Spencer *donated* time and money to this organization.

Past activity with relevance in the present: Finally, the present perfect tense can express an action that occurred at an unspecified time in the past but within a larger time frame that is considered part of the present, as in sentence H. Often there is a present result.

> He *has been* ill this week. (He is still ill now.)
> They've *closed* all the windows today. (The windows are still closed now.)
> The students *have arrived* this week.
> She *has* finally *completed* the drawings this afternoon.

Notice that none of these sentences uses a past time adverbial, such as *yesterday*, *last night*, or *two days ago*. You cannot use a past time adverbial with the present perfect tense. However, a present time adverbial can be used (*today*, *this week*, *this afternoon*). These time adverbials extend back into the past (before now) but view the time period as a present one. Contrast the sample sentences in the present perfect with similar sentences in the simple past tense.

> He *was* ill last week. (Last week is over. Perhaps he is no longer ill.)
> They *closed* all the windows yesterday. (Yesterday is past. Perhaps the windows are no longer closed.)
> The students *arrived* last week.
> She finally *completed* the drawings this morning. (It is now afternoon, so this morning is in the past.)

If an activity occurred at an *indefinite* time in the very recent past, the present perfect can be used with the adverb *just* between the HAVE auxiliary and the main verb.

> I *have just finished* the assignment.
> We *have just read* your report.

However, if a *definite* time in the recent past is intended, the past tense, not the present perfect, must be used.

> I *just finished* the assignment *at 2:00*.

11. *Already*, *yet*, and *still*:   The adverbs *already*, *yet*, and *still* are frequently used with the present perfect tense.

***Already*:**   Use *already* to show that an activity happened before a certain time, perhaps earlier than expected. *Already* is used in affirmative sentences and in questions; it is placed either between the HAVE auxiliary and the main verb or at the end of the sentence.

> We have *already* finished the assignment. (perhaps earlier than expected)
> We have finished the assignment *already*.
> Have you finished the assignment *already*? (I am surprised; you have finished earlier than I expected.)

Yet: Use *yet* in negative statements to show that an activity has not happened by a certain time and to imply that it may happen in the near future. *Yet* can also be used in questions. It is placed at the end of the sentence, before any other time adverbial.

> She hasn't studied *yet* today. (Perhaps she will study later today.)
> I haven't read the book *yet*. (But I intend to read it soon.)
> Have you read the book *yet*? (I don't know if you have read it, but if you
> haven't, I want you to know that I expect you to read it soon.)

Still: Use *still* to show that there has been no change in activity. It is often used with the present perfect tense in a negative sentence. *Still* is placed before the negative HAVE auxiliary.

> They *still* haven't written the letter.
> The mechanic *still* hasn't fixed the car.

EXERCISE 7.1-D   CHECKING FORM (ORAL)

using *still* with the present perfect tense

Use *still* to show that each situation has not changed. Use the present perfect tense in your response.

> **Example:** Howard didn't choose his topic yesterday.
> *He still hasn't chosen it.*

1. We didn't buy our groceries yesterday.
   We still haven't bought any groceries.
2. Janet didn't speak to us yesterday.

3. Eric didn't take his medicine yesterday.

4. Margaret didn't write a letter to her parents last week.

5. Jason didn't do his laundry last night.

6. Amy didn't sell her car last week.

EXERCISE 7.1-E   CHECKING FORM (ORAL)

using *already* and *yet* with the present perfect

Answer each question truthfully, using *already* with an affirmative statement and *yet* with a negative one.

> **Example:** Have you missed this class this term?
> *Yes, I've missed it several times already.*
> *No, I haven't missed it yet.*

1. Have you handed in yesterday's assignment?

2. Have you seen the news on television today?

3. Have you read today's newspaper?

4. Have you studied today?

5. Have you finished the assignment that is due tomorrow?

6. Have you chosen your major?

EXERCISE 7.1-F   DISCRIMINATING FORM

for **versus** *since*

Add *since* or *for* in each blank, or leave it empty, as appropriate.

1. They haven't gone out on the town _____ months.

2. We've spoken to our new neighbors several times _____ they moved in.

3. Has anyone seen Professor Al-Hamdan _____ today?

4. I haven't done the assignments _____ a month.

5. Sharon hasn't called us _____ last month.

6. Scientists have learned a lot about this illness _~~since~~_ 1980.

7. Joe hasn't ridden a bicycle _~~since~~_ he was a boy.

8. The newspaper has been late every morning _____ this week.

9. We have tried to help him _____ a long time.

10. Has anyone talked to Professor Butler _____ yesterday?

EXERCISE 7.1-G   MAKING PHRASES INTO SENTENCES

the present perfect tense

Create an affirmative or negative statement from each group of words and phrases, as indicated. Use the present perfect tense. If an adverb is given in parentheses, add it to the sentence.

> **Example:** I – eat – anything – this morning (negative statement, *still*)
> *I still haven't eaten anything this morning.*

1. the students – complete – the assignment (affirmative statement, *already*)
   The students have already completed the assignment.

2. the farmers – in this area – have – a good year (negative statement)

_____

3. we – reach – the halfway mark (negative statement, *yet*)

_____

4. Martha – drive – over 5,000 miles – on her trip (affirmative statement)

Martha drive over

5. we – write – our term project (negative statement, *still*)

We still havent our

6. we – mean – visit the Johansons – for several years (affirmative statement)

We have meant to visit the Johansons for several years.

7. my friends – see – that film – several times (affirmative statement, *already*)

_____

EXERCISE 7.1-H   ASKING QUESTIONS
● ·

the present perfect tense

Each sentence is in the present perfect tense. Change it to the question form indicated in parentheses.

> **Example:** The Johnsons have lived here for five years. (how long)
> *How long have the Johnsons lived here?*

1. Sam has written several letters to government agencies this week. (*what-do question*)

What has Sam done?

2. Ms. Samuels has taught the class this week. (who)

_____

3. Amanda has decided to buy the car with power steering. (which)

_____

4. The Ajax Company has marketed its products by mail since it was founded. (how long)

How long has the Ajax Company has marketed its products by mail?

5. The lecture has already started in the auditorium. (yes-no question)

_____

6. Tom has won the poetry contest that is sponsored by the English department. (who)

_____

EXERCISE 7.1-I   DISCRIMINATING TENSES

the simple present, the simple past, and the present perfect

Fill in each blank with the simple present, simple past, or present perfect tense of the verb in parentheses. In some cases, there may be more than one correct choice.

1. I _____have learned_____ (learn) a lot about group behavior since we _____enrolled_____ (enroll) in this sociology course. But I _____don't understand_____ (understand, negative) why bystanders sometimes _____fail_____ (fail) to help crime victims. I _____asked_____ (ask) my professor about it yesterday, but he _____didn't give_____ (give, negative) me a very satisfactory answer. I guess that sociologists _____haven't been able to_____ (BE able to, negative) explain all types of behavior yet.

2. This _____is_____ (BE) the best report that you _____have written_____ (write) so far this term. You _____arranged_____ (arrange) your ideas logically and _____stated_____ (state) them clearly. I can honestly say that I _____enjoyed_____ (enjoy) reading your paper.

3. Cheryl _____lived_____ (live) in Seattle for several years, but then she _____moved_____ (move) to Detroit a year ago. She _____hasn't been_____ (BE, negative) happy in Detroit recently and _____wants_____ (want) to return to the West Coast.

4. The mayor _____has just announced_____ (announce, just) the name of the new director of finance. There _____have been_____ (BE) rumors (for) several months that the new appointee might be a woman, but it now _____appears_____ (appear) that those rumors _____are_____ (BE) incorrect. This appointment _____upset (has upset)_____ (upset) many people because the mayor _____still hasn't named_____ (name, still, negative) any women to top administrative positions.

5. The math department at that school _____has never had_____ (have, never) a very good reputation, and I _____understand_____ (understand) why. I _____took_____ (take) two math courses there last year, and the quality of instruction _____was_____ (BE) very poor. Apparently, the situation _____hasn't changed_____ (change, negative) since that time. My friends who _____are_____ (BE) students there now _____complain_____ (complain) about their math classes, too.

EXERCISE 7.1-J   RESPONDING TO INFORMATION

● ·

the present, the past, and the present perfect

Here is information about the nation of Kuwait. Read the information carefully, and decide how each piece of information should be reported: in the simple present tense, in the present perfect tense, or in the simple past tense. Then write sentences which report the information.

Geography

Northeast of Saudi Arabia, at northern end of Persian Gulf
6,880 square miles
Low-lying land, mostly sandy and barren

Government

Constitutional monarchy
Emir: Sheik Jaber al-Ahmad al-Sabah (1977)

History

1700: Arab nomads settle Kuwait Bay
Mid-1700s to present: Al-Sabah dynasty rules Kuwait
1899: Kuwait signs agreement with Britain for defense
1961: agreement with Britain ends; Kuwait gains independence
1936: drilling for oil begins
1946: Kuwait becomes a major oil exporter
1961: Kuwait seen as a model welfare state; offers citizens a wide range of
    benefits
1990: Kuwait invaded by Iraq.

People

Population: 1,815,000
1930s to present: population increases dramatically; draws many emigrants
    from Persian Gulf and beyond
Religion: Islam, 92 percent; Christian, 6 percent

1. Geography:

    _____

    _____

2. Government:

    _____

    _____

3. History:

_____

_____

4. People:

_____

_____

_____

EXERCISE 7.1-K EXPRESSING YOUR OWN IDEAS

the present, the past, and the present perfect

Write one or more paragraphs about your own country, including information about its geography, its government, its history, and its people. Use the
simple present tense to express current activities and facts of an unchang-
ing nature. Use the simple past to express past activities. Use the present
perfect tense to indicate activities and situations which started in the past
and continue today or are relevant to the present time.

SECTION 7.2   The Present Perfect Progressive Tense

THE PRESENT PERFECT PROGRESSIVE		
Statements:	**A.**	Robert **has been working** on his project all morning.
	B.	He **hasn't been doing** anything else.
Questions:	**C.**	**Has** Robert **been working** on his project all morning? Yes, he has. (No, he hasn't.)
	D.	**Who has been working** on his project all morning? Robert.
	E.	**What has** Robert **been working** on all morning? His project.

1. Statements in the present perfect progressive: The present perfect
tense can be made progressive by adding the past participle of the BE
auxiliary (_been_) and using the present participle (_Ving_) form of the main
verb, as in sentence A, _has been working_.

	HAVE	been	*Present Participle (Ving)*	
Robert	has	been	working	on his project all morning.
I	have	been	sitting	in this room for more than an hour.

Statements are made negative by making the first auxiliary, HAVE, negative, as in sentence B, *hasn't been doing*.

> We *haven't* been studying very hard lately.
> Professor Johnson *hasn't* been giving us much reading this term.

2. Question forms: When a verb tense has more than one auxiliary, the first one is used to form questions. To form a yes-no question, move the HAVE auxiliary to the beginning of the sentence, as in sample sentence C. Can you explain how the different types of WH questions are formed in sentences D and E? How would you form a tag question in the present perfect progressive?

3. The use of the present perfect progressive: The present perfect progressive emphasizes the duration of an activity from a point in the past to the present moment. It is most commonly used in two situations.

a. Activity beginning in the past and occurring continuously until now: The present perfect progressive tense is most often used to express an activity or state that started in the past and continued until the moment of speaking, as in sentence A. The activity may still be occurring at the moment of speaking, or it may have just been completed.

> Robert has been working on his project all morning. (He started earlier this morning, and he worked continuously until now.)
> I've been typing my report for two hours. (I started two hours ago, and I typed steadily until now.)

Ever since is sometimes used with this meaning of the present perfect progressive to emphasize that the activity has been in progress until the moment of speaking.

> We have been planning to visit New York *ever since* we moved to the East Coast.

Some English verbs naturally suggest continuity: *lie, live, rain, sit, sleep, stand, study, wait,* and *work,* among others. With these verbs, there is little difference between the present perfect and the present perfect progressive tenses.

> It has rained all morning.
> It has been raining all morning.

But with other verbs, the use of the present perfect implies that the action is completed, whereas the present perfect progressive implies that the action is not completed yet.

> Helen has painted the room this morning. (She has finished the job.)
> Helen has been painting the room this morning. (The job is not finished yet.)

b. Frequently repeated activity in the past: When an activity has been repeated frequently in the past and the repetition is itself continuous, the present perfect progressive tense can be used. Adverbs of time with *every* are often used with this meaning. However, do not use an adverb of time with the word *time*.

Correct	*Incorrect*
She has been calling me every night this week.	She has been calling me several times this week.
I've been writing home once a month this year.	I've been writing home a number of times this year.

4. Stative verbs: Stative verbs (see Section 5.1) can be used in the present perfect tense but not in the present perfect progressive.

Correct	*Incorrect*
I have understood Spanish since I was a child.	I have been understanding Spanish since I was a child.

EXERCISE 7.2-A   CHECKING FORM (ORAL)

statements in the present perfect progressive

Use each group of words to create an affirmative statement or a negative statement in the present perfect progressive tense.

> **Example:** study – all day
> *I've been studying all day.*

1. sleep – well – lately
2. not write – to my family – very often this year
3. make – a lot of phone calls home – this month
4. not pay – attention – in class – this week
5. not work – hard – for the past few weeks
6. look for – you – all morning

7. plan my vacation – for weeks now

8. not keep up – with my work – ever since I was sick last month

EXERCISE 7.2-B   CHECKING FORM (ORAL)

WH questions in the present perfect progressive

For each sentence, ask the question indicated by the WH word in paren-theses.

> **Example:** Michael has been worrying all morning. (how long)
> *How long has Michael been worrying?*

1. Dean has been looking for the answer for two days. (how long)

2. Emily has been working on the computer. (who)

3. Bob has been asking Helen about the lab assignment. (what)

4. The English teachers have been meeting every day in order to revise the curricu-lum. (why)

5. Some family problems have been upsetting Nancy lately. (what)

6. Joe and Don have been living at the YMCA for the past two weeks. (where)

EXERCISE 7.2-C   ANSWERING QUESTIONS (ORAL)

the present perfect progressive tense

Answer each question in the present perfect progressive tense.

1. How long have you been living here?

2. How long have you been studying English?

3. What have you been studying in this class this week?

4. How have you been getting to class in the mornings?

5. What have you been doing in the evenings this week?

6. What have you been doing on the weekends this term?

7. How long have you been sitting down?

8. Who have you been studying with this term?

EXERCISE 7.2-D MAKING PHRASES INTO SENTENCES

●· ·

the present perfect progressive tense

Create a meaningful statement from each group of words, phrases, and clauses. Use the present perfect progressive tense in the main clause. If an adverbial clause is included, choose an appropriate tense.

> **Example:** the new record store – have – a sale / / since – it – open – last month
>
> *The new record store has been having a sale since it opened last month.*

1. Sam and his brother – fight about – money / / since – they – BE – children

     _____

     _____

2. the Youngs – stay – at the Imperial Hotel / / since – they – arrive – last week

     _____

     _____

3. locusts – destroy – the farm crops – this season

     _____

     _____

4. George – do – very well – in school – this year

     _____

     _____

5. the project – progress (negative) – quickly / / because – we – have (negative) enough money

     _____

     _____

6. the population in this area – grow – since the mid-1980s

     _____

     _____

EXERCISE 7.2-E COMPLETING SENTENCES

●· ·

perfect tenses

Complete each sentence on page 178 with your own ideas. Use the present perfect tense or the present perfect progressive tense in the main clause. Use an appropriate tense in all adverbial clauses.

1. I _____ since last year.

2. The superpowers _____
   since _____

3. The students in this class _____
   for _____

4. _____ since I
   _____ ago.

5. Science _____
   since the turn of the century.

6. Nuclear power _____
   since _____

EXERCISE 7.2-F　RESTATING INFORMATION

the present perfect progressive tense

Read each situation. Then write a sentence expressing the same information, using the present perfect progressive tense. Use the verb suggested in parentheses.

> **Example:** In 1970 a total of 43.2 percent of the Egyptian population lived in urban areas. Now over 50 percent of the population does. (increase)
> *The percentage of Egyptians in urban areas has been increasing since 1970.*

1. The U.S. budget deficit was approximately $45 billion in 1977. It is over $200 billion now. (grow)

   _____

   _____

2. Total world oil production was over 60 million barrels per day in 1978. It is under 54 million barrels per day now. (decrease)

   _____

   _____

3. The percentage of women in the U.S. work force was 31.9 percent in 1950. It is approximately 50 percent now. (get jobs each year)

   _____

   _____

4. The Latin American countries spent 2.2 percent of their total gross national product on education in 1960. They spend close to 4 percent of their GNP on education today. (spend . . . each year)

_____

_____

5. In 1850 the life expectancy for American men was 35 years. It has gotten longer every year since. Now it is almost 72 years. (increase)

_____

_____

EXERCISE 7.2-G   DISCRIMINATING TENSES

**the simple past, the present perfect, and
the present perfect progressive**

Fill in each blank with the appropriate form of the verb in parentheses. Use the simple past, the present perfect, or the present perfect progressive tense. In some cases there may be more than one possibility.

1. Scientists _____ (_talk_) about artificial intelligence ever since they _____ (_construct_) the first generation of superfast computers in the 1970s. Unfortunately, there _____ (BE, negative) much progress in the past few years.

2. We _____ (_visit_) our relatives in San Francisco several times since we _____ (_move_) to California. In fact, we _____ (_visit_) them last weekend.

3. The students are in the library right now. They _____ (_work_) on their group project since lunch, but they _____ (_get_, negative) very far. They _____ (_understand_, negative) their professor's instructions very well when he _____ (_give_) them yesterday, but they _____ (BE) hesitant to ask him for clarification.

4. I _____ (_go_) to that restaurant a few times, but I _____ (_like_, _never_) it very much. The last time that I _____ (_go_), the waitress _____ (BE) very rude. Since that time, I _____ (_tell_) my friends not to go.

5. It _____ (_rain_) for three days straight, and it doesn't look like it will ever stop. Several rivers _____ (_start_) to flood, and last night our basement _____ (_begin_) to fill up with water.

SECTION 7.3   The Past Perfect Tense and the Past Perfect Progressive Tense

. . . .

THE PAST PERFECT TENSE

A. The instructor **had** already **handed out** the test papers when I arrived.

B. But the students **hadn't started** the exam yet.

C. I didn't do well on the exam because I **hadn't studied** the night before.

---

1. The past perfect tense: Sentences A, B, and C use the past perfect tense. The past perfect shows that an activity occurred *before* another activity or time in the past. It is formed with the past tense of the HAVE auxiliary, *had*, and the past participle form (*Ven*) of the main verb. To make a statement negative, *had* is made negative.

	had	*Past Participle (Ven)*	
The instructor	had	handed out	the test papers when I arrived.
The students	hadn't	started	the exam yet.

2. Contractions: The auxiliary *had* can be contracted with subject pronouns or with *not*. Contractions with subject pronouns are usually avoided in formal writing.

I had	=	I'd		had not	=	hadn't
you had	=	you'd
she had	=	she'd
he had	=	he'd
we had	=	we'd
they had	=	they'd

3. The use of the past perfect tense: The past perfect tense shows that a past activity or state occurred *earlier* than another activity or time in the past. The earlier activity uses the past perfect tense. When a later activity is stated, it uses the simple past tense.

Situation: Sara called me at 9:00 P.M. I heard the news at 8:00 P.M.
I *had* already *heard* the news when Sara *called*.
I *had heard* the news by 9:00 P.M.

The later activity or point in time does not have to be stated in every sentence that uses the past perfect tense. It can be implied in the situation or stated just once.

> Sam was exhausted and upset when he got home last night. Work *had not gone* well at all. He *had made* several serious mistakes calculating costs for a new project, and his boss *had reprimanded* him for arguing with his co-workers.

4. Clauses with *before* and *after*:   The past perfect tense is not necessary if an adverbial subordinator such as *before* or *after* makes it clear which activity occurred before the other. The simple past tense can be used instead.

> She changed her course schedule *after* she *had spoken* to her adviser.
> She changed her course schedule *after* she *spoke* to her adviser.

5. Clauses with *when*:   However, the past perfect *must* be used with the subordinator *when* in order to show earlier action. Compare these sentences.

> Howard *had left* when we arrived. (He left before we arrived.)
> Howard *left* when we arrived. (He left immediately after we arrived.)
> Howard *was leaving* when we arrived. (He was in the process of leaving at the time we arrived.)

6. Questions: Use the HAVE auxiliary to form questions. Examine the following statement and the corresponding questions. How is a yes-no question formed in the past perfect tense? How are WH questions formed?

> The painters had completed the entire job by last Thursday.
>> *Had* the painters *completed* the entire job by last Thursday?
>>> Yes, they had. (No, they hadn't.)
>> *Who had completed* the entire job by last Thursday?
>>> The painters.
>> *What had* the painters *completed* by last Thursday?
>>> The entire job.

EXERCISE 7.3-A   CHECKING FORM (ORAL)

● . . . .

the past perfect progressive tense

Each item on page 182 tells you about a classmate's past activity. Indicate that you completed the same activity earlier. Use the past perfect tense in your response.

Example: (Student X) went to the library at 7:00 last night.
I had already gone to the library by then.

1. (X) talked to me about the assignment at 3:00 yesterday afternoon.

2. (X) bought her/his books last Wednesday.

3. (X) finished the assignment at midnight last night.

4. (X) ate dinner at 6:00 P.M. yesterday.

5. (X) started to study for the exam last Wednesday.

6. (X) wrote her/his essay last Saturday.

7. (X) decided to study here a year ago.

THE PAST PERFECT PROGRESSIVE TENSE

D. Margaret **had been working** for the telephone company for three years when she took this job with the university.

E. She **hadn't been looking** for a new job very long when she got it.

---

7. The past perfect progressive tense: The past perfect tense can be made progressive in order to emphasize the duration of the earlier activity. It is formed with the past tense of the HAVE auxiliary (*had*), followed by the past participle of the auxiliary BE (*been*), and finally the present participle of the main verb (*Ving*). To make a statement negative, make the auxiliary *had* negative.

	had	been	*Present Participle (Ving)*	
Margaret	had	been	working	for the telephone company for three years.
She	hadn't	been	looking	for a new job very long when she got it.

8. The use of the past perfect progressive: The past perfect progressive tense shows that an earlier activity continued up to the moment of a later past time or activity. The duration of the earlier activity is often indicated.

Situation: Margaret was working for the telephone company from 1985 to 1988. In 1988 she got this job with the university.
Margaret *had been working* for the telephone company *for three years* when she got this job with the university.

9. Questions: Examine the following statement and the corresponding questions. How is a yes-no question formed with the past perfect progressive tense? How are WH questions constructed?

> Howard had been trying for weeks before he succeeded.
> > *Had* he *been trying* for very long before he succeeded?
> > > Yes, he had. (No, he hadn't.)
> > *Who had been trying* for weeks?
> > > Howard.
> > *How long had* Howard *been trying* before he succeeded?
> > > For weeks.

EXERCISE 7.3-B   CHECKING FORM (ORAL)

the past perfect progressive tense

Restate each situation, using the past perfect progressive.

> **Example:** Don was sleeping from noon until 5:00 P.M. I woke him up
> at 5:00.
> *Don had been sleeping for five hours when I woke him up.*

1. The Johnsons were living in Chicago from 1980 until 1988. I met them in 1988.

2. Barbara was working for the Ajax Company from 1983 to 1985. She quit her job in 1985.

3. Howard wasn't feeling very well for more than a week. Finally, he went to see a doctor.

4. John and Jessica were traveling from Tuesday to Saturday. Jessica became ill on Saturday.

5. I was waiting for Julie at the airport for three hours. Then her plane landed.

6. City buses weren't operating during July and August. Finally, the bus drivers ended their strike.

EXERCISE 7.3-C   ANSWERING QUESTIONS (ORAL)

the past perfect and the past perfect progressive

Answer each question on page 184 in the past tense. Then add a statement about an earlier activity (in the past perfect or the past perfect progressive) which explains your answer.

Example: Were you hungry when you got home last night?
No, I wasn't. I had eaten a lot during the day.

1. Were you tired when you got up yesterday morning?

2. Were you tired when you got home yesterday?

3. Did you get wet in the rain yesterday?

4. Were you worried when you finished the test last week?

5. Were you in a good mood when you got home last night?

6. Were you discouraged when you handed in your assignment yesterday?

7. Were you relaxed when you came to class Monday morning?

8. Were you surprised when you got your grade on the last exam?

EXERCISE 7.3-D   MAKING PHRASES INTO SENTENCES

the past perfect and the past perfect progressive

Create a meaningful statement from each group of words and phrases. Use the past perfect or the past perfect progressive tense in the main clause. Use an appropriate tense in all adverbial clauses. You may have to add a second subject.

Example: the students – finish – work / / before – their time – BE – up
The students had finished working before their time was up.

1. by the time – Joe – fix – the roof / / water – damage – already – the ceiling

   _____

   _____

2. the Coopers – travel – more than ten hours / / when – their car – break down

   _____

   _____

3. the agency – change – its employment policy / / when – Emily – start – work – there

   _____

   _____

4. Ms. Hinman – grade – the term papers / / when – she – leave – for – her vacation

   _____

   _____

5. the store – lose – money – for months // when – it – finally – close – last year

_____

_____

6. Brian – decide – take the job // before – I – talk – to him

_____

_____

EXERCISE 7.3-E COMPLETING SENTENCES

the past perfect and the past perfect progressive

Complete each sentence, using your own ideas. Use the past perfect or the past perfect progressive tense in the main clause.

1. I _____
when I came to class today.

2. I had studied English _____
by the time that _____

3. Before my instructor _____ , I

_____

4. _____ when I heard the news.

5. Before I was ten years old, I _____

6. _____ by 1987.

EXERCISE 7.3-F DISCRIMINATING TENSES

**the simple past, the past progressive, the past perfect,
and the past perfect progressive**

Fill in each blank with the appropriate form of the verb in parentheses. Use the simple past, the past perfect, the past perfect progressive, or the past progressive tense. In some cases there may be more than one possibility.

1. We _had finished_ (finish) discussing the surprise party when John
came (come) in, so I don't think that he _heard_ (hear) any
of the plans.

2. The students _had___ed_ (master) the grammar patterns by the day
of the exam. Nevertheless, they _looked_ (look) very nervous

(handwritten top margin: ✗ had studied)

(handwritten left margin: were studying)

_____ when they _____ed (enter) the test room. Many of them

2. (had been — ing) (study) for hours the night before.

3. By the time that Sheila _____ed (graduate) from the university last
   June, she _had taken_ (take) every history course offered by the
   department. When she _____ed (decide) to return to school for a
   second major in sociology, we _were_ (BE) very surprised. She
   had never told (tell, never) us that she _was_ (BE)
   interested in studying another field.

4. When I _left_ (leave) for work this morning, it _was raining_ (rain)
   very hard. The storm _had — ed_ (start) in the middle of the night, and the
   river _already flooded_ (flood, already).

5. The hiring committee _was ing ~~the~~_ (spend) months interviewing candidates for this position when they finally _____ed (agree) on the
   best person for the job. Most of the applicants _had not done_ (do,
   negative) this type of work before.

(handwritten notes near item 4–5: had / ✗ had been spending / ✗ had spent)

EXERCISE 7.3-G RESPONDING TO INFORMATION

relating past activities

Here is information about the life of Jomo Kenyatta, the African statesman
who eventually became president of Kenya. The information is in chrono-
logical order. Read it carefully; then write sentences about Kenyatta's life
that show the time relationships between events. Use the simple past, the
past progressive, the past perfect, and the past perfect progressive tenses.

From 1906 to 1916 Kenyatta studied religion, English, and mathematics at the
    Church of Scotland mission.
In 1916 he went to Nairobi and took a job as a clerk and an interpreter.
In 1922 he began to protest against the domination of Kenya by white British
    settlers.
In the 1930s he studied at the University of Moscow and the London School of
    Economics and met other black nationalists.
During the early 1940s he helped organize the fifth Pan-African Congress.
Kenyatta returned to Kenya in 1946 and became the leader of the Kenya Afri-
    can Union.
In 1952 the British jailed him for involvement in the Mau Mau rebellion.
He got out of prison in 1961 and negotiated the independence of Kenya from
    British rule.
In 1964 he became president of Kenya. He remained in that position until he
    died in 1978.

1. Kenyatta _____ religion, English, and mathematics
at the Church of Scotland mission for _____ when he
_____ in 1916.

2. While Kenyatta _____ ,
he met other black nationalists.

3. Soon after Kenyatta _____ the fifth Pan-African
Congress, _____

4. _____
_____

5. _____
_____

6. _____
_____

7. _____
_____

SECTION 7.4   The Future Perfect Tense

. . . .

THE FUTURE PERFECT
A. Medical science **will have made** many advances by the year 2000.
B. It **will** probably **have unraveled** the mysteries of the human immune system before the twentieth century ends.
C. But it **will not have discovered** a cure for all diseases.

1. The future perfect tense: The future perfect tense expresses a future activity or state in relation to another future time. It is formed with the auxiliary *will*, the simple form of the HAVE auxiliary (*have*), and the past participle (*Ven*) of the main verb. To make a negative statement, make *will* negative.

	will	*have*	*Past Participle (Ven)*	
Science	will	have	made	many advances by the year 2000.
Scientists	will not	have	discovered	a cure for all diseases.

2. The use of the future perfect: The future perfect tense describes an activity or state in the future that will be completed before another activity or time in the future. The earlier future activity uses the future perfect. The later future time, if it is expressed in an adverbial clause of time, uses the simple present tense.

> *Situation:*   We will meet with you next Friday. We will make a decision before Friday.
>
> When we *meet* with you next Friday, we *will have made* a decision.

The later point in time can be expressed with an adverbial clause of time or with an adverb phrase.

Earlier Activity	*Later Activity or Point in Time*
They will have already left	when you come tonight.
	by the time (that) you come tonight.
	before you arrive this evening.
	by nine o'clock this evening.
	before midnight.

Compare the meaning of the future perfect tense with that of the future progressive.

Future Perfect

We *will have prepared* the meal when they arrive. (The preparation will be completed before they come.)

Future Progressive

We *will be preparing* the meal when they arrive. (The preparation will be going on at the time they come.)

3. Questions: The future perfect tense has two auxiliaries, *will* and *have*. How are questions formed in this tense? Examine the following statement and its corresponding questions; then explain how the different question types are created.

> Janice will have written her report by next Tuesday.
>> *Will* Janice *have written* her report by next Tuesday?
>>> Yes, she will. (No, she won't.)
>> *Who will have written* her report by next Tuesday?
>>> Janice.
>> *What will* Janice *have written* by next Tuesday?
>>> Her report.

EXERCISE 7.4-A   CHECKING FORM (ORAL)

the future perfect tense

Answer each question in the negative; then indicate that you will have completed the activity (future perfect tense) *by the time I see you next week.*

> **Example:** Have you read the book yet?
> *No, but I will have read it by the time I see you next week.*

1.   Have you finished the assignment yet?

2.   Have you called everyone yet?

3.   Have you drawn the plans yet?

4.   Have you talked to all the committee members yet?

5.   Have you written the report yet?

6.   Have you sold your car yet?

7.   Have you listened to the tapes yet?

8.   Have you paid the bills yet?

EXERCISE 7.4-B   ANSWERING QUESTIONS (ORAL)

the future perfect tense

Answer each question in the future perfect tense.

1.   How long will you have studied English by the end of the term?

2.   How many chapters in this book will we have completed by the end of the week?

3.   How much money will you have spent on your education by the time you graduate?

4.   How many hours will you have spent in this room when you finish this course?

5.   What will you have accomplished by the time you are 50?

6.   How many years of school will you have completed by the end of this year?

EXERCISE 7.4-C   MAKING PHRASES INTO SENTENCES

the future perfect tense

Create a meaningful statement from each group of words and phrases on page 190. Use the future perfect tense in the main clause and an appropriate tense in adverbial clauses of time.

Example: we – complete – the report / / by the time – it – BE – due – next week

We will have completed the report by the time it is due next week.

1. we – waited – for more than six hours / / when – the plane – finally – arrive – this evening

    _____

    _____

2. people – stop – use – fossil fuels – by the end of the next century

    _____

    _____

3. the new governor – lower – taxes / / by the time that – he – leave – office – four years from now

    _____

    _____

4. Sharon – BE – back from her vacation – for a week / / when – we – have – our meeting – on Tuesday

    _____

    _____

5. Greg and Sam – drive – more than 1,000 miles / / when – they – reach – Atlanta – tonight

    _____

    _____

EXERCISE 7.4-D   DISCRIMINATING TENSES

the simple present, the future progressive, and the future perfect

Fill in each blank with the appropriate form of the verb in parentheses. Use the simple present, the future perfect, or the future progressive tense.

1. The Grendalls _____ (*live*) in the same house for more than half a century when they _____ (*retire*) next year.

2. Do you think that human beings _____ (*travel*) to Mars before they _____ (*learn*) how to live in peace here on earth?

3. I _____ (*interview*) someone when you _____ (*arrive*) tomorrow. I hope you don't mind waiting a few minutes to see me.

4. The department _____ (*revise*) its entire curriculum by the end of the year. Faculty members _____ (*meet*) every Tuesday and Thursday to plan the new offerings and requirements.

5. When the show _____ (*start*) this evening, we _____ (*sit*) in the front row. We _____ (*want*) to have the best seats possible.

6. By the time that the university _____ (*build*) a new library five years from now, the current students _____ (*graduate*) and _____ (*leave*) campus.

7. I _____ (*work*) in the computer room at noon tomorrow, so don't try to call me at that time. But I _____ (*finish*) by late afternoon, and perhaps we can talk then.

EXERCISE 7.4-E RESPONDING TO INFORMATION

predictions with the future perfect

Here are an empty time line and a list of predictions for the future. Add a few predictions of your own. Then decide when you think these predictions will come true, and write them at the appropriate place on the time line. Finally, write sentences, using the future perfect tense, that express your ideas. (See the example on page 192.)

2000

2025

2050

2075

2100

Predictions

Scientists discover a cure for the common cold
Humans reach Mars

Peace prevails throughout the world
The superpowers agree to complete nuclear disarmament
Solar power becomes most used energy source
People control the earth's climate
World population stops growing
Americans elect a woman president

_____

_____

_____

Example: *Humans will have reached Mars by the middle of the twenty-first century.*
We will have reached Mars before scientists discover a cure for the common cold.

8 Modals

Modals and related verb phrases add meaning to the main verb of a sentence. This chapter reviews the basic grammar of modals and several related verb phrases and then examines the meanings these auxiliaries can have. The last section of the chapter presents the use of the perfect aspect with modals.

SECTION 8.1   Overview of Modals and Related Verb Phrases

MODALS		*(See page 194.)*
can	**A.**	Sue and Barbara **can ski** very well, but they **cannot skate.**
may	**B.**	We **may go** to the art show, but we **may not go** to the reception afterward.
might	**C.**	It **might snow** today. It **might not rain.**
should	**D.**	I **should study** now. I **should not go** to a movie.
ought to	**E.**	Edgar **ought to read** the textbook before the lectures.
must	**F.**	Helen **must leave** soon. She **must not be** late for her exam.
will	**G.**	Our plane **will leave** at 8:00 P.M. It **will not leave** at 7:00.
could	**H.**	I **could hear** Jonathan, but I **could not see** him.

1. Modals in affirmative statements: Modals are auxiliaries that add meaning to the main verb of the sentence. Sentences A through H on page 193 each contain a modal auxiliary. Modals have only one form; no ending is added for person or number. Modals are followed by the simple form of the verb. *Ought to* is the only modal that contains *to*.

Correct	*Incorrect*
Tim can go now.	Tim cans go now.
We should study harder.	We should to study harder.
They ought to see that film.	They ought see that film.
Dena may leave early.	Dena may leaves early.
I could hear Howard.	I could heard Howard.

2. Negative statements: Sentences with modals are made negative by adding *not* after the modal auxiliary. Notice that the negative of *can* is written as one word, *cannot*, as in sentence A. *Ought to* is usually not made negative; instead, *should not* is used. Some modals are commonly contracted with *not*:

cannot	=	can't
should not	=	shouldn't
must not	=	mustn't
will not	=	won't
could not	=	couldn't

3. Questions: Because modals serve as auxiliaries, they are used to form questions. Examine the following statement and its corresponding questions. Can you explain how the different types of questions are formed?

Graduating seniors should hand in the final assignment tomorrow.
    Should they *hand in* the final assignment tomorrow?
        Yes, they should. (No, they shouldn't.)
    Who should hand in the final assignment tomorrow?
        Graduating seniors.
    What should graduating seniors *hand in* tomorrow?
        The final assignment.
    What should graduating seniors *do* tomorrow?
        Hand in the final assignment.
Graduating seniors *should* hand in the final assignment tomorrow,
    shouldn't they?
        Yes, they should. (No, they shouldn't.)

4. Making modals progressive: Sentences with modal auxiliaries can be made progressive by adding the simple form of BE (*be*) after the modal and using the present participle (*Ving*) form of the main verb.

	Modal	be	Present Participle (Ving)	
John	might	be	studying	when we arrive.
You	should not	be	working	now.
I	may	be	going	this evening.

RELATED VERB PHRASES		
have to	I.	We **have to read** the article, but we **don't have to answer** the questions.
BE *able to*	J.	Brian **was able to work** on Monday, but he **was not able to work** on Tuesday.
had better	K.	You **had better clean up** this mess. You **had better not leave** it like this.
BE *allowed to*	L.	Ellen **is allowed to leave** at 5:00. She **is not allowed to leave** at 4:00.

5. Related verb phrases: Sentences I through L use four different verb phrases that have meanings similar to certain modals. All four, *have to*, BE *able to*, *had better*, and BE *allowed to*, are followed by a simple form of the verb.

In the expression *have to, have* functions as a regular verb. It must agree in number and person with the subject. The DO auxiliary is used to form negatives and questions.

> Sam *has to* read this article.
> He *doesn't have to* answer the questions.
> *Does* Sam *have to* read this article?
>   Yes, he does. (No, he doesn't.)
> *Who has to* read the article?
>   Sam.
> *What does* Sam *have to* read?
>   This article.

BE in the expressions BE *able to* and BE *allowed to* functions as the BE auxiliary. It must agree in number and person with the subject, and it is used to form negatives and questions.

> Sharon *was able to* work on Monday.
> She *wasn't able to* work on Tuesday.
> *Was* she *able to* work on Monday?
>   Yes, she was. (No, she wasn't.)

Examine how the expression *had better* is made negative and how it is used in questions.

> You *had better* go now.
> You *had better not* stay.
> *Hadn't* you *better* go now?
> *When had* they *better* arrive?

EXERCISE 8.1-A   CHECKING FORM (ORAL)

modals in statements

Make an affirmative statement from each group of words.

> **Example:** the boys – should – study – this evening
> *The boys should study this evening.*

1. Janice – can – join – us – this evening

2. Josh – could – hear – me – talking

3. you – should – leave – tomorrow

4. the answer – must – be – wrong

5. the children – ought to – ask – more questions

6. Margaret – will – call – this evening

Now restate each of the sentences you have just made in the negative. Use a negative contraction if possible.

> **Example:** The boys should study this evening.
> *The boys shouldn't study this evening.*

EXERCISE 8.1-B   CHECKING FORM (ORAL)

questions with modals

For each sentence, ask the question indicated by the WH word that is provided.

> **Example:** Bob might ask for an extension. (what)
> *What might Bob ask for?*

1. Howard can drive us to John's house at 8:00 P.M. (when)

2. George might go to school in Florida next year. (where)

3. Gary ought to write the final report. (who)

4. Bob should check these figures because they might be inaccurate. (why)

5. Professor Butler will talk about supply and demand tomorrow. (what)

6. Jane could use her sister's car if necessary. (whose)

EXERCISE 8.1-C   CHECKING FORM (ORAL)

related verb phrases in statements

Make an affirmative statement from each group of words.

> **Example:** Gilbert – have to – study – this evening
> *Gilbert has to study this evening.*

1. Emily – had better – speak to Joyce

2. the children – BE allowed to – walk to the store – by themselves

3. the store – have to – refund – your money

4. Thelma – BE able to – work – tonight

5. you – had better – change – your answer

6. George – BE allowed to – make a mistake

Now restate each of the sentences you have just made in the negative. Use a negative contraction if possible.

> **Example:** Gilbert has to study this evening.
> *Gilbert doesn't have to study this evening.*

EXERCISE 8.1-D   CHECKING FORM (ORAL)

questions with related verb phrases

For each sentence, ask a question using the WH word in parentheses.

> **Example:** Bob has to ask for an extension because he was ill. (why)
> *Why does Bob have to ask for an extension?*

1. Sharon is allowed to spend $50. (how much)

2. Howard has to have more time to finish this assignment. (who)

3. The Thompsons have to drive to Mobile this weekend. (where)

4. Phil had better leave at 8:00 this evening. (when)

5. Karen is able to speak five languages. (how many)

6. Michael is allowed to watch only wholesome television shows. (which)

EXERCISE 8.1-E   FOCUSING ON THE VERB PHRASE

modals and related verb phrases

Fill in each blank with the proper form of the verb phrase. In some cases you may have to make the verb progressive.

1. The Coopers _____ (*should*, *try*) to come this evening, but they certainly _____ (*have to*, *bring*, negative) anything.

2. We _____ (BE *able to*, *find*, negative) the right kind of paper for the computer. _____ we _____ (*should*, *go*) to another store?

3. Enid _____ (*may*, *talk*) on the telephone right now. _____ you _____ (*could*, *wait*) a minute while I check?

4. _____ we _____ (*have to*, *leave*) so early? We _____ (*will*, BE *able to*, *talk*, negative) to these people again anytime soon, and we _____ (*should*, *introduce*) ourselves at the very least.

5. Freshman students _____ (*must*, *allow*, negative) themselves to get too far behind in their work. They _____ (*ought to*, *keep up*) with their reading even if they _____ (*have to*, *turn in*, negative) homework papers every day.

SECTION 8.2   Expressing Ability, Availability, and Permission

ABILITY
A. I **can speak** Chinese, but I **can't speak** Arabic.
B. Sandra **could speak** Spanish when she was young, but she **couldn't speak** English.
C. I **am able to run** one mile easily, but not five.   I **was able to pass** my history course last term, but not my math class.   I **will be able to get** a good job when I graduate next year.

1. Expressing ability: *Can*, *could*, and BE *able to* can be used to show ability.

Future time: Only BE *able to* expresses ability in the future time.

I *will be able to* get a good job when I graduate next year.
Dennis broke his leg. He *won't be able to* walk for at least six weeks.

Do not use *can* for future ability.

Correct	*Incorrect*
I will be able to speak some Chinese after I finish this course.	I can speak some Chinese after I finish this course.

Present time: BE *able to* and *can* express ability in the present.

I *can* speak Chinese, but I *can't* speak Arabic.
I *am able to* run one mile easily. I'*m not able to* run five.

Past time: BE *able to* and *could* express *general* ability in the past.

Sandra *could* speak Spanish when she was young, but she *couldn't* speak English.
I *was able to* understand my history professor last term, but I *wasn't able to* understand my math professor.

However, *could* in the affirmative cannot be used to express ability for a *specific* past event. You must use BE *able to*.

Correct	*Incorrect*
I was able to win the race yesterday.	I could win the race yesterday.

EXERCISE 8.2-A   ANSWERING QUESTIONS (ORAL)

ability with *can*, *could*, and BE *able to*

Answer the following questions about ability in full sentences, using the same modal or related verb phrase as in the question.

1.   What languages can you speak?

2.   What languages could you speak when you were a child?

3.   What sports can you play well?

4.   What sports can't you play well?

5.   What were you able to do when you were a child that you can't do now?

6.   What won't you be able to do twenty years from now that you can do now?

AVAILABILITY

D. Margaret **can work** on Thursdays.
      She **can work** tomorrow night but not on Saturday.

E. Sharon **could** usually **work** on Saturdays last month.
      But she **couldn't work** last Saturday.

F. Barbara **is** often **able to work** in the evenings.
      She **was able to work** last night.
      She **will be able to work** tomorrow night, too.

---

2. Expressing availability: *Can*, *could*, and BE *able to* can be used to express availability, the idea that a person has time to do something.

Future time: BE *able to* and *can* express availability in the future.

> Margaret *can* work tomorrow night, but she *can't* work next Tuesday.
> Fred *will be able to* come tonight, but he *won't be able to* come tomorrow.

Present time: BE *able to* and *can* express availability in the present.

> Margaret *can* always work on Thursdays, but she *can't* work on Wednesdays.
> Fred *is able to* meet today, but he *'s not able to* meet tonight.

Past time: BE *able to* and *could* express availability for *general* situations in the past.

> Sharon *could* work Saturdays last month, but she *couldn't* work Mondays.
> Howard *was able to* take classes last term, but he *wasn't able to* work.

However, *could* in the affirmative cannot be used to express ability for a *specific* past event. You must use BE *able to*.

Correct	*Incorrect*
Sam was able to work in the cafeteria last night.	Sam could work in the cafeteria last night.

EXERCISE 8.2-B   ANSWERING QUESTIONS (ORAL)

availability with *can*, *could*, and BE *able to*

Answer the following questions about availability in full sentences.

1. Which days can you usually come to class?

2. Which days can you come to class next week?

3. Which days couldn't you come to class last week?

4. Which days were you able to come to class last week?

5. What time will you be able to study tonight?

PERMISSION

G. **May I use** a telephone?
Of course. You **may use** this phone if you wish.

H. **Can** I **speak** to you privately?
Certainly. You **can talk** to me now if you want to.

I. **Could** I **borrow** a pen?
Yes, you **can use** this one.

J. **Am** I **allowed to work** on the next section of the test now?
No, you **are not allowed to** (**work** on it).

---

3. Expressing permission: *May, can, could,* and BE *allowed to* can be used to express permission. *May* and *can* are used in both questions and statements in the present, as in sentences G and H, or in the future. *Could* is used to indicate permission in the past. However, *could* is also used in polite questions for the present, as in sentence I, or in the future. BE *allowed to* expresses permission in any time frame, past, present (sentence J), or future.

EXERCISE 8.2-C   RESPONDING TO SITUATIONS (ORAL)

stating permission

Respond to each situation, stating affirmative or negative permission with the modals *may, can,* or *could* or the related verb phrase BE *allowed to.*

> **Examples:** I want to borrow your pen.
> *You can borrow it. (You can't borrow it.)*
>
> I wanted to borrow your car yesterday, but you said no.
> *You weren't allowed to borrow my car.*

1. I want to leave the room now.

2. I want to talk with you after class.

3. I wanted to read (X's) notes yesterday, and she/he said yes.

4. I want to ask you for some advice now.

5. I want to call you this evening.

EXERCISE 8.2-D   MAKING PHRASES INTO SENTENCES

ability, availability, and permission

Create a meaningful statement from each group of words and phrases. Use the modals *may*, *can*, or *could* or the related verb phrases BE *able to* or BE *allowed to* in the main clause. Use appropriate tenses in adverbial clauses. Then change the statement to the negative or a question form, as indicated.

> **Example:** Dave – pass – the certifying exam / / after – he – finish – this course – next month (ability)
> *Dave will be able to pass the certifying exam after he finishes this course next month.*
>
> Change to a yes-no question.
> *Will he be able to pass the certifying exam after he finishes this course next month?*

1. Susan – come – to dinner – next Saturday (availability)

    _____

    Change to a WH question with *when*.

    _____

2. researchers – use – human subjects – without authorization / / when – Professor Nichols – BE – in charge – last year (permission)

    _____

    _____

    Change to a negative statement.

    _____

    _____

3. Enid – get – financial aid – last semester (ability)

    _____

    Change to a yes-no question.

    _____

4. the committee – reserve – the conference room – in the library – next Thursday (permission)

    _____

    Change to a WH question with *when*.

    _____

    _____

5. John – usually – meet – Sharon / /after – he – teach – his last class (availability)

    _____

    Change to a WH question with *when*.

    _____

EXERCISE 8.2-E   DISCRIMINATING MEANING

● ·

ability, availability, and permission

Decide if each blank requires the meaning of ability, availability, or permission. Then fill in the blank with the modal *may, can,* or *could* or the related
verb phrase BE *able to* or BE *allowed to* and the correct form of the verb in
parentheses. In many cases there will be more than one correct possibility.

1. I _____ (*go,* negative) to the lecture yesterday because I
    had to finish my history project. I _____ (*attend,* negative)
    this evening either, but I _____ (*go*) tomorrow.

2. The mechanic _____ (*fix*) the engine
    problems last week, but he _____ (*repair,*
    negative) the car's transmission because he didn't have the correct parts. He has
    ordered the necessary parts and _____
    (*finish*) the job next Friday.

3. Our   new   manager   is   very   cooperative.   He   says   that   we
    _____ (*put*) up these signs on the bulletin
    board   if   we   remember   to   take   them   down   later.   Last   year,   we
    _____ (*place,* negative) any notices in
    public areas.

4. George   and   Martha   weren't   working   last   Thursday,   so   they
    _____ (*help*) arrange the ceremony for
    that evening. I'm hoping that they _____
    (*assist*) us next Thursday, too.

5. Since the course schedule wasn't ready when I met with my adviser last week, she
    _____ (*tell,* negative) me specifically which courses to
    register for next term, but she _____ (*give*) me some
    good ideas about the types of classes that I might enjoy.

EXERCISE 8.2-F   RESPONDING TO INFORMATION

● ·

availability

Page 204 shows the calendar for November. Pretend that it is November 17
today and that the days that are underlined are days you are available to
work as a student employee in the English Department office.

Make statements about your availability to work, using *can, could,* or BE *able
to.* Use the time frames indicated.

Sun.	Mon.	Tues.	Wed.	Thurs.	Fri.	Sat.
	1	2̲	3	4̲	5	6
7	8	9̲	10	11̲	12	13
14	15	16̲	**17**	18̲	19	20
21	22̲	23̲	24	25̲	26	27
28	29	30̲				

Examples: November 2
I was able to work on November 2.

the week before last (negative)
I couldn't work on Monday, Wednesday, Friday, or Saturday the week before last.

1. next week (affirmative)

_____

2. next week (negative)

_____

3. November 15

_____

4. last week (affirmative)

_____

5. every Thursday

_____

6. November 30

_____

EXERCISE 8.2-G   RESPONDING TO INFORMATION

ability

Here is information about the capabilities of the Soviet Union's space program in the past, the present, and the future. Read the information carefully; then write statements which express these abilities using *can*, *could*, or BE *able to*.

1961–1965: place six cosmonauts in earth orbit
1971: use Proton rocket to launch Salyut I, an orbiting space station
1975: dock a Soyuz 19 spacecraft with American Apollo spacecraft
Present: spend more than 200 days in orbit aboard a Salyut space station

Present: conduct ongoing scientific experiments in outer space
1992: send large satellite to Mars to sample soil and map the land surface
1996: bring samples of Mars soil back to earth for study

Example: *The Soviet Union was able to place six cosmonauts in earth orbit between 1961 and 1965.*

SECTION 8.3 Expressing Possibility, Advisability, and Expectation

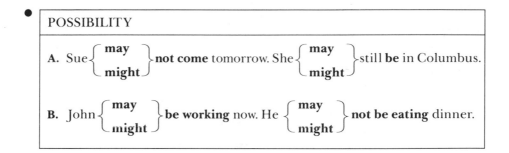

POSSIBILITY

A. Sue {**may** / **might**} **not come** tomorrow. She {**may** / **might**} still **be** in Columbus.

B. John {**may** / **might**} **be working** now. He {**may** / **might**} **not be eating** dinner.

1. Expressing possibility: The modals *may* and *might* can be used to express possibility in the present or in the future, as in sentence A. The negative forms of *may* and *might* mean that an activity will *possibly not* occur. To indicate that the activity is *impossible*, use *cannot*.

> Michael *may not* finish this evening. (It is possible that he will not finish.)
> George *cannot* finish this evening. (It is impossible for him to finish.)

May and *might* can be made progressive, as in sentence B. The progressive use of *may* and *might* for possibility often indicates continuing activity at the moment of speaking or at a moment in the future.

> They *might be arriving* right now. (at the moment of speaking)
> We *may be practicing* when you come tomorrow. (at a moment in the future)

2. Questions: Usually *may* and *might* are not used in yes-no questions to convey possibility. Instead, a question beginning with *Do you think* is used.

> *Do you think* the McGorys will miss their plane?
> They may. (They might.)

May is usually not used in WH questions, but *might* sometimes is. Questions formed with *do you think* are more common.

> *When might* they finish the project?
> *When do you think* they will finish the project?

3. *Maybe* versus *may be*: Do not confuse the modal *may* followed by the main verb *be* (*may be*) with the adverb *maybe*. *Maybe*, which is similar in meaning to *perhaps*, is generally placed at the beginning of a sentence.

> Rachel *may be* here early tomorrow.
> *Maybe* Rachel will be here early tomorrow.
> *Perhaps* Rachel will be here early tomorrow.

EXERCISE 8.3-A   ANSWERING QUESTIONS (ORAL)

possibility

Answer the following questions, using *may* or *might* to express possibility.

1. What do you think you will do this evening?

2. When do you think you will finish studying English?

3. How long do you think it will take to complete the assignment tonight?

4. What do you think you will be doing at this time on Saturday?

5. What job do you think you will be doing twenty-five years from now?

6. Where do you think you will go on your next vacation?

ADVISABILITY

C. Rob { **should** / **ought to** } **take** only two courses. He **should not take** three.

D. We { **should** / **ought to** } **be studying** now. We **should not be wasting** time.

E. You **had better turn in** the tax forms this week. You **had better not forget.**

F. Michael **had better be working** when I return. He **had better not be talking** on the phone.

4. Expressing advisability: Both *should* and *ought to* can express advisability, the notion that something is a good idea. Sentences C and D demonstrate this meaning. *Should not* indicates that an activity is not a good idea. *Ought to* is usually not used in negative statements or in questions.

Awkward	*Better*
Bob *ought not to* drive.	He *shouldn't* drive tonight.
Ought Don *to* memorize this list?	*Should* he memorize this list?

Should and *ought to* can be made progressive, as in sentence D.

5. Strong advice or warning: *Had better* expresses very strong advice in the present or the future, often a type of warning, as in sentence E. *Had better* implies that a harmful consequence may follow if the advice is not taken.

> You *had better* put some gasoline in the car. (If you don't, you will run out of gas on the highway.)
> John *had better not* drive so fast. (If he does, he will get a speeding ticket.)

Had better is usually not used in questions. However, it is found in *negative* yes-no questions to make suggestions.

> *Hadn't* you *better* leave soon? Your plane leaves in an hour. (I suggest that you leave soon.)

Had better can be made progressive, as in sentence F.

EXERCISE 8.3-B   EXPRESSING YOU OWN IDEAS (ORAL)

advisability

Listen to the statements about your classmates, and give them advice using *should*, *ought to*, or *had better*.

> **Example:** (Student X) is tired every morning.
> *She/he should get more sleep at night.*

1. (X) fails almost every exam we have.

2. (X) wants to buy a new car.

3. (X) needs to get up at 5:00 A.M. tomorrow.

4. (X) needs to find an apartment.

5. (X) often runs out of money by the end of the month.

6. (X) looks like she/he is catching the flu.

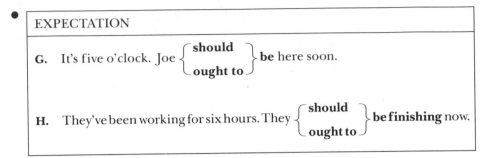

6. Expressing expectation: It is also possible to use *should* and *ought to* to express expectation in the present, as in sentence G, or in the future. This use of *should* and *ought to* can be made progressive, as in sentence H.

> She has studied for weeks. She *should be* ready for the test now. (I expect that she is ready.)
>
> They left over an hour ago. They *should be arriving* soon. (I expect that they will be arriving soon.)
>
> Everyone says that the exam is easy. You *shouldn't have* any difficulty. (I expect that you will not have any difficulty.)

EXERCISE 8.3-C   ANSWERING QUESTIONS (ORAL)

expectation

Respond to each question with a statement of expectation, using *should* or *ought to*.

> **Example:** Greg started working on the project three months ago. When do you think he will finish?
> *He should finish by the end of this month.*

1. The weather is going to be beautiful tomorrow. Do you think the park will be crowded?

2. All the students in this class have been working very hard. How do you think they will do on the final examination?

3. George is an expert on this subject. Do you think he can help us?

4. They left for New York several hours ago. Where do you think they are now?

5. I've been preparing for my interview for a week now. How do you think I'll do?

6. Margaret has been studying Spanish since the sixth grade. Is she very fluent yet?

EXERCISE 8.3-D   MAKING PHRASES INTO SENTENCES

possibility, advisability, and expectation

Create a meaningful statement from each group of words and phrases. Use
the modals *may, might, should,* or *ought to* or the related verb phrase *had better*
in the main clause. Use the progressive where appropriate. Then change the
statement to the negative or to a question form as indicated. Remember that
may and *might* are generally not used in question forms.

> **Example:** Henry – study / / when – we – arrive – tonight (possibility)
> *Henry may be studying when we arrive tonight.*
>
> Change to a yes-no question.
> *Do you think that Henry will be studying when we arrive tonight?*

1. the Davidson's – make – their reservations – at least a day in advance (advisability)

_____

_____

Change to a WH question with *how far in advance.*

_____

2. you – get – ready – now (strong advisability or warning)

_____

Change to a yes-no question (negative).

_____

3. the mayor – run (negative) – for another term / / because – his health – fail
(possibility)

_____

Change to a WH question with *why.*

_____

4. the runners – reach – the finish line – in about two minutes (expectation)

_____

Change to a WH question with *when.*

_____

5. when – his leg heals / / Eric – start – walk – as much as possible (advisability)

_____

Change to a *what-do* question.

_____

EXERCISE 8.3-E   DISCRIMINATING MEANING

possibility, advisability, and expectation

Decide if each blank requires the meaning of possibility, advisability, or expectation. Then fill it with *may, might, should, ought to,* or *had better* and the correct form of the verb in parentheses. Use the progressive aspect where appropriate. There may be more than one possibility in some cases.

1. You _____ (begin) working harder. I'm afraid that you won't pass this course if you don't.

2. I don't know where Herb and Sam are now. They _____ (talk) with Professor Bajouda, or they _____ (BE) on their way to the library. In any event, they _____ (BE) right here for our scheduled meeting.

3. The movie started more than three hours ago. It _____ (BE) over by now, so George and Martha _____ (walk through) the door any minute. However, they _____ (BE) late if they stopped to get something to eat before coming home.

4. Students _____ (try, negative) to cheat on the exam. If they are caught cheating, they will be thrown out of school. And a student who sees anyone else cheating _____ (tell) the proctor immediately.

5. The new superintendent has dealt with labor problems in his previous job. He _____ (BE *able to*) handle similar problems here. He _____ (have, negative) any difficulty knowing what to do.

EXERCISE 8.3-F   RESPONDING TO INFORMATION

possibility, advisability, and expectation

Here is information about the ozone layer which surrounds the earth and the harm that humans may be doing to it. Read the information carefully; then write statements of possibility, advisability, or expectation in response to the questions. Use *may, might, should, ought to,* or *had better.*

Approximately fifteen miles above the surface of the earth is a thin layer of ozone, a form of oxygen that is opaque to ultraviolet light from the sun. The ultraviolet portion of sunlight can be extremely harmful to plant and animal life on earth, causing skin cancer and cataracts in humans and killing microscopic life in the soil and on the surface of the oceans. But most of it is stopped by the ozone layer. Thus we are able to.walk in the sunlight with little damage.

In the early 1970s, scientists at the University of California at Irvine discovered that substances called chlorofluorocarbons, or CFCs, break down ozone. CFCs are used extensively in spray cans, refrigerators, and automobile air conditioners. More than ten million tons of CFCs have already leaked into the air, and more is added each day. In 1985 it was discovered that the ozone layer over Antarctica had a large hole, possibly caused by CFCs. If the same trend occurs elsewhere, the ozone layer above us will grow too thin to protect us from ultraviolet light.

Example: What do you think is causing the thinning of the ozone layer above Antarctica?
The use of CFCs may be causing the thinning of the ozone layer.

1. What are the possible dangers to human beings if the ozone layer disappears?

    _____

2. What are the possible dangers to other life forms?

    _____

3. Do you think that life on earth will continue in its present form if the ozone layer becomes too thin?

    _____

4. What do you think it is advisable for scientists to be doing about this danger?

    _____

5. What do you think it is advisable for governments to do?

    _____

6. If CFCs are prohibited all around the world, what do you expect will happen?

    _____

7. If CFCs are not prohibited, what do you expect will happen in the future?

    _____

SECTION 8.4 Expressing Necessity, Prohibition, and Logical Deduction

NECESSITY   (*See page 212.*)
A. The city council members **must meet** again tonight.
B. They **have to discuss** some new legislation.
C. They **had to make** several recommendations last night.
D. They **will** probably **have to meet** one more time next week.

1. Expressing necessity: *Must* and *have to* are both used to express necessity, as in sentences A through D on page 211. *Have to* is used more frequently in conversation and is considered more informal.

Must and *have to* can be used in present or future situations to express necessity. *Have to* can also follow *will* to emphasize the future aspect, as in sentence D. *Must* and *have to* are generally not made progressive to convey necessity.

To express necessity in the past, use *had to*, as in sentence C. Do not use *must*.

Must and *have to* indicate that there is no choice. *Should* and *ought to* express advisability, where a choice is possible.

> You *must* study harder. (You have no choice. If you don't study harder, you will fail.)
> You *should* study harder. (This is my advice to you. I realize that you may not take my advice.)

LACK OF NECESSITY

E.   You **don't have to write** the essay. It's optional.

F.   You **didn't have to write** the book report, either.

G.   You **will not have to take** the final exam if you are a graduating senior.

---

2. Expressing lack of necessity: *Have to* in the negative expresses lack of necessity, the idea that there is a choice. Examine sentences E, F, and G. The negative of *have to* can be used in the present, the past, or the future. It is generally not made progressive.

> You *don't have to go* this evening. (It is not necessary for you to go. You can go, or you can stay home; it is your choice.)

EXERCISE 8.4-A   ANSWERING QUESTIONS (ORAL)

necessity and lack of necessity

Answer each question with a full sentence, expressing either necessity or lack of necessity with *must* or *have to*.

1.   What do you have to do this evening?

2.   When do you have to take final examinations this term?

3. Why must you come to English class every day?

4. Is there anything that you will have to do next week?

5. Will you have to study tonight?

6. Do you have to take an English course next term?

PROHIBITION

H. You **must not call** me at the office, either now or in the future.

I. I'm **not allowed to take** personal calls during working hours.

---

3. Expressing prohibition: The negative of *must* expresses prohibition, the idea that something is not allowed, as in sentence H. Notice how different this is from the negative of *have to*.

> You *don't have to go* this evening. (It is not necessary; you have a choice.)
> You *must not go* this evening. (It is prohibited; you are not allowed to go. You have no choice.)

Prohibition with *must not* is used for present or future situations. It is usually not made progressive. *Cannot, may not,* and *not* BE *allowed to* have a similar meaning, indicating that something is not permitted. To express prohibition in the past, *could not* and *not* BE *allowed to* are often used.

> You *must not swim* in this lake.
> You *cannot swim* in this lake.
> You *may not swim* in this lake.
> You *are not allowed to swim* in this lake.
> You *could not swim* in this lake last year.
> You *were not allowed to swim* in this lake last year.

EXERCISE 8.4-B   ANSWERING QUESTIONS (ORAL)

prohibition

Answer each question with a full sentence, expressing prohibition with *must not*.

1. Can you drive a car without a license?

2. Am I allowed to cross in the middle of a street?

3. Are students permitted to bring notes to the final examination?

4. Is it legal for a person to vote more than once in an election?

5. Can I drive as fast as I want to on the highways?

6. Is it legal to use someone else's credit card?

LOGICAL DEDUCTION

J. Maria **must be** talented in languages. She never studies very hard, but she gets good grades in her English courses.

K. It's five o'clock. George **must be getting off** work about now.

L. Sam **must not like** his job. He never wants to talk about it.

---

4. Expressing logical deduction: *Must* can also be used to express logical deduction, the idea that there is only one logical possibility. Read sentences J, K, and L; then examine the situations that might lead to these logical deductions.

Situation: We know that Maria never seems to study English very hard, but she does well in her English classes. The speaker can think of only one explanation for this fact.
Maria must be talented in languages.

Situation: George usually finishes work at five o'clock. It is five now, so the logical deduction is that he is leaving work at this time.
George must be getting off work now.

Situation: We know that Sam never talks about his job. A logical conclusion is that he doesn't like it very much.
Sam must not like his job.

Must can be used in the affirmative and in the negative to express logical deduction. It can also be made progressive, as in sentence K. It is important to remember that logical deduction is not fact and that different people may reach different conclusions about the same situation.

Situation: Janet looks tired all the time and has been doing poorly in school.
She must be ill.
She must not be getting enough sleep.
She must spend too much time going out and having a good time.
She must be upset about a family problem.

EXERCISE 8.4-C   RESPONDING TO SITUATIONS (ORAL)

logical deduction

Listen to each situation. State a logical deduction with *must*.

1. John just came in the door, and he's soaking wet.

2. Dena cries all the time lately.

3. I've been calling Tim all day, but no one answers.

4. There's a lot of music and shouting coming from the apartment next door.

5. Gary's eyes are watering and his face is pale.

6. Julie was up all night studying.

EXERCISE 8.4-D   RESPONDING TO SITUATIONS (ORAL)

necessity, prohibition, and logical deduction

Respond to each statement with a statement of necessity, lack of necessity, prohibition, or logical deduction.

1. I just dropped a stack of dishes!

2. I drove over 80 miles per hour down Main Street today.

3. I really don't want to go to the lecture this evening.

4. I always get the highest grades in the class.

5. I'm going to fly first class when I go to Boston.

6. I'm failing my calculus class.

7. I'm going to borrow George's car without telling him.

EXERCISE 8.4-E   MAKING PHRASES INTO SENTENCES

necessity, prohibition, and logical deduction

Create a meaningful statement from each group of words and phrases on page 216. Use *must* or *have to* in the affirmative or in the negative in the main clause and an appropriate tense in any adverbial clauses.

> **Example:** we – turn in – our term papers – this week (lack of necessity)
> *We don't have to turn in our term papers this week.*

1. all department heads – meet – individually – with the vice president – last week (necessity)

   _____

   _____

2. you – use – other people's ideas – without giving them credit (prohibition)

   _____

   _____

3. Joy and Ann – enjoy – themselves – in Hawaii – this week (logical deduction)

   _____

   _____

4. you – give – a donation // when – the volunteer – ask – for one (lack of necessity)

   _____

   _____

5. job candidates – pass – a security clearance – before – get – a job (necessity)

   _____

   _____

6. you – discuss – this conversation – with anyone else (prohibition)

   _____

   _____

EXERCISE 8.4-F   DISCRIMINATING MEANING

necessity, prohibition, and logical deduction

Decide if each blank requires the meaning of necessity, prohibition, or logical deduction. Then fill it in with *must* or *have to* in the affirmative or in the negative and with the correct form of the verb in parentheses. Use the progressive aspect where appropriate. There may be more than one possibility in some cases.

1. Before you can be considered for a job with that company, you
   _____ (*complete*) an application form.
   You also _____ (*give*) several personal and professional
   references, but you _____ (*submit*) a resume. If you are
   called for an interview, you _____ (BE) late, and you
   _____ (*make*) a good appearance.

2. Arnold and Sally have been on the road for seven hours. It takes more than ten
   hours to reach Buffalo, so they _____

(*drive*, *still*). They _____ (BE) exhausted by now. They feel that they _____ (*complete*) the trip in one day, but they really _____ . WE _____ (*convince*) them to stretch the drive over two days next time.

3. You _____ (*fail*) to submit your tax return by April 15. The Internal Revenue Service _____ (*receive*) your tax form postmarked no later than that date. If they don't you may _____ (*pay*) a penalty.

4. George _____ (*finish*) the report today; he can turn it in tomorrow if he wants to. But he _____ (*forget*) to include the necessary illustrations with the report. The instructor _____ (*see*) them in order to evaluate the project.

5. It's been snowing for hours now. The roads _____ (BE) slippery, and the driving _____ (BE) dangerous. But most businesses and schools are closed, so not many people _____ (BE) on the highways.

EXERCISE 8.4-G   RESPONDING TO SITUATIONS

logical deduction

Read each situation. Then state a logical deduction in the present or in the future using *must*.

> **Examples:** The doors and windows are all shut at the Thompson house, and the lights are all off. There is a stack of newspapers piled on the front steps.
> *The Thompsons must be out of town.*   OR
> *The Thompsons must be on vacation.*

1. There are no students or teachers at the schools, and the banks are closed. The highways leading out of town are extremely crowded.

_____

2. The walls of Nathan's apartment are covered with art prints, and he has endless volumes of art history books on his shelves.

_____

3. I'm not sure exactly where Martha is right now. When I saw her an hour ago, she was wearing a sweat suit and walking toward the gym.

_____

4. John's answer doesn't match the one given in the back of the math book. He made sure to read the problem several times, and he checked and rechecked his calculations.

_____

EXERCISE 8.4-H   EXPRESSING YOUR OWN IDEAS

necessity, lack of necessity, and prohibition

Imagine that you are creating a new society where people can live more comfortably and happily than is possible anywhere else. In order to make your new society work, you need to construct guidelines, or rules, for the members of the society. What behavior is necessary? What behavior is prohibited? What behavior is not necessary? Write statements expressing the rules of your new society.

Examples: Behavior that is necessary:
People in my society have to serve ten hours each week helping others who are less fortunate.

Behavior that is prohibited:
Members of my society must not criticize others or show contempt.

Behavior that is not necessary:
Individuals do not have to serve in the military if it is against their beliefs.

1. Behavior that is necessary for everyone:

_____

_____

_____

2. Behavior that is prohibited for everyone:

_____

_____

_____

3. Behavior that is not necessary:

_____

_____

_____

SECTION 8.5   Modal Perfects

· ·

●
MODAL PERFECTS
A.   Rachael **may have spoken** to Joan earlier this morning, but she **could not have talked** to Sandra.
B.   Sam **must not have been working** in the library when I tried to find him last night, but he **may have been driving** home.

1. Modal perfects: Some modals can be given past meaning by adding the perfect aspect with the simple form of the HAVE auxiliary (*have*) followed by the past participle of the main verb, as in sentence A. The negative is formed by placing *not* after the modal.

	Modal	*have*	*Past Participle (Ven)*	
Rachael	may	have	spoken	to Joan earlier this morning.
She	could not	have	talked	to Sandra.

2. The modal perfect progressive: The modal perfect can sometimes be made progressive by adding the past participle form of the BE auxiliary (*been*) after the HAVE auxiliary, followed by the present participle form of the main verb (*Ving*), as in sentence B. The negative is formed by placing *not* after the modal.

	Modal	*have*	*been*	*Present Participle (Ving)*	
Sam	may	have	been	driving	home at that time.
He	must not	have	been	working	in the library.

3. Questions: The modal is used to construct question forms of various types.

> Horton could have come at 8:00 this morning.
> *Could* he *have come* at 8:00?
> *Who could have come* at 8:00?
> *When could* Horton *have come* this morning?

4. Pronunciation: In rapid speech, *have* in a modal perfect sounds more like "of" or even "a."

> You should *have* come yesterday. (correct written form)
> You should *of* come yesterday. (fast speech)
> You should*a* come yesterday. (very fast speech)

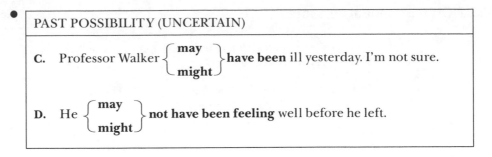

PAST POSSIBILITY (UNCERTAIN)

C.   Professor Walker { **may** / **might** } **have been** ill yesterday. I'm not sure.

D.   He { **may** / **might** } **not have been feeling** well before he left.

5. Past uncertain possibility: *May have* and *might have* are used to express possibility in the past when the outcome is uncertain, that is, when the speaker isn't sure if the activity happened or not. Modal perfects with *may* and *might* can be made progressive.

> *Situation:*   It is possible that Professor Walker was ill yesterday. I'm not sure if he was or not.
> Professor Walker may/might have been ill yesterday.

The negative of *may have* or *might have* indicates that it is possible that an event did not happen. It does not mean that an event was impossible.

> *Situation:*   It is possible that Professor Walker was not feeling well before he left. I don't know if he was or not.
> Professor Walker may/might not have been feeling well before he left.

EXERCISE 8.5-A   ANSWERING QUESTIONS (ORAL)

past uncertain possibility

Answer each question with a statement of past possibility, using *may have* or *might have*.

> **Example:** Did (student X) do the assignment last night?
> *She may have done the assignment, but I'm not sure.*

1.   Did (X) eat breakfast this morning?

2.   Did (X) read the newspaper this morning?

3.   Was (X) studying at the library last night?

4.   Did (X) return home during the last break?

5.   Was (X) upset when she/he left class yesterday?

6.   Did (X) want to see me yesterday afternoon?

PAST ABILITY OR POSSIBILITY (UNFULFILLED)

E. George **could have behaved** more politely to Martha, but he still **couldn't have pleased** her.

F. Joe **could have been working** more efficiently when I came in, but he **couldn't have been working** any harder.

---

6. Past unfulfilled ability or possibility: *Could have* is used to express ability or possibility in the past that was not fulfilled or achieved. *Could have* can be made progressive.

> *Situation:*   George didn't behave very politely toward Martha. It was possible for him to behave more politely, or he had the ability to do so. George could have behaved more politely to Martha.

7. Negative use: Use the negative of *could have* when you believe that the ability or the possibility did *not* exist in the past, and thus you believe that the event did *not* take place.

> *Situation:*   George wasn't able to make Martha happy. Either it just wasn't possible, or he didn't have the ability. George could not have pleased her.

8. Uncertain versus unfulfilled outcomes: Notice how *could have* (with an unfulfilled outcome) differs from *may* or *might have* (with an uncertain outcome).

> Harold *could have written* a letter. (The possibility existed. He had the ability, but for some reason, he didn't write one.)
> Harold *may have written* a letter. (It is possible, but I don't know if he did or didn't.)

Could not and *could not have* differ slightly in meaning, although both indicate impossibility in the past (unfulfilled outcomes).

> They *couldn't go* yesterday. (It is a fact that it was impossible for them to go.)
> They *couldn't have gone* yesterday. (It is my belief that it was impossible for them to go.)

In some situations, especially in speech, *could have* can indicate past ability or possibility with an uncertain outcome rather than an unfulfilled outcome.

> They *could have left* this morning, but I'm not certain if they did or not.

EXERCISE 8.5-B   ANSWERING QUESTIONS (ORAL)

past ability and possibility (unfulfilled)

Answer each question with a statement of past ability or possibility un-fulfilled. Use *could have* or *could not have*.

> **Examples:** Did (student X) read the chapter last night?
> *She could have read it, but she didn't.*   OR
> *She couldn't have read it. She lost her book.*

1.   Did (X) go to the language lab yesterday?

2.   Did (X) visit his/her friends last night?

3.   Was (X) preparing for the exam this morning?

4.   Did (X) attend the lecture last night?

5.   Did (X) get the information I needed?

6.   Did (X) see a movie last night?

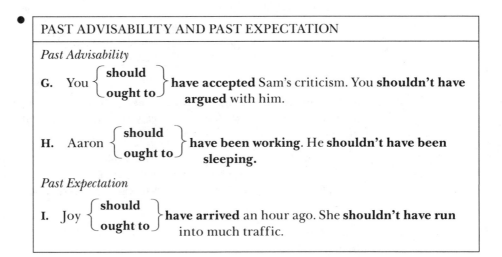

PAST ADVISABILITY AND PAST EXPECTATION

Past Advisability

G.   You { **should** / **ought to** } **have accepted** Sam's criticism. You **shouldn't have argued** with him.

H.   Aaron { **should** / **ought to** } **have been working**. He **shouldn't have been sleeping**.

Past Expectation

I.   Joy { **should** / **ought to** } **have arrived** an hour ago. She **shouldn't have run** into much traffic.

9. Past advisability and past expectation: *Should have* and *ought to have* express advisability or expectation in the past, usually with the meaning that the advice was not taken or the expectation did not prove true (un-fulfilled outcome).

> *Situation:*   It was advisable for you to accept Sam's criticism, but you did not. You should/ought to have accepted his criticism.

10. Negative use: *Should not have* usually indicates that a past activity was not advisable or was not expected, but it occurred anyway. *Ought to have* isn't usually made negative.

> *Situation:* It was not advisable for you to argue with John, but you did.
> You should not have argued with him.

Look at some other examples.

> You ought to have entered the race. (It was advisable, but you didn't.)
> You shouldn't have entered the race. (It was not advisable, but you did.)

In certain situations, *should* and *ought to* can express past advisability or expectation with an uncertain outcome.

> They should have made a reservation, but I don't know if they did or not.
> She shouldn't have had any difficulty, but I don't know what happened.

11. Progressive use: Modal perfects with *should have* and *ought to have* are frequently made progressive when the meaning involves past advisability, as in sentence H, but generally not when the meaning involves past expectation.

EXERCISE 8.5-C   RESPONDING TO SITUATIONS (ORAL)

. . . .

past advisability

Respond to each statement with advice about the past. Use *should have* or *ought to have* in the affirmative or in the negative.

> **Example:** I got a speeding ticket yesterday.
> *You shouldn't have been driving so fast.*

1. I forgot to bring my umbrella this morning, and now it's pouring.

2. I haven't sent in my tax return yet, and it was due last week.

3. I was late for an important meeting this morning.

4. I'm exhausted this morning.

5. My back aches from lifting furniture.

6. I didn't lock my apartment door before I left home this morning.

> ### PAST LOGICAL DEDUCTION
>
> **J.** Doris received a low grade on her essay. She **must have been** careless. She **must not have spent** much time on it.
>
> **K.** Howard's room was quiet when I passed his door. He **must have been sleeping**. He **must not have been talking** on the telephone.

12. Past logical deduction: *Must have* expresses past logical deduction. It does not indicate necessity in the past. *Must have* can be made progressive.

> *Situation:*   Doris usually receives good grades on her work. However, she received a low grade on her last essay. You make a conclusion based on this information.
> Doris must have been careless on her essay.
> She must not have spent much time on it.

EXERCISE 8.5-D   RESPONDING TO SITUATIONS (ORAL)

past logical deductions

Make a past logical deduction about each situation. Use *must have* in the affirmative or in the negative.

> **Example:** Traffic is tied up for miles.
> *There must have been an accident ahead.*

1. I fell down on the ice yesterday.

2. George had to borrow fifty dollars from me yesterday.

3. They left without finishing their meal.

4. Martha got a speeding ticket this morning.

5. My boss wants to see me immediately.

EXERCISE 8.5-E   MAKING PHRASES INTO SENTENCES

modal perfects

Create a meaningful statement from each group of words and phrases. Use a modal perfect in the main clause.

> **Example:** George – forget – ask – his parents – about the trip (past possibility, uncertain)
> *George may have forgotten to ask his parents about the trip.*

1. the mayor – make (negative) – so many campaign promises (past advisability)

_____

_____

2. your discussion – with Martha – BE (negative) – very pleasant (past possibility, unfulfilled)

_____

_____

3. the evidence – against him – BE (negative) – very convincing (past logical deduction)

_____

_____

4. Jones – have to (negative) – report – his extra income – to the tax officials (past possibility, uncertain)

_____

_____

5. the receptionist – BE able to – give – you – all the information (past expectation)

_____

_____

6. Anne – explain – the situation – more clearly (past ability, unfulfilled)

_____

_____

EXERCISE 8.5-F   DISCRIMINATING MEANING

● ·

modal perfects

Decide if each blank requires the meaning of past advisability (uncertain), ability or possibility (unfulfilled), advisability, expectation, or logical deduction. Then fill it in with a modal perfect in the affirmative or in the negative and the correct form of the verb in parentheses. Use the progressive aspect where appropriate. There may be more than one possibility in some cases.

1. The mechanic _____ (_repair_) the car by now, but I just got off the phone and he says that he's been too busy to get to it. He _____ (_tell_) me that he couldn't work on it when I took it to the shop this morning. I _____ (_take_) it to another mechanic.

2. Professor Pederson _____ (*present*) her proposal very effectively; the committee approved it quickly and with very little discussion. The committee members _____ (*reject*) it because of the high cost, but they _____ (*feel*) that the quality of the proposal justified the expense.

3. I'm not sure what the building inspectors were doing here last month. They _____ (*examine*) the building to see if it meets safety codes. They _____ (*find*, negative) any problems because we haven't received any warnings from them. But I'm upset that the inspectors didn't tell us they were coming. They _____ (*notify*) us ahead of time.

4. It takes six hours to drive to Cincinnati from here, so Sharon _____ (*get*, negative) there in only three hours. You _____ (*misunderstand*) her. She _____ (*arrive*, negative) in Cincinnati until at least four in the afternoon.

5. Pat is very upset about your conversation with him yesterday. You _____ (*criticize*, negative) him so harshly. He always tries his hardest, so he _____ (*try*) to do a good job for you. You _____ (BE) more encouraging when you talked with him.

EXERCISE 8.5-G   RESPONDING TO SITUATIONS

logical deduction in the present and in the past

Read each situation; then make a logical deduction either in the present or in the past. Use *must* or *must have* in the affirmative or in the negative.

> **Example:** Sue fell and broke her wrist when she stepped off the bus last Monday.
> *It must have been very painful.*   OR
> *She must be wearing a cast now.*   OR
> *The step must have been slippery.*

1. Gary has been very nervous all week.

_____

2. Burglars broke into my house last night.

_____

3. The results of the latest experiment seem to contradict earlier findings.

_____

4. Fewer than two in ten students were able to identify these countries on a map.

_____

5. Not very many people showed up for the eight o'clock lecture this morning.

_____

6. John is broke again this week.

_____

EXERCISE 8.5-H   RESPONDING TO INFORMATION

● ·

modal perfects

Read the paragraph; then create sentences from the phrases provided. Use appropriate modal perfects, either in the affirmative or in the negative.

> In 1876 Alexander Graham Bell patented the telephone in the United States. A few years later a Toronto publisher named George Brown was offered exclusive rights to market the telephone in Canada and throughout the British Empire. The rights would have cost Brown a total of $150. He turned down the offer because he thought the price was too high. By 1982 American Telephone and Telegraph, the company which had rights to the telephone in the United States, was worth $148 billion and had over one million employees. Imagine what George Brown let slip between his fingers.

> **Example:** pay $150 for the exclusive rights
> _Brown should have paid $150 for the exclusive rights._

1. BE rich

_____

_____

2. buy the rights to the telephone

_____

_____

3. turn down the offer

_____

_____

4. BE very shrewd

_____

_____

5. understand the potential of the telephone

_____

_____

6. BE very shortsighted

_____

_____

EXERCISE 8.5-I   RESPONDING TO INFORMATION

modal perfects

Read the paragraphs about a college student who designed an atomic bomb. Then create sentences from the phrases provided. Use appropriate modal perfects, either in the affirmative or in the negative.

> When John Phillips was a senior at Princeton University in 1976, he drew complete plans for an atomic bomb that could actually work. He used information from unclassified sources that are available to anyone in a university library. It took him only four months to finish his design. Phillips never actually built the bomb, but he estimated that if he did, the bomb would weigh 125 pounds and cost no more than $2,000. It would be one-third as powerful as the atomic bomb dropped on Hiroshima during World War II.

> Phillips says that he drew the plans because he wanted people to realize that terrorist organizations could do the same thing. In fact, several foreign governments contacted him for information, but he refused to talk with them. Eventually, the government classified Phillips' design as secret. Because he worked from unclassified documents, his actions were not illegal.

> **Example:** design the bomb
> _Phillips should not have designed the bomb._

1. BE available in the library

_____

_____

2. want publicity

_____

_____

3. BE illegal

_____

_____

4. work for a terrorist organization

_____

_____

5. BE very talented

_____

_____

6. BE punished

_____

_____

9 The Passive Voice

This chapter examines the use of the passive voice to change the emphasis of a sentence. First you will practice the passive with simple tenses and progressive tenses, then with the perfect tenses and with modal auxiliaries. The last section of the chapter discusses participial adjectives, which have either an active or a passive direction.

SECTION 9.1   The Passive of Simple Tenses and Progressive Tenses

SECTION 9.2   The Passive of Perfect Tenses and Modal Auxiliaries

SECTION 9.3   Participial Adjectives

SECTION 9.1   The Passive of Simple Tenses and Progressive Tenses

SIMPLE TENSES		
Active Voice:	**A.**	Floods **destroy** the crops in this area every few years.
Passive Voice:	**B.**	The crops in this area **are destroyed** by floods every few years.
Active Voice:	**C.**	Friends **donated** the money for the operation.
Passive Voice:	**D.**	The money for the operation **was donated** by friends.

1. The active voice: All the sentences we have examined in previous chapters have been in the active voice. In an active sentence, the subject is the *agent*, the *doer* or *performer* of the activity. The object of the sentence is the *receiver* of the activity. Examine sentence A. *Floods* is both the subject and the agent (it causes the destruction). *The crops in this area* is the object and the receiver (it receives the destruction). Read the other active sentence, C. What is both the subject and the agent of this sentence? What is both the object and the receiver? (The answers are on the next page.)

Subject		Object
Friends (agent)	donated	the money for the operation. (receiver)

2. The passive voice: In a passive sentence, the agent and the receiver change position. The receiver becomes the subject, and the agent becomes the object. *By* is placed in front of the agent. The verb phrase also changes. A form of the verb BE is added before the main verb, and the main verb is changed to the past participle form (*Ven*).

	Subject	Verb Phrase	Object
Active:	John (agent)	introduced	the speaker. (receiver)
Passive:	The speaker (receiver)	*was* introduced	*by* John. (agent)

Compare the active and passive sentence pairs A and B, C and D. The agent and the receiver have reversed position in the passive sentences, and *by* has been added before the agent. What has happened to the verb phrases? The main verb is changed to its past participle form. Notice that the form of BE that is added in front of the main verb is different in each case. It is the same as the form of the main verb in the active verb phrase. In the simple present, it will be *am*, *is*, or *are*. In the simple past, it will be *was* or *were*.

3. The use of the passive: Passive sentences emphasize the receiver of the activity by placing it in the subject position. The agent is *de-emphasized* by placing it in the object position at the end of the sentence. In fact, the agent is often omitted in passive sentences if it is not considered important, if its exact identity is unknown, if it is obvious, or if the speaker wants to hide the identity of the agent.

> The building is being renovated. (It is not important to know who is doing the work.)
> My car was built in Japan. (I don't know the exact identity of the workers who built it.)
> Wheat and corn are grown in this region. (The agent is obvious; farmers grow the corn and wheat.)
> The lights were left on last night. (I don't want to say who did it.)

4. Negative statements and questions: Negative statements and questions in the passive are formed with the first auxiliary of the passive verb phrase.

Active	*Passive*

John introduced the speaker   The speaker was introduced by John.

John didn't introduce the speaker.   The speaker wasn't introduced by John.

Did John introduce the speaker?   Was the speaker introduced by John?

5. Second subjects: A second subject, which acts as the object of the first verb, can be placed in the subject position in a passive sentence.

Active: We persuaded *John* to come along with us.

Passive: *John* was persuaded to come along with us.

Active: They saw *her* leaving the building.

Passive: *She* was seen leaving the building.

6. Intransitive and linking verbs: Active sentences that do not have objects cannot be made passive. Therefore, intransitive verbs and linking verbs are never made passive.

Many people die in fires every year. (never *is* or *are died*)

The solution came many years later. (never *was* or *were come*)

Accidents like this one occur often. (never *is* or *are occurred*)

A tragedy happened here years ago. (never *was* or *were happened*)

My brother became an engineer. (never *was* or *were became*)

PROGRESSIVE TENSES		
Active Voice:	E.	The city **is repairing** the broken pavement.
Passive Voice:	F.	The broken pavement **is being repaired** by the city.
Active Voice:	G.	Several organizations **were distributing** the pamphlets.
Passive Voice:	H.	The pamphlets **were being distributed** by several organizations.

7. The passive of progressive tenses: To make a progressive tense passive, add the present participle of BE (*being*) before the main verb, and change the main verb to the past participle form (*Ven*), as in sentences F and H. Remember that the first auxiliary must agree in person and number with the subject of the sentence, as in the following examples.

Active: Several students *are* writing the report.

Passive: The report *is* being written by several people.

8. The passive in the future with BE *going to*:   How is the future with BE *going to* made passive? Look at these examples.

Active: Someone *is going to send* the information tomorrow.

Passive: The information *is going to be sent* tomorrow.

What form of BE is added before the main verb?

EXERCISE 9.1-A   CHECKING FORM (ORAL)

from passive to active in simple tenses and progressive tenses

Change each passive sentence to the active voice.

1.   The window was broken by the children.

2.   Radiation is given off by the sun.

3.   Tonight's concert is going to be cancelled by the management.

4.   The computer wasn't being used by Tim.

5.   The accident was seen by a large crowd of people.

6.   Direct address is indicated by quotation marks.

7.   Free meals were not provided by the restaurant.

8.   The report is going to be written by three people.

EXERCISE 9.1-B   CHECKING FORM (ORAL)

from active to passive in simple tenses and progressive tenses

Change each active sentence to the passive voice. Include the agent in a phrase with *by*.

1.   The university employs a lot of people.

2.   Gary didn't finish the job yesterday.

3.   Her friends are helping her.

4.   Workmen didn't repair the roof yesterday.

5.   His club is going to organize the trip.

6. The secretary announces the meetings.

7. Dena won the lottery.

8. John is checking all the calculations.

9. Professor Madden gave the instructions.

EXERCISE 9.1-C   CHANGING ACTIVE TO PASSIVE

including or omitting the agent

Change each statement to the passive voice. Omit the agent (*by*) phrase if it is not necessary.

> **Example:** Some workers are painting the classrooms this week.
> *The classrooms are being painted this week.*

1. People speak both French and English in Canada.

_____

_____

2. The police were not investigating the incident.

_____

_____

3. Someone broke the windows and smashed the furniture.

_____

_____

4. The Food and Drug Administration is going to test the new vaccine over a two-year period.

_____

_____

5. Fishermen catch a tremendous quantity of fish off this coast every year.

_____

_____

6. Someone founded Buddhism about 2,500 years ago.

_____

_____

7. Prince Siddhartha Gautama founded Buddhism about 2,500 years ago.

_____

_____

EXERCISE 9.1-D   CHANGING ACTIVE TO PASSIVE

questions

Change each question to the passive voice. Omit the agent (*by*) phrase if it is not necessary.

> **Example:** When did he write the report?
> *When was the report written?*

1. When is the committee going to announce the results?
   <u>When are the results going to be announced?</u>

2. Why did they publish only part of the report?
   <u>Why was only part of the report published?</u>

3. Did anyone ever post the notices on the bulletin board?
   <u>Were the notices posted on the bulletin board?</u>

4. Who did people blame for the accident?
   <u>Who was blamed for the accident?</u>

5. Where do we send the forms after we fill them out?
   <u>Where are the forms sent after we fill them out.</u>

EXERCISE 9.1-E   DISCRIMINATING FORM

choosing the active or the passive

Fill in each blank with either the active form or the passive form of the verb in parentheses. Use the simple present, the simple past, the present progressive, the past progressive, or the future with BE *going to*. There may be more than one possibility in some cases.

1. A tunnel beneath the English Channel <u>was propose</u> (*propose*) by Thomas de Gamond in the middle of the nineteenth century, and the idea <u>was greeted</u> (*greet*) enthusiastically by the citizens of England

and France. Both governments _____ consider _____ (consider) the cost too high, however. Today, a similar project _____ is being discuss _____ (discuss). Government support _____ was announced _____ (announce) in 1986 for a tunnel running between Dover and Calais. The project _____ was financed _____ (finance) privately and _____ was completed _____ (complete) in 1993.

2. The largest modern supertankers _____ are called _____ (call) ultralarge crude carriers, but they are much lighter in weight than you might think. The world's largest ship in the 1980s, the oil tanker *Seawise Giant*, _____ was built _____ (build) in Japan. Although it is more than a quarter of a mile long, it _____ is designed _____ (design) to weigh only 90,000 tons when empty. But when it _____ is loaded _____ (load) with oil, it _____ weighs _____ (weigh) over 700,000 tons.

3. Every eleven years the weather and radio transmissions on earth _____ have been disrupted _____ (disrupt) by sunspots. These giant magnetic disturbances on the surface of the sun _____ were discovered _____ (discover) accidentally in the nineteenth century. Heinrich Schwabe _____ was searching _____ (search) for a new planet when he _____ noticed _____ (notice) dark spots on the surface of the sun that appeared and disappeared periodically. Schwabe _____ was keeping _____ (keep) careful records, and by 1843 the pattern of the spots _____ was worked _____ (work) out. We now know that a concentration of sunspot activity _____ occurs _____ (occur) every eleven years and that the northern and southern lights on earth _____ are influenced _____ (influence) by this activity.

4. Henry Wistanley _____ erected _____ (erect) the first modern lighthouse on the dangerous Eddystone Rocks in the English Channel in 1698. He _____ built _____ (build) the structure 80 feet high originally, but it _____ was raised _____ (raise) to a height of 200 feet two years later. Five years after it _____ was completed _____ (complete), the lighthouse _____ was swept _____ (sweep) away in a storm. Despite this tragedy, more modern lighthouses _____ are constructed _____ (construct), and today they _____ are found _____ (find) all over the world.

5. A new generation of supercomputers _____ is being developed _____ (develop) now for the 1990s. In 1985 only seventy-five supercomputers _____ existed _____ (exist) in all the world. Most of them _____ were used _____ (use) to solve complex scientific problems and to design weapons and aircraft. The new generation of supercomputers _____ is being designed _____ (design) in Japan and the United States and will be capable of more than one billion calculations per second. The computer race between the two countries is fierce, and only one of them _____ is going to be declared _____ (declare) the winner.

EXERCISE 9.1-F   MAKING PHRASES INTO SENTENCES

the passive voice and the active voice

Create a meaningful statement from each group of words and phrases. Use the tense indicated in the main clause, and use an appropriate tense in any adverbial clauses. Use the appropriate voice, active or passive.

> **Example:** the best seats – take – the people – who arrive early (BE *going to*)
> *The best seats are going to be taken by the people who arrive early.*

1. the new highway plans – discuss (negative) – yet / / when – we arrive (past progressive)

    _____

    _____

2. this book – recommend – my history professor (simple present)

    _____

    _____

3. George – like – that picture / / because – it – paint – a good friend (simple present)

    _____

    _____

4. the life cycle – of that species – study (negative) – extensively – until the 1950s (simple past)

    _____

    _____

5. Joe's colleagues – receive – job promotions / / while – he – get – nowhere (past progressive)

    _____

    _____

6. new treatments – for this disease – develop – at this very moment (present progressive)

    _____

    _____

EXERCISE 9.1-G   RESTATING INFORMATION

choosing the active voice or the passive voice

Read the paragraphs. All the sentences are in the active voice. Which ones could be changed to the passive voice to improve the paragraph?

(1) The bubonic plague struck Europe in 1347. (2) People called it the Black Death, and they regarded it as the single greatest disaster ever to happen to humanity. (3) It wiped out towns and cities. (4) About 30 million people (more than a quarter of the European population) died. (5) The plague killed another 45 million people in Asia. (6) Epidemics of the plague followed at intervals over the centuries.

(7) In 1900 someone discovered the cause of the plague. (8) Bacteria caused the disease. (9) Infected rat fleas were carrying these bacteria. (10) But people did not develop a vaccine for the disease until many years later. (11) The last major outbreak of the plague came in 1910. (12) Over 60,000 people died in eastern Siberia in just seven months.

Eight of the sentences in these paragraphs can be made passive. Which ones are they?

_____   _____   _____   _____

_____   _____   _____   _____

Write the passive counterparts of those sentences. Are the paragraphs improved by making all eight sentences passive? Should only some be made passive?

SECTION 9.2   The Passive of Perfect Tenses and Modal Auxiliaries
· ·

(See box on page 240.)   **1. The passive of perfect tenses and modals:**   Active sentences in the perfect tenses and those with modal auxiliaries can be made passive in the same way as sentences in the simple tenses and the progressive tenses. The form of BE that is added before the main verb is the same as the form of the active main verb. For simple modals, use *be*, as in sentence F. For perfect tenses and for modal perfects, use *been*, as in sentences B, D, and H.

2. The passive of *have to*:   The phrase *have to* is frequently made passive.

> Someone *has to send* a message.
> A message *has to be sent.*

> The committee *didn't have to grant* our request.
> Our request *didn't have to be granted.*

3. The passive of perfect progressive verbs and modal progressives: Passive sentences can also be constructed from perfect progressive

---

PERFECT TENSES AND MODALS

Perfect Tenses

Active Voice: **A.**   The college **has changed** its requirements since I was a student.

Passive Voice: **B.**   The requirements **have been changed** since I was a student.

Active Voice: **C.**   Someone **had located** some extra chairs by the time we arrived.

Passive Voice: **D.**   Some extra chairs **had been located** by the time we arrived.

Modals

Active Voice: **E.**   Professor Naumoff **will not proctor** our exam tomorrow.

Passive Voice: **F.**   Our exam **will not be proctored** by Professor Naumoff tomorrow.

Active Voice: **G.**   John **must have written** this note.

Passive Voice: **H.**   This note **must have been written** by John.

---

tenses and modal auxiliaries in the progressive, but they are uncommon and often awkward. It is advisable to avoid these constructions.

They have been publicizing tonight's ceremony for weeks now.
Awkward: Tonight's ceremony *has been being publicized* for weeks now.
Better: Tonight's ceremony *has been publicized* for weeks now.

Doctors had been observing the effects of the new drug for several years before the government approved it.
Awkward: The effects of the new drug *had been being observed* for several years before the government approved it.
Better: The effects of the new drug *were observed* for several years before the government approved it.

The committee might be awarding the contract tomorrow.
Awkward: The contract *might be being awarded* tomorrow.
Better: The contract *might be awarded* tomorrow.

The agency should have been considering our request last week.
Awkward: Our request *should have been being considered* last week.
Better: Our request *should have been considered* last week.

EXERCISE 9.2-A   CHECKING FORM (ORAL)

from the passive to the active

Change each passive sentence to the active voice.

1. All the problems have been solved by Tim. *Tim has solved all the problems*

2. This product can be used by anyone. *Anyone can use this product.*

3. These books must not have been left here by the students. *The students must not have left their books here.*

4. Both experiments had already been duplicated by other researchers.
    Other researchers had already duplicated both experiments.

5. The best essay has been written by Dena.
    Dena wrote the best essay

6. The winners will not be chosen by the committee.

7. A less effective approach had been taken by scientists before that time.

8. The results should have been checked by Judy before she reported them.
    Judy should have checked the results before she reported them

EXERCISE 9.2-B   CHECKING FORM (ORAL)

from the active to the passive

Change each active sentence to the passive voice. Omit the agent if appropriate.

1. Someone has made a mistake in the final calculations. *A mistake has been made it in the final calculations.*

2. You must not lock the door this evening.

3. Workmen had already installed the new phones when we moved in.

4. Someone may have left these books here by mistake.
    These books may have been left by mistake.

5. The students didn't have to list the answers in the correct order.

6. The manufacturer has introduced improvements.

7. You cannot send the package more cheaply.

8. Someone had proposed similar ideas years before.

EXERCISE 9.2-C   CHANGING ACTIVE TO PASSIVE

omitting the agent

Change each active statement on page 242 to the passive voice. Omit the agent (*by*) phrase if it is not necessary.

Example: Someone had already made the announcement when we arrived.
The announcement had already been made when we arrived.

1. Someone must have entered the data incorrectly.

   _____

2. You don't have to send a reply until next week.

   _____

3. No one has performed this operation before.

   _____

4. People ought to turn off the lights when they close the office.

   _____

5. No one has changed the rules for the competition.

   _____

6. No one can persuade Arnie to change his mind.

   _____

EXERCISE 9.2-D   CHANGING ACTIVE TO PASSIVE

question forms

Change each active question to the passive voice. Omit the agent (*by*) phrase if it is not necessary.

Example: Why has he written this book?
Why has this book been written?

1. How many pages will you have written by the end of the month?

   _____

2. Why should we cancel the appointment?

   _____

3. What have you accomplished so far?

   _____

4. When did you have to submit the application form?

   _____

5. What had people done to increase profits in the past?

   _____

EXERCISE 9.2-E DISCRIMINATING FORM

active verbs and passive verbs

Fill in each blank with either the active form or the passive form of the verb in parentheses. Use an appropriate tense. There may be more than one possibility in some cases.

1. Computers _____ (can, use, now) to read to the blind. A machine that _____ (use) synthetic speech _____ (develop) by Raymond Kurzweil at the Massachusetts Institute of Technology. It _____ (will, read) almost any typeface from a book or a magazine. Then the print _____ (convert) into speech, using digitally stored sounds. The machine _____ (can, learn) the characteristics of an unfamiliar typeface, and it _____ (claim) to make fewer mistakes than a human reader.

2. Almost 1,300 scientific patents _____ (grant) to Thomas Alva Edison by the time he died in 1931. Surprisingly, he _____ (attend) school for only three months, when he was seven years old. After he _____ (call) stupid by one of his teachers, he _____ (run) away. He eventually _____ (invent) the phonograph, a practical electric light, the microphone, and sound films. He _____ (consider) one of our greatest practical scientists ever since.

3. Some scientists now _____ (believe) that certain sounds _____ (can, recognize) by babies soon after birth. Furthermore, babies _____ (BE able to, imitate) certain patterns of speech before they _____ (can, form) intelligible words. In one series of tests, babies _____ (show) to respond to a speaker's tone of voice at only four months. Generally, by six months, infants _____ (can, mimic) the rhythm and intonation of adult speech.

4. The life of the Polish physicist Marie Curie _____ (may, save) by the drafty condition of the laboratory where she _____ (work). She and her husband, Pierre, _____ (attempt) to isolate the radioactive element radium. It is now assumed that the drafts _____ (must, prevent) her from inhaling deadly amounts of the radioactive dust. By 1898 she _____ (isolated) radium, along with another element, polonium, which _____ (named) after Curie's native Poland.

5. The world's oldest trees _____ (find) growing in the White Mountains of California in the 1960s. They _____ (call) bristlecone pines and _____ (determine) to be over 4,600 years old. Even older life forms _____ (discover) in sandstone rocks in a dry valley in Antarctica, however. In this location _____ (live) a colony of tiny lichens. They _____ (calculated) to be at least 10,000 years old.

EXERCISE 9.2-F   MAKING PHRASES INTO SENTENCES

active and passive

Create a meaningful statement from each group of words and phrases. Use the tense indicated in parentheses in the main clause and an appropriate tense in any adverbial clauses. Use the appropriate voice, active or passive.

> **Example:** by the time that – dinner – serve / / I – run out of – conversation
> (past perfect)
> *By the time that dinner was served, I had run out of conversation.*

1. these corrections – should – make / / before – you – give – me – the report (modal perfect)

_____

_____

2. her ideas – will (never) – accept – the general population (simple modal)

_____

_____

3. several investigations – make / / since – the accident – occur (present perfect)

_____

_____

4. when – I – first – learn – of his behavior / / the damage – do – already (past perfect)

_____

_____

5. the development of new plastics – could (negative) – accomplish – without advances in theoretical chemistry (modal perfect)

_____

_____

6.   we – will – provide – you – with the documents / / as soon as – authorization –
         receive – from the main office (simple modal)

_____

_____

EXERCISE 9.2-G   CHANGING ACTIVE TO PASSIVE

reporting information

Read the paragraphs. All the sentences are in the active voice. Which ones
could be changed to the passive voice to improve the paragraph?

> (1) People have used mirrors for thousands of years. (2) In Egypt, people were
> constructing mirrors from highly polished metal, usually bronze, by 2500 B.C.
> (3) But they were only for the very wealthy because they were so valuable. (4)
> By the middle of the sixteenth century, craftsmen had produced the first com-
> mercial glass mirrors in Venice. (5) Craftsmen blew molten glass into a spherical
> shape, flattened it, and then coated it with an amalgam of mercury and tin. (6)
> In 1840 Justus Liebig developed the methods of mirror making that we still use
> today.
>
> (7) A regular mirror cannot produce a perfect image. (8) But for certain scien-
> tific uses such as in telescopes, precision is necessary. (9) Therefore, people
> have to make these mirrors in a special way, with a coating of aluminum and
> chromium on both sides of the glass.

Seven of the sentences in the paragraphs can be made passive. Which ones
are they?

_____   _____   _____   _____

_____   _____   _____

Now write the passive counterparts of those sentences. Are the paragraphs
improved by making all seven sentences passive? Should only some be made
passive? Which ones?

SECTION 9.3   Participial Adjectives

(See box on
page 246.)   **1. The stative passive:**   Recall from Chapter 1 that adjectives can follow the
verb BE or other linking verbs (such as *seem* and *become*), as in sentence A.
Certain past participles can also function as adjectives after BE or other
linking verbs. Examine sentence B. *Crowded* acts as an adjective here to
describe the subject, *it*. Although this sentence may appear to be passive, it

---

ADJECTIVES AFTER *BE* AND *GET*

BE + *Adjective*

A. The room is **dark**.

B. It is **crowded**.

C. It is **located** *in* the basement.

Get + *Adjective*

D. George is getting **careless.**

E. He gets **tired** all the time.

F. He doesn't get **excited** *about* his work anymore.

---

shows no activity, so we can consider it a past participle adjective. This construction is sometimes called the stative passive.

Now examine sentence C. It also contains a past participle adjective, *located*. Notice that *located* is followed by the preposition *in* and a noun phrase. Certain past participle adjectives can be followed by specific prepositions and an object. (See the box on page 247.)

> The students are finished.
> The students are finished *with the work*.
>
> She is married.
> She is married *to George*.

2. Adjectives after *get*:   Adjectives can also follow the verb *get* when it means "become," as in sentence D. Adjectives that commonly follow *get* include these:

angry	full	sick
busy	hot	sleepy
careless	hungry	sloppy
cold	late	thirsty
dark	nervous	upset
dizzy	old	warm
fat	overweight	well

Here are some sentences with adjectives after *get:*

> The students *were getting hungry*.
> He *gets upset* whenever I mention the problem.

Get can also be followed by certain past participle adjectives, as in sentences E and F. (See the box on page 247.)

COMMON PAST PARTICIPLE ADJECTIVES AFTER *BE* AND *GET*

Past participles that are often used after BE and *get* are listed below. All can follow BE. The ones that have an asterisk (*) can also follow *get*.

acquainted (with)*	exhausted (from)*	made (of)
bored (by, with)*	finished (with)*	married (to)*
broken*	frightened (by, of)*	opposed (to)
closed	gone	prepared (for)*
crowded (with)*	interested (in)*	satisfied (with)
decorated (with)	involved (in, with)*	scared (of)*
disappointed (in, with)*	limited (to)	shut
done (with)*	located (in, on, etc.)	tired (from, of)*
excited (about)*	lost*	worried (about)*

Examples: We *are acquainted with* Professor Thorensen.
                We *got acquainted with* Professor Thorensen.

3. Preposition + Gerund: Recall that a gerund is a present participle that functions as a noun. Some of the Past Participle Adjective + Preposition combinations can be followed by a gerund.

> We are *excited about* the trip tomorrow.
> We are *excited about leaving* on our trip tomorrow.

> He is *opposed to* the project.
> He is *opposed to participating* in the project.

Notice that *to* is a preposition in these expressions, so it is followed by the gerund rather than the simple form of the verb.

4. BE *used to* and BE *accustomed to*:   Two very common expressions appear to be similar to the past participle adjectives: BE *used to* and BE *accustomed to*. Both expressions indicate that something is familiar or customary. *To* is a preposition in these expressions and so can be followed by a gerund.

> They *are used to* the long drive home.
> They *are accustomed to* the long drive home.
> They *are used to driving* for an hour to get home.
> They *are accustomed to driving* for an hour to get home.

Notice that BE *used to* is different in meaning and in grammar from the habitual past expression *used to*.

> He *used to come* every day. (He did in the past; he doesn't anymore.)
> He *is used to coming* every day. (It has become customary for him.)

Expressions that mean "used to" can follow *get* as well as BE.

> I'm getting used to living in a small town.
> She hasn't gotten accustomed to getting up so early.

MORE PARTICIPIAL ADJECTIVES

G. Tom's jokes **embarrass** me.
I am **embarrassed**.
His jokes are **embarrassing**.

H. The news **disappointed** the children.
The children are **disappointed**. They are **disappointed** children.
The news is **disappointing**. It is **disappointing** news.

---

5. Present participle adjectives and past participle adjectives: Both the present participle and the past participle of some verbs can be used as adjectives. These participial adjectives show an active direction or a passive direction. Look at sentence G, *Tom's jokes embarrass me.* The present participle of the verb, *embarrassing*, describes the subject (the agent that causes the embarrassment); hence, *His jokes are embarrassing.* The past participle, *embarrassed*, describes the receiver; hence, *I am embarrassed.*

These directional participial adjectives can follow the verb BE and linking verbs. Sometimes they can also be placed before a noun, as in sentence H.

VERBS USED AS BOTH PRESENT PARTICIPLE ADJECTIVES AND PAST PARTICIPLE ADJECTIVES

The following verbs can be used as adjectives in both the present participle form and the past participle form.

alarm	disappoint	interest
amaze	disturb	please
amuse	embarrass	satisfy
astonish	excite	shock
bore	fascinate	surprise
confuse	frighten	tire
damage		

Examples: The novel that I'm reading is *fascinating*.
I'm *fascinated*.

EXERCISE 9.3-A   COMPLETING SENTENCES (ORAL)

● ·

past participle + preposition combinations

Finish each sentence, using a noun phrase or a gerund after the preposition.

1. I'm acquainted with . . .

2. I sometimes get bored with . . .

3. This room is crowded with . . .

4. I'm disappointed with . . .

5. I get excited about . . .

6. Last week, I was exhausted from . . .

7. Next week, I will be finished with . . .

8. I've never been frightened of . . .

9. Lately, I've gotten interested in . . .

10. This class is limited to . . .

11. This room is located in . . .

12. My (article of clothing) is made of . . .

13. I am opposed to . . .

14. When I was a child, I got used to . . .

15. I am not prepared for . . .

16. I am not satisfied with . . .

17. I have gotten tired of . . .

18. I never get worried about . . .

19. I am getting accustomed to . . .

EXERCISE 9.3-B   RESTATING SENTENCES (ORAL)

● ·

present participle adjectives and past participle adjectives

Listen to each statement carefully. Then make two statements, one about the subject of the sentence (using a present participle adjective) and another about the object of the sentence (using a past participle adjective).

> **Example:** His behavior alarms me.
> *His behavior is alarming. I am alarmed.*

1. Her knowledge amazes me.

2. Dena's jokes didn't amuse me.

3. English classes never bore me.

4. English grammar sometimes confuses me.

5. Restaurant food often disappoints me.

6. The latest news report disturbed me.

7. Learning about other cultures excites me.

8. Driving too fast frightens me.

EXERCISE 9.3-C   DISCRIMINATING PREPOSITIONS

past participle adjective + preposition combinations

Fill in each blank with the proper preposition.

1. Judy is disappointed _____ her new office. It's located _____ the top floor, and she gets tired _____ walking up five flights of steps. She's not accustomed _____ so much exercise.

2. We are acquainted _____ the work your company does, and we are not satisfied _____ the firm that is handling our business now. So we are interested _____ getting an estimate from you.

3. I am opposed _____ this new health plan because it is limited _____ only certain employees, not open to all. I'll send you my own proposal as soon as I am finished _____ it.

4. My brothers are exhausted _____ all the extra work they have been forced to do during the past few months, but at the same time they are excited _____ the prospect of a new project. They have gotten very involved _____ this new line of research, and they would like to continue with it.

5. Chuck is finally done _____ his paper, but he's worried _____ his instructor's reaction. He thinks that Professor Stanley might not be prepared _____ such radical ideas or used _____ his type of approach to the topic.

EXERCISE 9.3-D   COMPLETING SENTENCES

past participle adjectives

Fill in each blank with BE or *get* and an appropriate past participle adjective from the list. Add the proper preposition where necessary. Use an appropriate tense.

bored	limited	crowded
disappointed	satisfied	worried
made	frightened	opposed
married	tired	interested

1. The neighbor's children _____ our dog.
    They run whenever they see it.

2. The ballroom _____ people. You can
    hardly move!

3. George _____ political issues more than
    ever before. Now he wants to run for state representative.

4. I _____ (negative) your answer. You
    haven't really explained why you behaved so poorly.

5. We _____ coming to class at 8:00 every
    morning. What's more, we _____ with
    the class. The lectures are so dull that it's hard to stay awake.

6. Martha and George _____ last week.
    They went to Hawaii on their honeymoon.

7. Henry _____ our plan completely. He
    wants us to think of a totally different way to achieve our goal.

8. I _____ the exam that I have to take
    tomorrow. I don't know the material very well, and if I fail it, I'll fail the entire course.

9. The front of the new building _____ brick
    and stone.

10. The advanced seminar _____ seniors
    and graduate students. Other students cannot register for it.

EXERCISE 9.3-E   DISCRIMINATING FORM

present participle adjectives and past participle adjectives

Fill in each blank with either the present participle adjective or the past
participle adjective of the verb in parentheses.

1. This radio was ___damaged___ (*damage*) when I bought it. But the clerk
    didn't believe me when I returned it to the store, and the situation was very
    ___embarrassing___ (*embarrass*).

2. Henry's jokes are not at all ___amusing___ (*amuse*). I will never stop
    being ___surprised___ (*surprise*) at his childish sense of humor.

3. The instructor of my history course is a _____distinguish_____ (distinguish) professor. Her lectures are always _____fascinated_____ (fascinate), and her personal anecdotes are _____astonishing_____ (astonish). I am never _____bored_____ (bore) in her class.

4. The children are _____confused_____ (confuse). They were looking forward to an _____exciting_____ (excite) day, but now they have been told that the trip is cancelled.

5. The children are _____confused_____ (confuse). First they tell you that they are _____excited_____ (excite) about going to a baseball game, but as soon as they get there, they quickly become _____bored_____ (bore).

6. This is a very _____interesting_____ (interest) book, but it contains some _____alarming_____ (alarm) facts. I am _____shocked_____ (shock) by some of the information.

7. It is an extremely _____tiring_____ (tire) trip from here to London, and the time change may be _____confusing_____ (confuse) to you.

EXERCISE 9.3-F   DISCRIMINATING AMONG EXPRESSIONS

BE *used to*, BE *accustomed to*, and *used to*

Fill in each blank with BE *used to*, Be *accustomed to*, or *used to*, plus the appropriate form of the verb in parentheses, if there is one. Use either the affirmative or the negative, as appropriate. Use the simple past tense or the simple present tense.

1. This is too much food for me. I generally eat only a small snack for dinner. I _____ (have) such a big meal.

2. The students in the class _____ (get along) very well together, but now they have become very competitive.

3. When Judy first arrived, she was upset about how far her apartment is from campus, but now she _____ (walk) that distance every day.

4. The city _____ (permit) swimming in that lake when I was a child. Now it's crowded with swimmers in the summer.

5. When I was a child, I lived in the South and _____ very hot weather. But I _____ it anymore. I need air conditioning now!

10 Nouns and Determiners

This chapter examines the distinction between count and noncount nouns and how they can be marked in different ways to show features such as definiteness, possession, number, and quantity.

SECTION 10.1   Count Nouns and Noncount Nouns

COUNT NOUNS AND NONCOUNT NOUNS

Count Nouns

A.   Sue tried to find *some* **articles** for her report last night.

B.   She found *an* **article** in a science journal and *two* **articles** in a newsmagazine.

C.   But *the* **article** in the science journal was too technical for her to understand.

Noncount Nouns

D.   Sue needed to find *some* **information** about her topic.

E.   She also wanted **advice** about writing a bibliography.

F.   *The* **advice** was easy to find, but *the* **information** wasn't.

---

1. Count nouns: Nouns which have both a singular and a plural form are called count nouns. Sentences A, B, and C contain the count noun *article* (*articles*). The plural form of most count nouns adds either *-s* or *-es*, following the same spelling rules as the third person singular verb ending for the simple present tense (see Section 2.2).

Singular	*Plural*
article	articles
watch	watches

Some count nouns have irregular plural forms (see Appendix D for a list of the common irregular noun plurals).

Singular	*Plural*
man	men
knife	knives
child	children

Singular count nouns *must* be preceded by a determiner, a word such as *a/an*, *one*, or *the*. Plural count nouns can be preceded by determiners such as *some*, *several*, *the*, a cardinal number (*two*, *three*, etc.), or no determiner at all (∅). They cannot be preceded by an *a/an*.

Singular Count Nouns (after a/an, one, the*)*

Jane bought *a pen*.
Joe found *one book* on his topic.
We met *the* new *librarian*.

Plural Count Nouns (after some, several, two, three, the, ∅*)*

Jane bought *several pens*.
Joe found *three books* on his topic.
We met *the* new *librarians*.
I need *articles* on my topic.

2. Subject-verb agreement with count nouns: The verb which follows a count noun subject must agree with it in number. Remember that a count noun is either singular or plural.

A librarian *was* behind the reference counter.
Several librarians *were* behind the reference counter.

3. Noncount nouns: Nouns that are not counted and have no plural form are called noncount nouns. In sentences D, E, and F you will find the noncount nouns *information* and *advice*. No plural ending is used. Noncount nouns can be preceded by the determiners *some* or *the* or by no determiner at all (∅). Noncount nouns cannot be preceded by counting words such as *several* or the cardinal numbers. Do not use *a/an* with a noncount noun.

Noncount Nouns (after some, the, Ø)

We bought *equipment* from the Randolph Corporation.
The importance of his work has been overlooked.
John needs *some encouragement* in order to keep working.

4. Subject-verb agreement with noncount nouns: Noncount nouns are grammatically singular, so the verb which follows must be singular.

The new equipment *is* broken already.
Encouragement *has* been shown to be an effective motivator.

5. Identifying noncount nouns: Concepts which are countable in one language may not be countable in another language. Therefore, the best way to learn which English nouns are countable and which are noncountable is to learn the distinction as you learn new vocabulary. However, there are several categories of noncount nouns which may help you.

Wholes Made Up of Separate Parts

furniture	homework	equipment
money	fruit	machinery

Solids, Liquids, and Gases

air	water	soap
smoke	gasoline	glass

Categories of Food

bread	butter	cheese
food	meat	rice

Abstract Qualities

beauty	happiness	peace
help	equality	ignorance

Gerunds

understanding	dancing	studying
waiting	smoking	clothing

Natural Phenomena

rain	sunshine	darkness
electricity	fire	heat

Names of Languages and Fields of Study

English	Arabic	history
psychology	physics	philosophy

6. Nouns that can be either count or noncount: Some nouns have both countable and noncountable meanings.

    Count: She is a great *beauty*. (a very beautiful person)

    Noncount: *Beauty* is only skin deep. (the quality of beauty)

    Count: A *war* has broken out between the two rival factions. (a fight)

    Noncount: *War* is an inevitable human activity. (the concept of war)

    Count: This is a very dark *bread*. (type of bread)

    Noncount: I forgot to buy *bread* at the grocery. (bread as food)

    Count: We have visited them several *times*. (different occasions)

    Noncount: We don't have *time* to visit them this weekend. (time in general)

7. Counting noncount concepts: Many noncount nouns can be measured or classified (and thus counted) using expressions with *of*.

    some bread / a *slice of* bread / two *slices of* bread
    some coffee / a *cup of* coffee / three *cups of* coffee
    some equipment / a *piece of* equipment / several *pieces of* equipment
    some paper / a *sheet* (or *piece*) *of* paper / two *sheets* (or *pieces*) *of* paper
    some information / a *piece of* information / several *pieces of* information

EXERCISE 10.1-A IDENTIFYING FORM

count nouns and noncount nouns

Read the following paragraph carefully. Determine if the underlined nouns are countable or noncountable. Write them under the appropriate heading on page 257. Are any used in both ways?

    Pearls, which are treasured throughout the world as jewelry, are the products of a fight against an invader. Mollusks with double shells (such as clams and oysters) normally produce pearl as an inner layer of their shells. Pearl consists largely of calcium carbonate, the same substance that chalk is made of. When foreign matter, such as a grain of sand, gets into a body of a mollusk, the mollusk will build a sac around it and isolate it. Then the mollusk builds layer upon layer of calcium carbonate around the sac, creating a pearl.

Count Nouns   *Noncount Nouns*

_____   _____

_____   _____

_____   _____

_____   _____

_____   _____

_____   _____

EXERCISE 10.1-B IDENTIFYING FORM

● ·

count nouns and noncount nouns

Read the following paragraph carefully. As in Exercise 10.1-A, determine if the underlined nouns are countable or noncountable and write them in the appropriate column. Are any used in both ways? In some cases, you will have to pay close attention to the meaning of the noun; the use of determiners will not always help you.

In the endless blackness of the deep oceans, far from the warmth of the sun, certain animals owe their existence to the heat of the earth. Temperatures at the bottom of the oceans' abysses are usually near freezing and cannot support life. But where there are cracks in the earth's crust, the heat from the earth's core escapes and warms the water. In these places, sometimes 8,000 feet below water, scientists have found densely populated colonies of earth-heated life forms, including bacteria, crabs, fish, and ten-foot-long worms.

Count Nouns   *Noncount Nouns*

_____   _____

_____   _____

_____   _____

_____   _____

_____   _____

_____   _____

EXERCISE 10.1-C DISCRIMINATING FORM

●···

nouns that can be both count and noncount

Complete each sentence with the noun indicated. The usage will be count-able in one sentence and noncountable in the other. Write the proper form of the noun, and add *a* or *an* for singular count nouns if necessary. Circle the correct verb if a choice is given. Circle *C* if the noun is countable and *N* if it is noncountable.

1. *glass*
   a. _____ (is/are) a fragile material and must be handled with care. (C/N)
   b. My new _____ (is/are) very uncomfortable; they need to be adjusted. (C/N)

2. *noise*
   a. The car is making a lot of different _____. We should take it to the mechanic. (C/N)
   b. The _____ from the engine (is/are) so loud that I can't hear myself think. (C/N)

3. *food*
   a. The price of _____ has increased dramatically during the past few years. (C/N)
   b. Meat and poultry are _____ that contain high amounts of protein. (C/N)

4. *fire*
   a. Faulty electrical wires started _____ in the basement. (C/N)
   b. _____ (is/are) dangerous and should be handled with care. (C/N)

5. *light*
   a. The small window at the other end of the room lets in some ___light___. (C/N)
   b. Please turn on some ___light___. It's too dark in here. (C/N)

6. *room*
   a. There (isn't/aren't) a lot of _____ in the lobby. Can we find a larger area? (C/N)
   b. The ___room___ on this floor (is/are) too small. Can we find larger ones? (C/N)

7. *time*
   a. We will have ___time___ to finish if we hurry. (C/N)
   b. He has been here several ___time___ before. (C/N)

EXERCISE 10.1-D DISCRIMINATING FORM

choosing determiners

For each sentence, from the choices provided in parentheses, choose a proper determiner for the noun that follows. There may be more than one correct choice in some items. $\emptyset$ means no determiner.

1. The laboratory needs _____ ($\emptyset$, *an, some, two*) new equipment.

2. Professor Shih has received _____ ($\emptyset$, *a, several*) proposals already.

3. _____ ($\emptyset$, *a, several*) homework is important because it gives you a chance to practice concepts you learn in class.

4. She needs to buy _____ ($\emptyset$, *a, several, some*) gasoline before she begins her trip.

5. There are _____ ($\emptyset$, *a, several, one*) separate items under this heading.

6. _____ ($\emptyset$, *an, some, several*) increase in the size of _____ ($\emptyset$, *a, some*) population can be determined only with careful samplings.

7. I studied _____ ($\emptyset$, *a, several*) biology many years ago.

8. There is only _____ ($\emptyset$, *one, some, several*) factor that we should be considering at this time.

EXERCISE 10.1-E COMPLETING SENTENCES

counting noncount concepts

Use the words in the list to measure or classify the noncount nouns. Be sure to use *of*.

> **Example:** Could you pour me a _____ milk?
> *Could you pour me a glass of milk?*

piece	bar	pair
gallon	foot	box
glass	sheet	loaf

1. Mrs. Epstein gave me a _____ advice that I will never forget.

2. We need a new _____ soap in the bathroom.

3. Howard wore an old _____ jeans to a formal party last night.

4. How many _____ gasoline does your car hold?

5. I brought several _____ rope to tie down the boxes.

6. Please give me ten _____ paper.

7. Could you buy two _____ cereal while you're at the store?

SECTION 10.2   Articles

. . . .

	INDEFINITE AND DEFINITE ARTICLES	
	Indefinite Usage	
Count Nouns:	**A.**	Judy has **a** good *idea* for our project.
	B.	Judy has **some** good *ideas* for our project.
	C.	Judy has good *ideas* for our project.
Noncount Nouns:	**D.**	Mary gave us **some** sound *advice*.
	E.	Mary gave us sound *advice*.
	Definite Usage	
Count Nouns:	**F.**	**The** *computer* is malfunctioning again.
	G.	**The** *computers* are malfunctioning again.
Noncount Nouns:	**H.**	**The** *equipment* has been repaired.

1. English articles: English has four articles: *an, an, the,* and the zero article (∅). *Some* is an indefinite pronoun that functions in a manner similar to an article, so it is included in this section. Articles are used before nouns to indicate if the noun has been identified in the mind of the speaker and listener.

2. Definite usage and indefinite usage: When a noun is used in an indefinite sense, it refers to an object or a concept, but not to a specific object or concept that is known to both the speaker and the listener. Look at sentences A through C. In each of these sentences, the speaker assumes that the listener does not know *which* good idea or ideas Judy has. The same is true for sentences D and E: The speaker refers to *advice* but doesn't assume that the listener knows *which* advice.

When a noun is used in a definite sense, it refers to a specific object or concept that is known to both the speaker and the listener. Both the speaker and the listener know the *identity* of the noun. Look at sentences F and G. In these sentences the speaker assumes that the listener knows *which* computer is being referred to.

> *Indefinite Usage*
>
> I have *a book* that can help you.
> (You don't know the identity of the book.)
>
> *Definite Usage*
>
> But I lent *the book* to someone else.
> (You know which book I am referring to.)

3. Using articles to show definite usage and indefinite usage: Use *a, an, some,* or the zero article (∅) to show that a noun has an indefinite sense. Use *the* to show that a noun has a definite sense.

> *Indefinite Singular Count Noun:* a *or* an
> a good idea
>
> *Indefinite Plural Count Noun:* some *or* ∅
> some good ideas
> good ideas
>
> *Indefinite Noncount Noun:* some *or* ∅
> some sound advice
> sound advice
>
> *Definite Noun:* the
> the computer
> the computers
> the equipment

4. Establishing the identity of a noun: In order to decide if a noun is used in a definite sense, you need to determine if the noun has been identified by the speaker and the listener. The identity of a noun can be established in many ways. However, three situations usually indicate that the noun is being used in a definite manner and requires a definite article (*the*).

a. Previous mention: When the object or the concept has already been mentioned, the listener is aware of its identity. This is often called *second mention.*

> Jonathan made *suggestions* regarding the use of the laboratory by students. *The suggestions* were not well received. (The first mention is indefinite, *suggestions*; the second mention is definite, *the suggestions*.)

Julie needs to buy *a coat, some gloves,* and *a pair of boots* for her skiing trip. *The clothing* has to be warm for the frigid weather in the mountains. (The first mention is indefinite: *a coat, some gloves*, and *a pair of boots*. The second mention uses a different word, *clothing*, but it refers to the same objects, so it is definite, *the clothing*.)

b. A following identifying phrase: When a noun is identified as a specific object or a specific concept by a phrase or a clause that follows it, the definite article is used.

The ideas that they were discussing should be presented to the entire committee.
The object of this game is to get rid of all your cards.

Be careful! A phrase or a clause that follows a noun does not always identify it.

I am fascinated by *an idea that George mentioned to me*. (The listener isn't aware of the specific identity of the idea, only that Goerge mentioned it.)
A goal of this new program is to provide financial aid more fairly. (There are several goals; this is one of them.)

c. Shared knowledge: The speaker and the listener share knowledge of the identity of the noun. This situation can occur in many ways.

The sun has disappeared behind some clouds. (Both speaker and listener share the knowledge of the earth's sun.)
Can you help me find *the car?* I can't remember where I parked it. (Both speaker and listener know which car is being discussed; it is the car both of them arrived in.)
Please see who is at *the door*. (The speaker is referring to only one possible door, the one that someone is knocking at.)
Perhaps you should speak to *the director*. (Speaker and listener work in the same office; there is only one director.)

5. Choosing *a* or *an*:   *An* is used before a word that begins with a vowel *sound*, and *a* is used before a word beginning with a consonant *sound*.

a book
an essay
a university (the first sound in *university* is a consonant)
an honorable man (the first sound in *honorable* is a vowel)

6. Generic usage: There is another use of nouns called the *generic*, which is neither definite nor indefinite. Nouns are used generically when the speaker or writer refers to a *category* of concepts or objects, not to the concepts or objects themselves. This usage is common when we make generalizations or state definitions.

Language is humanity's highest achievement.
Elephants are the largest mammals that live on land.
A book should be treasured and cared for.
The avocado is a popular fruit which is grown in California.

Plural count nouns and all noncount nouns: Use the zero article for the generic.

Prejudice is humanity's greatest enemy. (noncount)
Laws are established to maintain order in societies. (plural count)

Singular count nouns: Use *a* or *an* to indicate a representative of a category. Use *the* to refer to the entire category.

A contract is an agreement between two or more parties. (*a contract* = a representative of the category *contracts*)
The whale is the largest mammal. (*the whale* = the entire category)

The second mention rule does not apply when the first mention is generic, because the specific identity of the noun has not been established.

Contracts are agreements between two parties. *Contracts* can be written documents or simply verbal agreements. It is the duty of the courts to decide if *contracts* are valid when the parties disagree.

SUMMARY OF THE USE OF ARTICLES

	Singular Count Nouns	*Plural Count Nouns*	*Noncount Nouns*
Indefinite:	a/an	∅, some	∅, some
Definite:	the	the	the
Generic:	a/an, the	∅	∅

EXERCISE 10.2-A IDENTIFYING ARTICLES

generic usage, indefinite usage, and definite usage

In each sentence, identify the italicized noun phrases as generic, indefinite, or definite. If they are definite, be prepared to tell how identity has been established.

1.   *The movie* that you suggested turned out to be excellent. _____

2.   *Peace and prosperity* should be the goals of all nations. _____

3.   I couldn't find *decent vegetables* at the grocery this morning. _____

4. Someone needs to tell *the students* about the test. _____

5. I don't understand *the answer* to this problem. _____

6. Thomas A. Edison is credited with inventing *the electric light.* _____

7. *A play by Shakespeare* contains difficult language. _____

8. Right now, I'm reading *a play by Shakespeare.* _____

EXERCISE 10.2-B CHOOSING ARTICLES

definite usage and indefinite usage

Write the appropriate article (*a, an, the, some,* or ∅) in each blank. You may have a choice in some cases.

1. I haven't seen _____ results of yesterday's election yet.

2. _____ animals such as _____ lobster and _____ shrimp are called _____ crustaceans.

3. I can't get _____ car started. I guess that we'll have to call for _____ taxi.

4. This is _____ excellent essay. _____ main points are clearly stated, and _____ examples are well chosen.

5. No one was very happy about _____ suggestions that she made. Do you think that she's trying to start _____ argument?

6. When you leave, please turn out _____ lights and lock _____ door. You can put _____ key under _____ doormat.

EXERCISE 10.2-C CHOOSING ARTICLES

definite usage and indefinite usage

Fill in each blank with an appropriate article (*a, an, the, some,* or ∅). You may have a choice in some cases. If so, how would the different articles change the meaning?

Since before _____ dawn of history, _____ human beings have used _____ energy sources to assist them in performing _____ difficult jobs. In fact, _____ ingenuity that humans have used to harness _____ animals, _____ water, _____ wind, and _____ natural resources is one of the characteristics of _____ human civilization. From _____ time of the ancient Greeks until _____ eighteenth century, many great empires were based to a large extent on _____ wind power—their merchant marines and navies were composed of _____ sailing ships. _____ introduction of steam power came in _____ eighteenth century, but was largely replaced by _____ electric power one hundred years later.

In _____ modern world, _____ nation's capacity to create _____ energy is _____ major factor in its economy and therefore in _____ standard of living of its people. Only _____ nation with substantial energy resources, or _____ ability to purchase energy, can develop _____ significant industrial base and _____ advanced economy.

EXERCISE 10.2-D CHOOSING ARTICLES

proper nouns

Fill in each blank with *the* or ∅. (See the box on page 266.)

1. I haven't lived in _____ Worthington since I was a child. My family had a house on _____ Stafford Avenue, right across from _____ Worthington Inn.

2. The continent of _____ Australia is the home of many unusual animal species. It is surrounded by _____ Pacific Ocean and _____ Indian Ocean. Its highest point is _____ Mount Kosciusko, and its lowest point is _____ Lake Eyre, 52 feet below sea level.

3. _____ Cayman Islands are located in _____ Caribbean Sea. They are a colony of _____ United Kingdom.

4. _____ Rocky Mountains run through several states, including _____ Montana, _____ Wyoming, and _____ Colorado.

5. _____ Ohio River meets _____ Mississippi near _____ Cairo, _____ Illinois.

6. _____ Johnsons have lived next to us on _____ Channing Way for years. But _____ Sandra Johnson who you know isn't the one who is my neighbor.

ARTICLES WITH PROPER NOUNS   (*See Exercise 10-2 D.*)

The indefinite articles are not used with proper nouns. The definite article *the* is used only in certain instances. Several generalizations are possible, although there are many exceptions.

Do not use *the* with people's names, except a family name in the plural.

> Ruth Hyatt   Professor Naumoff   *the* McGorys

The can be used to distinguish two people with the same name.

> *The* Sam Sloan you are talking about isn't *the* Sam Sloan I know.

Use *the* with the names of oceans, seas, rivers, and deserts.

> *the* Atlantic Ocean   *the* Nile River
> *the* Dead Sea   *the* Sahara

Use *the* with the names of plural mountains, lakes, and islands but not with singular names.

> *the* Andes Mountains   Lake Michigan
> Mount Everest   *the* Hawaiian Islands
> *the* Great Lakes   Easter Island

Do not use *the* with the names of continents, countries, states, provinces, or cities. However, use *the* with the name of a country if it is plural, if it contains the word *united* or *union,* or if you use an official name that includes an *of* phrase.

> Africa, China, Brazil
> *the* United States; *the* Netherlands; *the* Philippines
> *the* Soviet Union
> *the* Kingdom of Sweden; *the* People's Republic of China
> *the* state of Ohio
> *the* city of Columbus

Do not use *the* with the names of streets or parks.

> Fifth Avenue (exception: *the* Avenue of the Americas)   Central Park

Do not use *the* with the name of a college or university unless it contains an *of* phrase.

> Bard College   Northwestern University   *the* University of Iowa

Use *the* with the names of most buildings, but not if the name includes the word *hall.*

> *the* Empire State Building   *the* Marriott Hotel
> *the* Washington Monument   Bevis Hall

SECTION 10.3   Determiners

· ·

SIX CATEGORIES OF DETERMINERS		
Articles:	**A.**	We received **a** *letter* yesterday.
	B.	**The** *letter* was from some old college friends.
Possessive Adjectives:	**C.**	**My** *suggestions* were accepted.
	D.	**His** *suggestions* were not.
Possessive Nouns:	**E.**	I want to go to **Professor Helal's** *lecture.*
	F.	I don't want to rely on **Sam's** *notes.*
Demonstratives:	**G.**	**This** *equipment* can be repaired easily.
	H.	**Those** *machines* will have to be replaced.
Cardinal Numbers:	**I.**	We need **five** *copies* of the proposal.
	J.	**One** *copy* should be sent to the research office.
Ordinal Numbers:	**K.**	**The first** *goal* must be to improve efficiency.
	L.	**The second** *goal* is to improve staff morale.

1. Determiners: Determiners are words that are placed before nouns to identify them or to indicate quantity. The box shows six categories of determiners. If a noun is modified by an adjective, the determiner precedes the adjective.

2. Articles: The articles *a*, *an*, and *the* constitute one type of determiner. As discussed in Section 10.2, they indicate if a noun is definite or indefinite. Sentences A and B each contain an article that modifies the noun *letter*.

3. Possessive adjectives: The possessive adjectives *my*, *your*, *his*, *her*, *its*, *our*, and *their* function as determiners to show possession, as in sentences C and D. The possessive pronoun forms (*mine*, *yours*, *his*, *hers*, *its*, *ours*, and *theirs*) are used when the noun is not stated.

> I need *your* notes.   I need *yours.*

4. Possessive nouns: Possessive nouns can also function as determiners to show possession, as in sentences E and F. If the noun of possession is plural and ends in the letter *s*, only an apostrophe is added. In all other cases, add an apostrophe and *s*. Examples are given on page 268.

Noun of Possesion	*Possessive Noun*
(one) boy	the *boy's* books
(two) boys	the *boys'* books
children	the *children's* toys
Ms. Jones	*Ms. Jones's* new job
my son	my *son's* teacher

The possessive noun can itself have a determiner, as in *the boy's books* and *my son's books*. And the possessive noun can stand alone (without a following noun) if the meaning is understood.

> Of all the essays, I liked *John's* the most. (John's *essay*)

5. Demonstratives: The demonstratives *this, that, these,* and *those* serve as determiners, as in sentences G and H. *This* and *that* are used with singular count nouns and with all noncount nouns. *These* and *those* are used with plural count nouns. Demonstratives are similar to the definite article *the*; they show that the noun is identified. *This* and *these* are often used to indicate close distance, and *that* and *those* to show farther distance.

> *This* typewriter is mine, and *that* one belongs to George. (*This typewriter* is
> closer to the speaker than *that one*.)
> I don't want *these* pictures. I want *those*. (*These pictures* are closer than *those*.)

This and *that* can be followed by the pronoun *one* if the meaning is understood, as in the first example. *These* and *those* can act alone as pronouns if the meaning is clear, as in the second example. *These* and *those* should not be followed by *ones* unless there is a descriptive adjective.

Correct	*Incorrect*
these *new* ones	these ones
those *black* ones	those ones

6. Cardinal numbers: The cardinal numbers (*one, two, three, four, five,* etc.) can serve as determiners of count nouns (but not noncount nouns), as in sentences I and J. They can be preceded by articles, possessive pronouns, possessive nouns, or demonstratives.

> the
> her
> Martha's } three best friends
> those
> my child's

A cardinal number can stand alone if the meaning of the noun is clear.

> Howard needs to turn in *five copies* of the report, but he only made *three*.
> (three copies)

7. Ordinal numbers: The ordinal numbers (*first, second, third, fourth, fifth,* etc.) can function as determiners, as in sentences K and L. A definite determiner (*the, this, that, my, your, John's*) is generally placed before an ordinal number. It is possible to place a cardinal number after the ordinal.

> our *first* three choices
> John's *second* serious mistake
> these *first* ten answers

The ordinal numbers can be followed by the pronoun *one*, or they can stand alone if the meaning is understood.

> There will be a series of three lectures. This is
> { the first lecture.
> the first one.
> the first.

EXERCISE 10.3-A UNSCRAMBLING PHRASES

determiners and nouns

Unscramble each group of words in parentheses to create a meaningful sentence.

> **Example:** (second/paragraph/short/the) should be moved.
> *The second short paragraph should be moved.*

1. (two/roommate's/classes/my) meet in the morning.

_____

2. (official/the/three/first/acts/mayor's) involved budget reductions.

_____

3. (students/new/those/two) are from Brazil.

_____

4. I don't like these dishes, but I do like (ones/new/Joan's).

_____

5. I am envious of (new/two/my/cars/friend's).

_____

EXERCISE 10.3-B COMPLETING SENTENCES

possessive adjectives and possessive nouns

Fill in each blank on page 270 with an appropriate possessive adjective (*my, your,* etc.) or an appropriate possessive pronoun (*mine, yours,* etc.). There may be several choices in some cases.

1. I don't like _____ ideas, but I do like _____.

2. _____ plan is ridiculous, but it's better than _____.

3. I left _____ book at home. Could you share _____ with me?

4. Jim's sister never lends him any money; instead, she always wants to borrow _____.

5. _____ is probably the best report, and no one gave them any help.

6. _____ roommate's parents are coming this weekend, but _____ aren't.

FORMS OF *OTHER*

M.   Sharon has answered only one question. She needs to answer **another** *one.*

N.   There should be two manuals. I have one. Where is **the other**?

---

8. Meanings of the forms of *other*:   The forms of *other* can serve as determiners of nouns. When *other* is indefinite (*another* or *other/others*, without *the*) it means at least one more of something. When *other* is made definite with *the*, it means the remaining item or items.

> *Indefinite (another, other, others)*
>
> I have two volunteers to help me. I need *another* volunteer. (one more volunteer)
> There are several restaurants on State Street. You can find *other* restaurants on Mound Street. (several more restaurants)
>
> *Definite (the other, the others)*
>
> We have two cars. My wife drives one. I drive *the other* car. (the remaining car)
> There are five children in my family. One is away at school. *The others* live at home. (the remaining four children)

9. Uses of the forms of *other*:   *Another* is used only with singular count nouns. If the noun is countable, the pronoun *one* or *ones* can be substituted for the noun. Or *other* can stand by itself as a pronoun.

Indefinite Use

Singular Count: I've found two articles. I need to find $\begin{cases} \text{another article.} \\ \text{another one.} \\ \text{another.} \end{cases}$

Plural Count:	Some tests are taken here.	*Other tests* / *Other ones* / *Others* ⎬ are taken in the next room.

Noncount: Some advice is good. *Other advice* isn't worth listening to.

Definite Use

Singular Count:	There are two pens. One is John's.	*The other pen* / *The other one* / *The other* ⎬ is Martha's.

Plural Count:	Sue bought four gifts. Two are for me.	*The other gifts* / *The other ones* / *The others* ⎬ are for you.

Noncount: Some equipment is stored in this building. *The other equipment* is in the basement of the chemistry building.

Both definite and indefinite *other* are sometimes used together.

> He has four brothers. One is studying in France. *Another one* is studying in New York. *The others* are in business with their father.

Demonstratives, possessive adjectives, and possessive nouns can be placed before *other*. Cardinal numbers can be placed before or after *other*.

> my other car
> John's other two good answers
> those other three students (three specific students)
> three other students (not specific students)

EXERCISE 10.3-C DISCRIMINATING FORM

forms of *other*

Fill in each blank with an appropriate form of *other*.

1. The film that we want to see is being shown in only three theaters. One is around the corner. _____ are downtown.

2. I've made a mistake filling out this form. May I have _____?

3. Some people enjoy studying, but _____ do not.

4. The school hired seven new instructors. Two are history teachers. _____ is a math teacher. Two _____ will teach English classes. _____ will teach chemistry.

5. Sue broke a lens in her glasses, so she's going to get _____ pair at the optometrist's tomorrow.

6. Mary broke a lens in her glasses, so she's going to get _____ pair that she keeps for just such an emergency.

7. The advice that you gave me last week was excellent. Do you have any _____ suggestions for me?

8. There are a number of ways you can get there. Route 71 is one way. Interstate 80 is _____.

EXERCISE 10.3-D COMPLETING SENTENCES

forms of *other*

Complete each sentence, using a form of *other*.

> **Example:** She has two brothers. One is . . .
> *She has two brothers. One is in college, and the other is an accountant.*

1. Do you want this sandwich? I have _____

2. Some of these exercises are difficult, but _____

3. I am taking three classes this term. One is _____

   _____

4. Some statements are accurate, but _____

5. This housing project has been so successful that the city plans to _____

   _____

EXERCISE 10.3-E COMPLETING SENTENCES

determiners

Add a determiner or a group of determiners in each blank. You will have to use determiners as pronouns in certain sentences, or use the pronoun *one*. You might want to add adjectives in some cases. Use your own ideas, but make sure that each sentence makes sense. There are many possible answers for each item.

1. _____ suggestions were all rejected.

2. I would like to go to _____ party this evening, but I'm busy.

3. They didn't like _____ paintings, but they did like _____ .

4. I failed _____ my history test today, but I am allowed to take _____ tomorrow.

5. _____ goal is to finish studying English; _____ is to begin coursework toward a degree in engineering.

6. I can't find _____ newspapers. Have you seen them?

EXERCISE 10.3-F CORRECTING ERRORS

determiners

Each sentence has one or more mistakes. Write the corrected sentences.

1. The children's heavy other jackets are in the hall closet.

   _____

   _____

2. One of the mayor's two assistants is on vacation. Another one is in Los Angeles.

   _____

   _____

3. He didn't take my advice; instead, he took their.

   _____

   _____

4. Some coffee tastes delicious to me. Other tastes bitter.

   _____

   _____

5. The another packages should be delivered soon.

   _____

   _____

6. Professor Salvino hasn't given us back the other our test yet.

   _____

   _____

SECTION 10.4 Quantifiers

> **QUANTIFIERS WITH SINGULAR COUNT NOUNS**
>
> **A. Each** *student* has been given a test booklet.
>
> **B. Every** *test booklet* has a test number and a serial number.
>
> **C. Either** *number* can be used for identification.
>
> **D. Neither** *number* is on any of the other test booklets.

1. Quantifiers: Quantifiers form another group of determiners. They indicate quantity (how much) of a noun. If the noun is modified by an adjective, the quantifier is placed before the adjective.

Each new student should complete this data form.

2. Quantifiers with singular count nouns: Four quantifiers are commonly used with singular count nouns: *each, every, either,* and *neither.* Examine sentences A through D. Notice that these four quantifiers are followed by singular count nouns and that the singular form of the verb is used.

Correct	*Incorrect*
Every answer is wrong.	Every answers are wrong.
Neither article was very long.	Neither articles were very long.

3. Quantifiers with the pronoun *one*: The singular noun that follows the quantifiers *each, every, either,* and *neither* can be replaced with the pronoun *one* if the meaning is clear.

Have you examined the proposals yet?
    Yes, I've looked over *each one.* (each proposal)
I like both plans. *Either one* will do. (either plan)

4. Quantifiers with noncount nouns and with plural count nouns: The quantifiers *a lot of, most,* and *all* can be used with both noncount nouns and plural count nouns. The quantifiers *many, a great number of, few,* and *a few* are used only with plural count nouns. *Much, a great deal of, little,* and *a little* can be used only with noncount nouns.

Noncount Nouns	*Plural Count Nouns*	*Both*
much	many	a lot of
a great deal of	a great number of	most
little	few	all
a little	a few	

QUANTIFIERS WITH NONCOUNT NOUNS
AND WITH PLURAL COUNT NOUNS

Noncount Nouns	*Plural Count Nouns*
E. **How much money** was donated? **A lot of** *money* was donated. **Not much** *money* was donated. They did**n't** collect **much** *money*.	**How many** *people* came? **Many** *students* were there. **Not many** *teachers* came. There were**n't many** *teachers*.
F. We didn't have **a lot of** *time*.	But we had **a lot of** *assignments* to do.
G. I enjoy **most** *music*.	I go to **most** *classes*.
H. Joe has **a great deal of** *pride*.	And he has **a great number of** other good *traits*.
I. Bob refuses **all** *advice*.	And he rejects **all** *suggestions*.
J. Sue gave **a little** *advice*, but she received **little** *appreciation*.	She gave **a few** *examples*, but she was asked **few** *questions*.
K. Did you get **any** *information*? I got **some** *information*. I didn't get **any** *information*.	Did you attend **any** *concerts*? I went to **some** *concerts*. I didn't go to **any** *concerts*.

---

5. Expressing large quantities: *Many, much, a lot of, most, a great number of, a great deal of,* and *all* express large quantities.

***Much* and *many*:**   Use *much* with noncount nouns and *many* with plural count nouns, as in sentences E. Both are used in questions with *how* (*how much, how many*). *Many* is used in affirmative statements, but *much* is usually not (*a lot of* is used instead). Both *many* and *much* can be used in negative statements.

***A lot of*:**   Use *a lot of* with either noncount nouns or plural count nouns to indicate a large quantity, as in sentences F. Note that *a lot* is written as two separate words. In conversation and in very informal writing, *lots of* can be used instead.

> George gave us *a lot of* help.
> George gave us *lots of* help.

***Most*:**   Use *most* with either noncount nouns or plural count nouns, as in sentences G.

***A great number of* and *a great deal of*:**   Use *a great number of* to modify a plural count noun. Use *a great deal of* with noncount nouns. (See sentences H.)

All: *All* can be used with both noncount nouns and plural count nouns, as in sentences I.

6. Expressing small quantities: *Few, a few, little,* and *a little* express small quantities. Use *few* and *a few* for plural count nouns. Use *little* and *a little* for noncount nouns. (See sentences J.)

Few **and** *little*:   Use *few* and *little* (without *a*) to indicate a small quantity that is not enough (not adequate for some reason). *Very* can be placed before *few* and *little* to emphasize the lack of quantity.

>   John has *few* good friends. (not enough)
>   And he has *very little* money. (not at all enough)

A few **and** *a little*:   *A few* and *a little* also indicate a small quanitity, but without the implication that there should be more.

>   John has *a few* acquaintances but *few* good friends. (He has a small number
>   of acquaintances but not enough good friends.)
>   Mary gave us *a little* advice but *little* help. (We got a small amount of advice
>   but not enough help.)

Only can be placed before *a few* and *a little* (not before *few* or *little*) for emphasis.

>   *Only a few* students chose to write the optional paper.
>   That article gave me *only a little* information.

Placing *quite* in front of the quantifier *a few* changes its meaning. *Quite a few* means a fairly large quantity.

>   *Quite a few* students elected to write the optional paper. (I was surprised at the
>   number; it was larger than I had expected.)

7. Expressing indefinite quantities: *Some* and *any* are used to indicate an indefinite quantity of a noun. They are used with both noncount nouns and plural count nouns, as in sentences K. *Any* is usually used in questions and negative statements. *Some* is used in affirmative statements. However, if a questioner expects an affirmative answer, *some* can be used in the question.

>   Do you have *any* money? (I don't know if you do or not.)
>   Do you have *some* money? (I think that you do and expect that you will lend
>   me some.)

No can also be used as a quantifier to mean *not . . . any*, but it often sounds awkward and is best avoided.

Awkward   *Better*

I took *no* money from him.   I did*n't* take *any* money from him.

8. Omitting the noun after a quantifier: For all the quantifiers except *every* and *all*, it is possible to omit the following noun if its meaning is clearly understood.

> I need *some money*. I don't have *any*, and I need *a little* for lunch.
> I have not spoken with George or Martha this morning. *Neither* has arrived yet.

When a quantifier with *of* (*a lot of*, *a great deal of*, *a great number of*) stands alone without a noun, *of* is omitted.

> I don't want more *advice*. You've given me *a great deal* already, and *most* wasn't very good.
> She asked if I go to many plays. I admitted that I go to *a lot*.

If the noun following the quantifier *no* is omitted, the form *none* must be used.

> Did any students come?
>   No, *no students* came.
>   No, *none* came.

EXERCISE 10.4-A ANSWERING QUESTIONS (ORAL)

quantifiers

Answer each question with a quantifier. Your answer can be a full statement or a short reply.

> **Example:** Are there many students in this class?
>   *No, there are only a few students.*   OR
>   *No, there are only a few.*

1. Is there much crime in this city?

2. Do you spend much time studying?

3. Do you know many Americans at this school?

4. Are there any good restaurants near campus?

5. Do you play any sports?

6. Do you go to many films?

7. Did your family give you any advice before you left home?

EXERCISE 10.4-B ASKING QUESTIONS (ORAL)

· ·

how many* and *how much

Listen to each statement that your instructor makes. Then form a question with *how many* or *how much*, and ask your question to a classmate. Your classmate will answer your question.

> **Example:** I've seen two movies this month.
> *Student A: How many movies have you seen this month?*
> *Student B: I haven't seen any.*   OR
> *None.*   OR
> *Several.*

1. I spent a lot of time preparing for this class last night.

2. I know every student in this class.

3. I've never studied any chemistry or physics.

4. I live five miles from campus.

5. I've been to the library two times this week.

6. I've been to every restaurant in town.

7. I get a lot of advice from my parents.

EXERCISE 10.4-C EXPRESSING YOUR OWN IDEAS (ORAL)

· ·

quantifiers

Make affirmative or negative statements about the city or town you now live in, using each noun provided. Use a quantifier in your statement.

> **Example:** movie theaters
> *There are a lot of movie theaters in (name of city).*   OR
> *There aren't many movie theaters in (city).*   OR
> *There are few movie theaters in (city).*

1. friendly people
2. churches
3. pollution
4. inexpensive housing
5. nightlife
6. affluence
7. skyscrapers
8. schools
9. poverty
10. stores

EXERCISE 10.4-D DISCRIMINATING FORM

choosing quantifiers

Circle the correct quantifier in each sentence.

1. I don't have (*many*, *much*) faith in the weather report.

2. I didn't find (*either*, *a great deal of*, *a great number of*) new vocabulary in that article.

3. I found (*some*, *any*) information, but not (*a lot of*, *a lot*).

4. (*A few*, *A little*, *Each*) hard work is good for your character.

5. I read all the essays, and (*each*, *every*, *many*, *much*) is excellent.

6. I haven't seen (*any*, *no*, *none*) familiar faces since we've been here.

7. (*Either*, *Neither*, *None*) plan is a good one. You'll have to come up with a new idea.

8. It will take (*few*, *quite a few*, *little*, *a little*) time to complete this project. How are you going to fit it in with all your other work?

EXERCISE 10.4-E COMPLETING SENTENCES

choosing quantifiers

Fill in each blank with an appropriate quantifier. In most cases, there are several possibilities.

1. There are _____ reasons for his success, but _____ hard work is the primary one.

2. We didn't find _____ wrongdoing on the part of the governor.

3. She needs _____ encouragement, but you shouldn't give her _____ help.

4. You will have _____ trouble in the future if you don't take care of this problem now.

5. She has _____ confidence, but not as much as she should have.

6. Those countries export _____ oil but not _____ manufactured products.

7. _____ famous painters have lived in poverty throughout most of their lives.

EXERCISE 10.4-F RESTATING INFORMATION

using quantifiers

Read the information in each item. Then write an affirmative statement or a negative statement including the words in parentheses. Use an appropriate quantifier to modify the underlined word.

> **Example:** There are thirty students in the class. Three students came.
> (<u>students</u>/come)
> *Few students came.*

1. Martha has $2. She needs $100 for textbooks. (Martha/have/<u>money</u>)

   _____

2. Professor Lucus enjoys classical, popular, jazz, and folk music. She can't stand hard rock. (Professor Lucus/enjoy/<u>music</u>)

   _____

3. George spent twenty minutes on the assignment. Most students spent two hours. (George/spend/<u>time</u>/on the assignment)

   _____

4. Twelve children came to the party. Eleven children won prizes. (<u>children</u>/win/prize)

   _____

5. Ms. Moon didn't understand my question. Mr. Wolek didn't understand my question. (<u>teacher</u>/understand/my question)

   _____

6. I have free time now. It should be enough to talk about our plans. (I/have/<u>time</u>/to talk about our plans)

   _____

7. There are fifty pages. I read fifty pages. (I/read/<u>page</u>/carefully)

   _____

EXERCISE 10.4-G EXPRESSING YOUR OWN IDEAS

using quantifiers

Use each group of words to write a negative statement or an affirmative statement about yourself. Use a quantifier to describe the underlined noun.

> **Example:** enjoy – <u>sports</u>
> I enjoy most sports.   OR
> *I don't enjoy any sports.*

1. have – <u>self-confidence</u>

_____

2. see – <u>films</u> – this year

_____

3. possess – fine <u>qualities</u>

_____

4. read – <u>magazines</u> – last week

_____

5. notice – <u>pollution</u> – in this city – since – I – arrive

_____

6. want – develop – <u>expertise</u> – in my field

_____

SECTION 10.5   Predeterminers

· ·

(See the box on page 282.)

1. Predeterminers: Quantifiers can be used as predeterminers if the noun phrase is already definite. Look at sentences A through C. In each case, the quantifier is followed by *of* and then by a definite noun phrase.

Quantifier	*of*	*Definite Noun*	
Most	*of*	*the children*	can do the job.
A few	*of*	*your answers*	are incorrect.

The noun phrase must be made definite by using a definite determiner, such as *the*; a possessive noun, such as *John's*; a possessive adjective, such as *my*; or a demonstrative, such as *those*. Or the noun phrase may be an object pronoun (*them, us, it*), which is always definite.

Correct	*Incorrect*
some of the students	some of students
all of her ideas	all of ideas

2. Predeterminers with plural count nouns: Examine sentences A and B. The predeterminers in A are used with plural count nouns, and the verb is singular (*is*). The predeterminers in B are also used with plural count nouns, but the verb is plural (*are*).

Singular predeterminers: With the predeterminers *each, every one, either, neither, one,* and *none*, the noun phrase that follows is plural, but the verb is singular. See the examples below the box on page 282.

PREDETERMINERS

Plural Count Nouns

A. **Each (one)**
    Every one
    Either (one)   of   the children / my friends / those students / them / us   *is* capable of doing the job.
    Neither (one)
    One
    None

B. **Many**
    A lot
    (A) few
    A (great) number
    All
    Any/Some   of   the children / my friends / those students / them / us   *are* capable of doing the job.
    Most
    Three
    Several
    Both
    Neither (one)
    None

Singular Count Nouns and All Noncount Nouns

C. **Much**
    A lot
    (A) little
    A great deal   of   his information / this book / John's advice / the article / it   *is* accurate.
    All
    Some/Any
    Most
    None

Correct	*Incorrect*
Either one of them is correct.	Either one of them are correct.
Every one of the girls is here.	Every one of the girl is here.

Compare these quantifiers used as determiners and as predeterminers.

Determiner	*Predeterminer*
Each boy has done his best.	*Each of the boys* has done his best.
Neither report is adequate.	*Neither of the reports* is adequate.
Only *one person* can come.	Only *one of them* can come.

Notice that *each, either,* and *neither* can be followed by *one. Every* must be followed by *one* when it is used as a predeterminer.

Plural predeterminers: The predeterminers *many, a lot, (a) few, a (great) number, all, any, some, most, several, both,* and the cardinal numbers (*two, three,* etc.) can be used with plural noun phrases. When they are used this way, the verb that follows is also plural (see sentence B). In less formal usage, the predeterminers *neither* and *none* are sometimes followed by a plural verb instead of a singular verb.

Correct	*Incorrect*
Some of them are angry.	Some of them is angry.
A lot of John's friends are coming.	A lot of John's friends is coming.
None of them is angry.	
None of them are angry. (informal)	

3. Predeterminers with singular count nouns and with noncount nouns: The predeterminers *much, a lot, (a) little, a great deal, all, some, any, most,* and *none* can be used with singular count nouns and with noncount nouns (see sentence C). In both cases, the verb that follows is singular.

Correct	*Incorrect*
A lot of the information is wrong.	A lot of the information are wrong.
Some of the book is boring.	Some of the book are boring.

When these predeterminers are used with singular count nouns, the meaning is "part of the whole." For example, *most of the article* means "a large part of the article." Be sure to use *much,* not *many,* as a predeterminer with a singular count noun.

Plural Count Noun

Determiner: How *many books* did you read?
Predeterminer: How *many of the books* did you read?

Singular Count Noun

Predeterminer: How *much of the book* did you read?

4. *Both* and *all*:   *Both* and *all* can be used as predeterminers without the word *of* if the noun phrase is not a pronoun. There is no change in meaning.

Correct:	All of the money was lost.	Both of the boys were late.
	All the money was lost.	Both the boys were late.
	All of it was lost.	Both of them were late.
Incorrect:	All it was lost.	Both them were late.

EXERCISE 10.5-A ANSWERING QUESTIONS (ORAL)

using predeterminers

Answer each question with a full statement, using a predeterminer.

> **Example:** Do you know any of the students in this class?
> *Yes, I know all of them.* OR
> *Yes, I know quite a few of them.* OR
> *No, I don't know any of them.*

1. Do you enjoy your English classes?

2. Do you listen to your parents' advice?

3. Did you complete your assignment last night?

4. Do you spend your money on entertainment?

5. Did you watch the news on television last night?

6. Did you read the chapter last night?

EXERCISE 10.5-B ASKING QUESTIONS (ORAL)

***many* and *much* as predeterminers**

Listen to each statement. Then form a question with *how many* or *how much*, and ask your question to a classmate. Your classmate will answer your question.

> **Example:** I've attended every one of the classes this week.
> *Student A: How many of the classes have you attended this week?*
> *Student B: I've attended all of them.* OR
> *I've attended most of them.*

1. I read only some of the newspaper this morning.

2. I understand only some of this chapter.

3. I know every one of the people in this class.

4. I have done all of my assignments this week.

5. I wrote to all of my friends last month.

6. I didn't eat any of my breakfast this morning.

7. I'm going to spend most of this evening studying grammar.

EXERCISE 10.5-C EXPRESSING YOUR OWN IDEAS (ORAL)
● ·

predeterminers

Use each noun provided to make an affirmative statement or a negative statement about your native country. Include a predeterminer in your statement.

> **Example:** large cities
>> *A few of the large cities in my country are industrial centers.*   OR
>> *Most of the large cities in my country are growing rapidly.*

1.	people's religions	**6.**	restaurants
2.	people's occupations	**7.**	public transportation
3.	crime	**8.**	education
4.	schools	**9.**	stores
5.	housing	**10.**	music

EXERCISE 10.5-D DISCRIMINATING FORM
● ·

predeterminers

Circle the correct word or phrase in each sentence.

1. (*A great deal, A great number*) of the students plan to come to tonight's study session.

2. None (*pollution, the pollution, of the pollution*) (*is, are*) caused by that chemical factory.

3. Every one of (*they, them*) (*come, comes*) every day.

4. (*Both, Three*) the estimates are too high.

5. Each of the (*machine, machines, machinery*) (*has, have*) broken at least once this year.

6. Several (*repairs, the repairs*) have already been made.

7. They weren't happy with any (*the suggestions, of suggestions, of them*).

EXERCISE 10.5-E COMPLETING SENTENCES

determiners and predeterminers

Fill in each blank with an appropriate predeterminer or determiner. In most cases, there are several possibilities.

1. The city council cancelled _____ construction contracts.

2. _____ project wasn't done very well, but _____ it was.

3. _____ anger was directed at me.

4. _____ designs is good enough to use.

5. The university agreed to meet _____ student demands.

6. She has completed only _____ assignment.

7. We're not pleased with _____ results.

EXERCISE 10.5-F RESTATING INFORMATION

determiners and predeterminers

Read the information in each item. Then write an affirmative statement or a negative statement including each group of words in parentheses. Use an appropriate predeterminer or determiner to modify the underlined word.

> **Example:** Professor Johnson teaches a history class. There are thirty
> students in it. Only ten students came this morning.
> (students / come)
> *Only ten of Professor Johnson's students came this morning.*   OR
> *Most of Professor Johnson's students didn't come this morning.*

1. George has three daughters. Jane and Linda are in college. Betty is in high school.
   (daughters / BE / in college)

   _____

   (daughters / BE / in high school)

   _____

2. The university has two dormitories. Scott Hall is in bad repair. Taylor Hall isn't in good shape, either.
   (dormitories / BE / in good repair)

   _____

   (dormitories / BE / in bad repair)

   _____

3.   Martha inherited $3,000. She bought a computer for $2,000 and clothes for $500.
(Martha / spend / <u>inheritance</u> / on a computer)

_____

(she / spend / <u>inheritance</u> / on clothes)

_____

4.   The book that I have to read is over 400 pages long. I read 200 pages last week. I
(read another 50 pages this morning.
(I / read / <u>book</u> / last week)

_____

(I / read / <u>book</u> / this morning)

_____

5.   The department has four administrators. Professor Michaels is in charge of curriculum. Professor Hanson works with faculty matters. Professor Rupright and Mr.
Samuels handle budgets and scheduling.
(<u>administrators</u> / BE / professors)

_____

(<u>administrators</u> / work / on budgets and scheduling)

_____

(<u>administrators</u> / work / with curriculum)

_____

EXERCISE 10.5-G RESPONDING TO INFORMATION
● ·

predeterminers

Each item on page 288 gives statistics from which generalizations can be
made. Read the data in each item carefully. Then create statements which
generalize the data, incorporating each group of words in parentheses. Use
a predeterminer to modify the noun which is underlined.

1.   _Causes of Accidental Death in the United States, 1985_

Motor vehicles	45,600
Falls	11,300
Drowning	5,700
Burns	4,900
Firearms	1,600

Examples: (<u>accidental deaths</u> / cause / by firearms)
Few of the accidental deaths in the United States in 1985 were
caused by firearms.
(<u>accidental deaths</u> / cause / by burns)
Approximately 5,000 of the accidental deaths were caused by
burns.

(accidental deaths / cause / by motor vehicles)

_____

_____

(accidental deaths / cause / by falls)

_____

_____

(accidental deaths / cause / by drowning)

_____

_____

2. *Production of Petroleum by World Region, 1987*

North America	3,956,600,000 barrels
South America	1,809,670,000 barrels
Western Europe	1,504,530,000 barrels
Middle East	4,044,565,000 barrels
Asia, the Pacific	1,125,660,000 barrels
Africa	1,689,585,000 barrels
Communist bloc	5,652,025,000 barrels
Total	19,782,635,000 barrels

(total oil production / BE / from the Communist bloc)

_____

_____

(the world's oil / produce / by countries in Africa)

_____

_____

(the world's oil / come / from the Middle East)

_____

_____

3. *Immigration to the United States by Origin, 1986*

Europe	62,512
Asia	268,248
North and South America	249,588
Africa	17,463
Australia	1,792
Total	601,708

(immigrants to the United States / BE / from Australia)

_____

_____

(<u>immigrants to the United States</u> / come / from Asia)

_____

_____

(<u>immigrants to the United States</u> / BE / from Africa)

_____

_____

11 Adjectives and Adjective Clauses

Clauses which describe, or modify, nouns are called adjective clauses. In this chapter you will review different types of noun modification and then examine adjective clauses in detail.

SECTION 11.1   Modifying Nouns

> MODIFIERS OF NOUNS
>
> **A.**   George read *an* **article**.
>
> **B.**   George read *a long* **article**.
>
> **C.**   George read *a very long* **article**.
>
> **D.**   George read *a long journal* **article**.
>
> **E.**   George read *a long journal* **article** *about population growth*.
>
> **F.**   George read *a long journal* **article** *that Dr. Thomas had written*.

1. Modifying a noun: In Chapter 1 you learned that a noun can be modified by an adjective, another noun, a prepositional phrase, or an adjective clause. Adjectives and nouns are placed in front of the nouns that they modify. Prepositional phrases and adjective clauses are placed after the nouns that they modify.

2. Using adjectives and nouns as modifiers: In sentence B on page 291, the noun *article* is modified by the adjective *long*. The adjective itself can be modified by an adverb, such as *very, rather, unusually,* or *extremely*, as in sentence C.

> a very long article
> an extremely difficult course

When a noun modifies another noun, it must be used in the singular form.

> This is food for cats. It is *cat food*.
> He is a collector of stamps. He is a *stamp collector*.

If a noun modifier is used in combination with a cardinal number, a hyphen is placed between them.

> This building has three stories. It is a *three-story building*.
> That girl is five years old. She is a *five-year-old girl*.

When both an adjective and a noun modify another noun, the adjective comes first, as in sentence D. Predeterminers and determiners precede adjectives.

Predeterminer	Determiner	Adjective	Noun Modifier	Main Noun
all of	those	new	steel	shelves
many of	John's	old	school	friends

3. Using prepositional phrases and adjective clauses as modifiers: Prepositional phrases and adjective clauses follow the nouns that they describe. In sentence E, the prepositional phrase *about population growth* follows the noun *article*. In sentence F, the adjective clause *that Dr. Thomas had written* modifies *article*.

You will remember from Chapter 1 that an adjective clause is one type of dependent clause. It cannot stand alone but must be attached to a main, or independent, clause. In sentence F, what is the main clause? What is the adjective clause? Does the adjective clause have a subject and a verb?

EXERCISE 11.1-A   IDENTIFYING MODIFIERS

modifiers of nouns

For each sentence, circle the structures which modify each underlined noun. Label them as predeterminers, determiners, adjectives, prepositional phrases, or adjective clauses.

1. Many of the <u>assignments</u> from that class are too difficult.

2. The best <u>offer</u> that we can possibly make is $500.

3. Our school system can't afford to replace any of those aging buses.

4. A few of the candidates for the office of mayor have already made some promises
which they probably cannot keep.

5. The Eastern European dishes that are served by that restaurant are known for their
unusual spices.

6. Quite a few of Martha's predictions about the fall elections proved to be true.

7. Two of the news reports that I saw on television mentioned details of the tragedy.

EXERCISE 11.1-B COMBINING SENTENCES

nouns as modifiers

Combine the sentences in each item, using a noun from the second sentence
to modify a noun in the first sentence.

Example: He is a repairman. He fixes appliances.
He is an appliance repairman.

1. The Huntington Plaza is an old building. It has three stories.

   _The Huntington_____

2. Howard is a salesman. He sells used cars.

3. This is a book. It explains English grammar.

   _This is a English Grammar Book_____

4. Janice doesn't like her course. It concerns advanced chemistry.

5. Howard installed a new plug. It has three prongs.

6. George is a teacher. He is 37 years old.

EXERCISE 11.1-C UNSCRAMBLING NOUN PHRASES

nouns and their modifiers

On page 294, unscramble the modifiers of the underlined nouns in each set
of parentheses to create a meaningful sentence.

Example: (manuscripts/few of/of that period/valuable/the) have been found
Few of the valuable manuscripts of that period have been found.

1. people are upset about (<u>regulations</u>/new/that go into effect next week/the city's/some of/tax)

_____

_____

2. (<u>students</u>/with a lot of potential/young/who don't do well in school) need special instruction

Young students with a lot of potential who don't do well in well in school need special instruction.

3. Martha spoke to (<u>friends</u>/George's/who were here for the reunion/former/most of/college)

_____

_____

4. (<u>sculptures</u>/clay/three/in the collection/the other) are out on loan

_____

_____

5. (<u>policy</u>/welfare/that she helped establish/the/much of) has been modified

Much of the welfare policy that she helped established has been modified.

6. (<u>members</u>/the university's/with five or more years of service/each of/faculty) was given a bonus

_____

_____

SECTION 11.2   Adjective Clauses

1. Adjective clauses: You know that adjective clauses modify a noun. The noun that an adjective clause describes is called its antecedent. The word in the adjective clause that refers to the antecedent is called the relative pronoun. Read sentence A on page 295. This sentence contains an adjective clause, *who are in Dr. Danforth's class.* The antecedent in this adjective clause is *students.* The relative pronoun can be either *who* or *that.*

Antecedent	Relative Pronoun	
The students	who	*are in Dr. Danforth's class* speak highly of her.

—————Adjective Clause—————

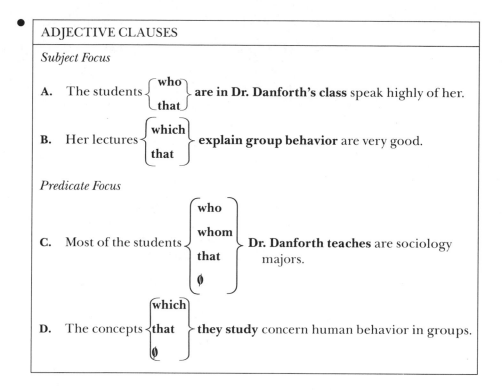

Examine sentence B. What is the adjective clause? What is its antecedent? What are the two possible relative pronouns? Note that *who* is used for human antecedents, *which* for nonhuman antecedents, and *that* for either human or nonhuman.

2. Subject focus adjective clauses: The adjective clauses in sentences A and B have a subject focus because the relative pronouns also serve as the subjects of the adjective clauses.

Relative Pronoun and Subject	*Verb*	
who	are	in Dr. Danforth's class
which	explain	group behavior

You might want to think of these complex sentences as combinations of two simple sentences. One sentence is changed to an adjective clause by substituting a relative pronoun for the subject and then placing the entire clause immediately after the antecedent, as on page 296.

In subject focus adjective clauses, *who, which,* and *that* can be used as relative pronouns. *Whom* cannot be used.

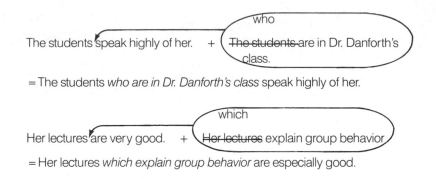

The students *speak highly of her.*   +   ~~The students~~ *who* are in Dr. Danforth's class.

= The students *who are in Dr. Danforth's class* speak highly of her.

Her lectures *are very good.*   +   ~~Her lectures~~ *which* explain group behavior.

= Her lectures *which explain group behavior* are especially good.

3. Predicate focus adjective clauses: Sentences C and D on page 295 contain predicate focus adjective clauses. Adjective clauses have a predicate focus when the relative pronoun serves as part of the predicate of the clause, usually the object. The subject and the verb of the adjective clause follow the relative pronoun.

Relative Pronoun and Object	*Subject*	*Verb*
whom	Dr. Danforth	teaches
which	they	study

These sentences can also be thought of as combinations of two simple sentences. One sentence is changed to an adjective clause by substituting a relative pronoun for the object and then moving it in front of the subject.

Most of the students *are* sociology majors.   +   Dr. Danforth teaches ~~those students~~ *whom*.

= Most of the students *whom Dr. Danforth teaches* are sociology majors.

The concepts *concern human behavior in groups.*   +   They study ~~those concepts~~ *which*.

= The concepts *which they study* concern human behavior in groups.

Be sure not to repeat the object in a predicate focus adjective clause.

Correct	*Incorrect*
This is the book that I have been reading.	This is the book that I have been reading it.

The relative pronouns that can be used in a predicate focus adjective clause are *who*, *whom*, *that*, *which*, or no relative pronoun (∅). (See sentences C and D on page 295.) *Who* is generally used in conversation. *Whom* should be used in formal writing. Remember that *whom* and ∅ are possible only in predicate focus clauses, not in subject focus clauses.

Correct	*Incorrect*
I'm the person who wrote to you.	I'm the person whom wrote to you.
	I'm the person wrote to you.

4. Adjective clauses as identifiers of nouns: An adjective clause defines its antecedent, and in many cases it identifies the antecedent closely enough to make it definite.

> I read *the* article *which you recommended to me.*
> *The* suggestions *that were given* were very helpful.

However, the antecedent of an adjective clause can sometimes be indefinite. In these cases, the adjective clause describes the antecedent but does not identify it as one specific item.

> I enjoy a movie that makes me cry. (any movie that makes me cry)
> Mammals are animals that have milk-secreting glands for feeding their young.
>   (any animals that have milk-secreting glands)

EXERCISE 11.2-A ANSWERING QUESTIONS (ORAL)

● ·

subject focus adjective clauses

Answer each question with a full statement containing a subject focus adjective clause. Use the information in parentheses for the adjective clause. What choices do you have for the relative pronoun?

> **Example:** Which book do you want? (explains Johnson's theories)
> *I want the book that explains Johnson's theories.*

1. Which students did you talk to? (are in the other English class)

2. Which bus are you going to take? (leaves at noon)

3. Which sweater did she buy? (is made of real cashmere)

4. Which travel agency did they call? (gave the best discounts)

5. Which question did you answer? (required an economic analysis)

6. Which restaurant did you go to? (is at the top of the Briggs Building)

7. Which English class did you register for? (meets at eight o'clock every day)

EXERCISE 11.2-B ANSWERING QUESTIONS (ORAL)

predicate focus adjective clauses

Answer each question with a full statement containing a predicate focus adjective clause. Use the information in parentheses for the adjective clause. What choices do you have for the relative pronoun?

> **Example:** Which book do you want? (You borrowed it last week.)
> *I want the book that you borrowed last week.*

1.   Which film are you going to go to? (George recommended it.)

2.   Which class did you drop? (Professor Haywood teaches it.)

3.   Which students have you talked to? (John interviewed them last week.)

4.   Which English class did you register for? (Martha took it last term.)

5.   Which sweater did she buy? (George liked it.)

6.   Which travel agency did they call? (I usually use that agency.)

7.   Which house did they buy? (The Hermanns used to own it.)

EXERCISE 11.2-C IDENTIFYING AND ANALYZING SENTENCES

adjective clauses

Underline the adjective clause in each sentence. Then decide if the adjective clause has a subject focus or a predicate focus. What is the antecedent? What other relative pronouns could be used?

> **Example:** Most of the problems which you mentioned have already been
> addressed.
> Focus: *predicate*   Antecedent: *problems*
> Other relative pronouns: *that, ∅*

1.   The answers which you gave on the last part of the exam are all incorrect.
     Focus: _____   Antecedent: _____
     Other relative pronouns: _____

2.   We didn't understand most of the terms she used in yesterday's lecture.
     Focus: _____   Antecedent: _____
     Other relative pronouns: _____

3.   A lot of the information that was given to us proved to be inaccurate.
     Focus: _____   Antecedent: _____
     Other relative pronouns: _____

4. A good portion of the housing that was constructed in the 1960s for lower-income families is now uninhabitable.
    Focus: _____   Antecedent: _____
    Other relative pronouns: _____

5. The budget problems we are facing at the present time will only worsen in the future.
    Focus: _____   Antecedent: _____
    Other relative pronouns: _____

6. Computers that use that type of operating system have been replaced by more sophisticated machines.
    Focus: _____   Antecedent: _____
    Other relative pronouns: _____

7. The computers which that company builds are usually very reliable.
    Focus: _____   Antecedent: _____
    Other relative pronouns: _____

EXERCISE 11.2-D COMBINING SENTENCES

adjective clauses with subject focus and with predicate focus

Each sentence contains an underlined noun that needs to be further defined. Use the information in parentheses to form an adjective clause that will define that noun.

> **Example:** The advice was excellent. (You gave us the advice.)
> *The advice that you gave us was excellent.*

1. George disputed some of the results. (Professor Judd reported the results.)

    _____

    _____

2. George disputed some of the results. (The results were reported by Professor Naumoff.)

    _____

    _____

3. The refreshments were consumed almost immediately. (The English Department provided the refreshments.)

    _____

    _____

4. Each of the <u>suggestions</u> was carefully considered. (You gave the suggestions to the committee.)

_____

_____

5. The new <u>laws</u> have been greeted with enthusiasm. (The laws restrict political campaign contributions.)

_____

_____

6. Most of the <u>children</u> are boys. (The children have trouble learning to read.)

_____

_____

7. The <u>equipment</u> is the best available. (Our laboratory uses that equipment.)

_____

_____

EXERCISE 11.2-E COMPLETING SENTENCES

adjective clauses

Fill in each blank with an adjective clause defining the underlined antecedents. Use the verb in parentheses and your own ideas. There are many possible answers for each item.

Example: I don't agree with the <u>answer</u> _____.
(*give*)
I don't agree with the answer that you gave.   OR
I don't agree with the answer that was just given.

1. Some of the <u>stories</u> _____ are unbelievable. (*tell*)

2. The <u>news</u> _____ contradicts earlier reports. (*hear*)

3. The <u>instructions</u> _____ don't make any sense. (*print*)

4. We've never encountered the <u>problems</u> _____ . (*describe*)

5. On the second page is the <u>information</u> _____ . (*explain*)

6. <u>Students</u> _____ will not have to take the final exam. (*do*)

7. <u>Adjective clauses</u> _____ can use *whom* as a relative pronoun. (BE)

EXERCISE 11.2-F ANSWERING QUESTIONS

● ·

using adjective clauses to specify

Answer each question with a full sentence, using an adjective clause to describe or identify the underlined noun.

> **Example:** Which apartment did you decide on?
> *I decided on the apartment that is next to John's.*

1. What kinds of books do you like to read?

   _____

2. Which restaurant do you often go to?

   _____

3. What kind of a meal do you enjoy?

   _____

4. What kind of teacher do you like the most?

   _____

5. What kind of advice do you value the most?

   _____

6. What kinds of people do you enjoy spending time with?

   _____

EXERCISE 11.2-G RESPONDING TO INFORMATION

● ·

adjective clauses

Read the paragraph about the discovery of penicillin. Then complete each item on page 302 with an adjective clause which identifies the underlined noun. Use the information from the paragraph.

> One of the key discoveries in modern medicine came about by accident. In the autumn of 1928, Alexander Fleming, a Scottish scientist, returned to his laboratory after a long absence. He noticed that a number of yeasts and molds had contaminated a culture dish of staphylococcus bacteria—the cause of many diseases, from boils to pneumonia. Fleming was immediately interested that one of the molds had killed the staphylococcus. On further investigation, he narrowed down the cause for this occurrence to an active ingredient which he named penicillin, after the name of the mold, *Penicillium notatum*. In 1940 Howard Florey and E. B. Chain isolated penicillin in their Oxford laboratories. All three men were awarded the Nobel Prize in Medicine for their work in 1945.

1. Alexander Fleming was the <u>scientist</u> _____

_____

2. Fleming found a number of molds and yeasts in a culture <u>dish</u> _____

_____

3. Fleming investigated a <u>mold</u> _____

_____

4. The staphylococcus had been killed by an active <u>ingredient</u> _which h_____

_named penicillin_____

5. Howard Florey and E. B. Chain were able to isolate the active <u>ingredient</u> _____

_____

SECTION 11.3   Using *Whose* and Prepositions in Adjective Clauses

●

WHOSE AS A RELATIVE PRONOUN
A. All the artists ***whose*** *paintings are on display* will be coming to the gallery tonight.
B. The sculptor ***whose*** *work you admire so much* will be there also.

1. *Whose* as a relative pronoun: The relative pronoun *whose* shows a posses-sive relationship between the subject or the object of the adjective clause and its antecedent.

Examine sentence A. *Whose painting*s means "the artists' paintings." This is a subject focus adjective clause because the *whose* + Noun combination serves as the subject of the clause.

Relative Pronoun and Subject	Verb	
whose paintings	are	on display

In sentence B, the *whose* + Noun combination serves as the object of the clause, so it has a predicate focus.

Relative Pronoun and Object	Subject	Verb	
whose work	you	admire	so much

If the meaning of these sentences is not clear, you might want to think of them as combinations of two simple sentences.

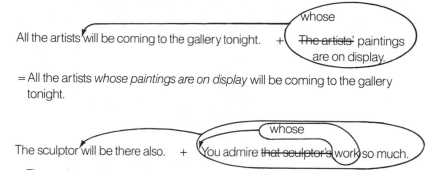

= All the artists *whose paintings are on display* will be coming to the gallery tonight.

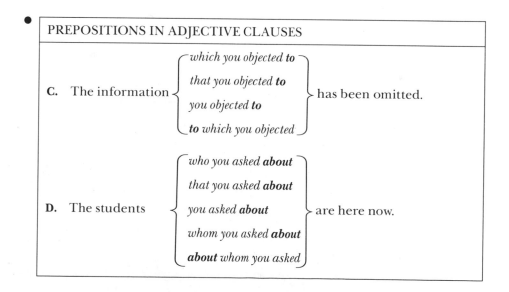

= The sculptor *whose work you admire so much* will be there also.

2. ***Whose* for nonhuman antecedents:** *Whose* can also be used to refer to nonhuman antecedents, although this is less commonly encountered.

> He comes from a country *whose government guarantees a free education.*
> That is one of the towns *whose residents are opposing the new tax law.*

PREPOSITIONS IN ADJECTIVE CLAUSES

C. The information
- *which you objected **to***
- *that you objected **to***
- *you objected **to***
- ***to** which you objected*

has been omitted.

D. The students
- *who you asked **about***
- *that you asked **about***
- *you asked **about***
- *whom you asked **about***
- ***about** whom you asked*

are here now.

---

3. Relative pronouns as objects of prepositions: In sentence C, the relative pronouns are objects of the preposition *to*. In sentence D, the relative pronouns are objects of the preposition *about*. Notice that when the preposition follows the verb, you can use any of the relative pronouns (*who, whom, that, which,* or ∅). However, if the preposition is moved to the beginning of the adjective clause, in front of the relative pronoun, only *whom* or *which* can be used.

Correct	*Incorrect*
The information he asked for can't be found.	The information for he asked can't be found.
The information for which he asked can't be found.	The information for that he asked can't be found.
The information that he asked for can't be found.	

EXERCISE 11.3-A COMBINING SENTENCES

whose as a relative pronoun

Each sentence contains an underlined noun that needs to be further defined. Use the information in parentheses to form an adjective clause with *whose* that will define that noun.

> **Example:** The instructor is a lot of fun. (I'm taking his math course.)
> *The instructor whose math course I'm taking is a lot of fun.*

1. The student is going to the police. (Her purse was stolen this morning.)

    _____

    _____

2. This is a special class for students. (The students' background in math is weak.)

    _____

    _____

3. Here is another applicant. (You should check this applicant's credentials.)

    _____

    _____

4. Ada is a small town. (Its residents are mostly farmers.)

    _____

    _____

5. The employees are listed on this page. (We have to verify their work hours.)

    _____

    _____

6. All the people were given temporary shelter, food, and clothing. (The people's homes had been destroyed by the flood.)

    _____

    _____

7. A <u>government</u> should be a popular one. (A government's officials are responsive to its people.)

_____

_____

EXERCISE 11.3-B COMBINING SENTENCES

● ·

relative pronouns as the objects of prepositions

Each sentence contains an underlined noun that needs to be further de-fined. Use the information in parentheses to form an adjective clause that will define that noun. What other relative pronouns could be used? In which cases can the preposition be placed at the beginning of the adjective clause?

> **Example:** This is all the <u>information</u>. (I am aware of it.)
> _This is all the information of which I am aware._   OR
> _This is all the information which I am aware of._   OR
> _This is all the information that I am aware of._   OR
> _This is all the information I am aware of._

1. The <u>company</u> has not been doing well for the past few years. (I work for the company.)

_____

_____

2. Most of the <u>policies</u> involved reducing educational benefits. (George is opposed to the policies.)

_____

_____

3. The other <u>teachers</u> rarely arrive before 9:00 A.M. (Martha shares an office with the other teachers.)

_____

_____

4. The <u>letter</u> should provide Sam with some important data. (He is waiting for the letter.)

_____

_____

5. The <u>person</u> doesn't want me to divulge his name. (I got the information from the person.)

_____

_____

6. My ideas weren't very popular among the <u>students</u>. (I talked to the students last week.)

_____

_____

EXERCISE 11.3-C CORRECTING ERRORS

adjective clauses

Each sentence contains one or more errors. Identify the errors, and write the corrected sentence on the line provided.

1. The company to that he sent the letter never replied.

    _____

2. The children whom we punished them began to behave better.

    _____

3. The man whose you borrowed his car wants to speak to you.

    _____

4. The people have formed a citizens' patrol whose homes were burglarized.

    _____

5. The students about she asked have all left already.

    _____

SECTION 11.4 Nonrestrictive Adjective Clauses

RESTRICTIVE CLAUSES AND NONRESTRICTIVE CLAUSES
Restrictive Clauses
A. *Seniors* **who graduate this term** have to take an early final exam.
B. *The professor* **who usually teaches this course** is on leave this term.
Nonrestrictive Clauses
C. *Seniors,* **who graduate this term**, have to take an early final exam.
D. *Professor Weber,* **who usually teaches this course**, is on leave this term.

1. Restrictive clauses: The adjective clauses that we have examined so far have all been restrictive clauses. Restrictive clauses are essential, or necessary, because they help to limit or restrict the meaning of the antecedent.

Look at sentence A. Who has to take an early final exam? Is it all seniors? No, only seniors *who graduate this term* have to take the early test. This sentence implies that some seniors graduate this term, and some do not. The adjective clause restricts which group is being referred to. Now examine sentence B. The restrictive adjective clause *who usually teaches this course* helps to identify *which* professor.

Restrictive clauses give necessary information that helps to identify the antecedent. If the adjective clause is omitted, the meaning of the main clause may change.

> People bother me. (All people bother me.)
> People who complain all the time bother me. (Only a restricted group of people bother me—those who complain all the time.)

2. Nonrestrictive clauses: When the antecedent is already identified, the adjective clause which follows it provides additional *but not essential* information. Read sentence C. The commas before and after the adjective clause indicate that it is a nonrestrictive clause. It gives extra information about the antecedent *seniors*, but it does not identify or restrict them. This sentence implies that *all* seniors have to take the early exam, and *all* seniors graduate this term. Now look at sentence D. The antecedent is a proper noun, *Professor Weber*. Propers nouns are definite and unique. We do not need further information to identify them. So the adjective clause is nonrestrictive; it only provides additional information about Professor Weber.

Compare the following pairs of sentences. Which one is restrictive? Which one is nonrestrictive? How do you know? What is the difference in meaning?

> He doesn't like his colleagues, who are extremely competitive. (All of his colleagues are competitive and he doesn't like them.)
> He doesn't like his colleagues who are extremely competitive. (Some of his colleagues are competitive; those are the ones he doesn't like.)

> My relatives, who live in New York, are coming for a visit. (All of my relatives live in New York; they are all coming for a visit.)
> My relatives who live in New York are coming for a visit. (Some of my relatives live in New York; those are the ones who are coming.)

3. Relative pronouns in nonrestrictive clauses: Nonrestrictive adjective clauses do not use *that*. In addition, they cannot omit the relative pronoun. However, all the other relative pronouns can be used in a nonrestrictive clause.

Correct	*Incorrect*
The Briggs Building, which is being renovated, is ninety years old.	The Briggs Building, that is being renovated, is ninety years old.
Mr. Wolek, whom I met with yesterday, doesn't approve of my plan.	Mr. Wolek, I met with yesterday, doesn't approve of my plan.

4. Using predeterminers with relative pronouns: Predeterminers can be placed before relative pronouns in nonrestrictive adjective clauses.

> The children, *some of whom* had never been to a play, reacted enthusiastically to the production.
> I didn't pay any attention to her advice, *most of which* was ill-intentioned.

EXERCISE 11.4-A IDENTIFYING STRUCTURE

restrictive clauses and nonrestrictive clauses

Each sentence contains one or more adjective clauses. Underline each adjective clause. Then place commas around it if it is nonrestrictive.

1. The proposals which were received before last Tuesday have already been read by Dr. Siddens. The proposals which have arrived since Tuesday will be read next week.

2. Five billion years from now, the sun which is 93 million miles from earth will become a giant red star which will engulf the planets.

3. Drivers who have been drinking alchohol cause the majority of serious automobile accidents every year.

4. Donna who has always been somewhat shy has managed to make a lot of new friends this year.

5. The mayor wasn't happy with the reporter's questions many of which were openly critical of the way in which he had handled the budget crisis.

6. Professor Newman enjoys working with students who are academically capable and highly motivated.

7. Professor Newman enjoys working with students who are generally more curious and open-minded than other people.

EXERCISE 11.4-B COMBINING SENTENCES

restrictive adjective clauses and nonrestrictive adjective clauses

Use the information in parentheses to form a restrictive adjective clause or a nonrestrictive adjective clause to modify the underlined noun.

> **Example:** I haven't had a chance to speak to the students. (Some of the students have already left for spring break.)
> *I haven't had a chance to speak to the students, some of whom have already left for spring break.*

1. Mayor Stratton will probably be reelected for another term. (She has held office for eight years.)

    _____

    _____

2. Mammals feed their young through milk-secreting glands. (Most of the mammals live on land.)

    _____

    _____

3. Mammals include whales and dolphins. (These mammals live in the sea.)

    _____

    _____

4. It has been three months since I've spoken with my father. (He is traveling overseas.)

    _____

    _____

5. I've interviewed several applicants. (I didn't like any of them.)

    _____

    _____

6. The comments have been very favorable. (I received these comments today.)

    _____

    _____

7. We enjoyed living in the South. (The South is known for its hospitality.)

    _____

    _____

EXERCISE 11.4-C CORRECTING ERRORS

restrictive clauses and nonrestrictive clauses

Each sentence contains one or more errors. Identify the mistakes, and write the corrected sentence on the lines provided.

1. My roommate, that comes from Peru, has learned English quickly.

    _____

2. The only answer, which he could give, was totally inadequate.

    _____

3. I've never met Professor Kaufman, John tells me is an excellent speaker.

_____

_____

4. The earth's atmosphere that extends many miles above the planet is vital to our existence.

_____

_____

5. Her children two of who are in college are all talented.

_____

6. Some of the topics, which you listed, need to be researched.

_____

EXERCISE 11.4-D EXPANDING SENTENCES

restrictive adjective clauses and nonrestrictive adjective clauses

Add a restrictive adjective clause or a nonrestrictive adjective clause to each basic sentence. Your adjective clause should modify the underlined noun. Use your own ideas.

> **Examples:** I just met Mr. Melching.
> _I just met Mr. Melching, who is our new supervisor._
>
> The _clerk_ couldn't give me a satisfactory answer.
> _The clerk that I spoke to couldn't give me a satisfactory answer._

1. The Empire State Building was the tallest building in the world for many years.

_____

_____

2. Professor Butler hasn't graded the tests.

_____

_____

3. The textbook for Chemistry 211 is very difficult to understand.

_____

_____

4. The students weren't very interested in the lecture.

_____

_____

5. George's <u>parents</u> both retire next month.

_____

_____

6. <u>IBM</u> is a giant international corporation.

_____

_____

EXERCISE 11.4-E RESPONDING TO INFORMATION

● ·

adjective clauses

Read the paragraph about the extinction of the dinosaurs. Then, to each sentence that follows, add a restrictive adjective clause or a nonrestrictive adjective clause which modifies the underlined noun. Use the information from the paragraph. (Sentence 5 is on the next page.)

> Luis and Walter Alvarez believe that an asteroid caused the extinction of the dinosaurs. The Alvarezes are researchers at the University of California at Berkeley. They say that an asteroid hit the earth about 65 million years ago. It was probably six or seven miles in diameter. The impact of the asteroid sent quadrillions of tons of rock dust into the earth's stratosphere. This dust formed a layer ten miles above the surface of the earth and blocked out most of the sunlight. Huge quantities of land plants and sea plants died. Without enough vegetation for their food supply, the dinosaurs starved and became extinct.

1. <u>Luis and Walter Alvarez</u> think they have found the cause of the extinction of dinosaurs.

_____

_____

2. Almost 70 million years ago an <u>asteroid</u> hit the earth.

_____

_____

3. <u>Rock dust</u> formed a layer ten miles above the earth.

_____

_____

4. <u>This layer of dust</u> killed huge quantities of land plants and sea plants.

_____

_____

5. The dinosaurs eventually starved and became extinct.

_____

_____

SECTION 11.5   Reduced Adjective Clauses

· ·

REDUCED ADJECTIVE CLAUSES

A. Most of the students **who are taking the test** plan to take another English course next term.

Most of the students **taking the test** plan to take another English course next term.

B. All of the papers **that were turned in late** will receive a lowered grade.

All of the papers **turned in late** will receive a lowered grade.

C. The paragraph **that is at the bottom of the first page** should be revised.

The paragraph **at the bottom of the first page** should be revised.

D. The equipment **that is available to us** isn't adequate.

The equipment **available to us** isn't adequate.

E. Professor Wagner, **who is chair of the humanities division**, is leaving the university.

Professor Wagner, **chair of the humanities division**, is leaving the university.

---

1. Reduced adjective clauses: In some cases, a subject focus adjective clause can be reduced to a phrase by omitting the relative pronoun and the verb BE. Look at sentences A. The first sentence contains a full adjective clause, _who are taking the test_. In the second sentence, the clause has been reduced to a phrase, _taking the test_.

2. Reduced restrictive clauses: Restrictive adjective clauses (those without commas) can be reduced if the relative pronoun and BE are followed by a present participle (sentences A), a past participle (sentences B), a prepositional phrase (sentences C), or an adjective phrase (sentences D). The present participle and the past participle are usually followed by an object or an adverb to complete the idea of the participle.

3. Reduced nonrestrictive clauses: Nonrestrictive adjective clauses (those with commas) can be reduced in the same way.

> Mr. Peterson, *who was working hard to meet his deadline*, asked not to be interrupted.
> Mr. Peterson, *working hard to meet his deadline*, asked not to be interrupted.

> The Briggs Building, *which was built in 1890*, is now being renovated.
> The Briggs Building, *built in 1890*, is now being renovated.

4. Appositives: In addition, a nonrestrictive clause can be reduced if the relative pronoun and BE are followed by a noun phrase, as in sentences E. In this example, the reduced phrase, *chair of the humanities division*, is called an appositive.

> The model 500, *which is our newest computer*, is causing a lot of excitement.
> The model 500, *our newest computer*, is causing a lot of excitement.

EXERCISE 11.5-A REDUCING CLAUSES

restrictive adjective clauses and nonrestrictive adjective clauses

Reduce the adjective clause in each sentence to a phrase.

1. The tall building which is nearing completion will eventually house the Department of Chemistry.

2. The number of crimes which are reported to the police has risen steadily each year.

3. You need to do something with that typewriter that is on the corner of the desk.

4. I spoke to the woman who is responsible for preparing transcripts.

5. Barley, which was first grown in Egypt 6,000 years ago, is now used primarily for cattle feed.

6. Gregor Mendel, who was an Austrian monk, discovered the principles of genetics.

7. Hammond College, which is trying to increase its enrollment, has started to offer evening and weekend courses.

8. The Pharos of Alexandria, which was the world's first lighthouse, stood over 400 feet high.

9. The taste buds, which are located on the surface of the tongue, can distinguish only four basic tastes.

EXERCISE 11.5-B COMBINING SENTENCES

• ·

reduced adjective clauses

Each sentence contains an underlined noun. Use the information in parentheses to form a reduced adjective clause, either restrictive or nonrestrictive, to modify that noun.

> **Example:** The people should have been more considerate. (They were whispering during the lecture.)
>
> *The people whispering during the lecture should have been more considerate.*

1. We just spoke to the man. (He is in charge of freshman orientation.)

   _____

   _____

2. In 1870 Maling Hansen marketed the first typewriter. (He was a Danish pastor and inventor.)

   _____

   _____

3. Please don't disturb the woman. (She is talking with those customers.)

   _____

   _____

4. Haymarket Square has become a successful retail mall. (It is in the center of town, near the lake.)

   _____

   _____

5. The painter's last work was donated to the art museum. (The work was judged to be worth over a million dollars.)

   _____

   _____

6. The building will be used for city service offices. (It is being constructed on the edge of town.)

   _____

   _____

7. Sir Isaac Newton formulated the general laws of planetary motion. (He was one of the greatest scientific minds of all time.)

   _____

   _____

EXERCISE 11.5-C DISCRIMINATION FORM

present participles and past participles in reduced adjective clauses

Fill in each blank with the present participle or past participle form of the verb in parentheses.

1. The news _____ (*report*) on television last night didn't mention the cause of the tragedy.

2. The student _____ (*hand out*) the papers is George.

3. Martha, _____ (*cross*) the street without a care in the world, failed to notice the car _____ (*come*) toward her.

4. This manuscript, _____ (*find*) in the attic of a house _____ (BE) demolished, has been talked about for years.

5. All students _____ (*plan*) to take English next term need to register this week.

6. The town, _____ (*destroy*) by a flood three years ago, has been largely rebuilt.

7. This line is for people _____ (*hope*) to get a refund.

8. Papers _____ (*write*) for this class must use the system of documentation _____ (*explain*) in the back of the textbook.

9. Anyone _____ (*look for*) an apartment should place a notice on the bulletin board _____ (*locate*) in the hallway.

EXERCISE 11.5-D RESPONDING TO INFORMATION

reduced adjective clauses

Using the information provided in each item, construct a sentence with a reduced adjective clause.

> **Example:** Cairo, Egypt: It was founded in A.D. 969. It was originally called al-Kahira.
>
> *Cairo, Egypt, founded in A.D. 969, was originally called al-Kahira.*

1. Islamabad, Pakistan: It was built in the early 1960s. It became the capital in 1967.

_____

_____

2. Amsterdam, Netherlands: It was started as a thirteenth-century fishing village. It was named for a dam at the mouth of the Amstel River.

_____

_____

3. Sigmund Freud: He was an Austrian neurologist. He was the founder of psycho-analysis.

_____

_____

4. Pythagorean theorem: It was named after the Greek philosopher Pythagoras. It had been known to the Babylonians 1,000 years earlier.

_____

_____

5. Anna Mary Moses: She was an American painter. She was also known as Grandma Moses. She didn't begin painting until age 76.

_____

_____

12 Intensifiers, Comparatives, and Superlatives

This chapter first examines the use of intensifiers to show result and then introduces the idea of comparison and the many ways that it is expressed in English. Finally, the superlative is reviewed and practiced.

SECTION 12.1 *Enough, Too, So,* and *Such*

ENOUGH
A. This room is **large enough** *to hold a few hundred people.*
B. But the chairs aren't **comfortable enough** for the audience *to sit through a long lecture.*
C. In addition, most speakers can't talk **loudly enough** for the people in the back *to hear.*
D. There is **enough light** for people *to take notes,* but there are not **enough chairs** for everyone *to sit down.*

1. Using *enough* to show adequacy: *Enough* indicates that something is adequate and that a particular result is possible. In sentence A, *large enough* means that the room is an adequate size, so it can hold a few hundred people. In sentence B, *aren't comfortable enough* means that the chairs are *not* adequately comfortable, so people will *not* be able to sit through a long lecture. What are the meanings of sentences C and D?

317

2. *Enough* **with adjectives and adverbs:**   *Enough* is placed after an adjective or an adverb. The result is expressed in an infinitive (*to* + Verb) phrase that follows. If the infinitive phrase has a subject different from the main subject, use a *for* phrase.

	Adjective or Adverb	*enough*	for *Phrase*	*Infinitive Phrase of Result*
The room is	large	enough	for us	to use.
He spoke	slowly	enough	for George	to understand.
She ran	quickly	enough		to win second place.

3. *Enough* **with nouns:**   *Enough* can also be used to modify a noun (plural count or noncount), as in sentence D on page 317. *Enough* is usually placed before a noun, but it is also possible to place it after.

> We have *enough time* to do all our shopping.
> We have *time enough* to do all our shopping.
> There aren't *enough seats* for everyone to sit down.
> There aren't *seats enough* for everyone to sit down.

EXERCISE 12.1-A COMBINING SENTENCES (ORAL)

enough

Combine each pair of sentences into one sentence, using *enough*.

> **Example:** Donna has some money. She can buy a car.
> *Donna has enough money to buy a car.*

1. They worked very quickly. They were able to finish by three o'clock.

2. There are a lot of pencils. We can give one to each student.

3. She isn't very perceptive. She can't understand the situation.

4. He speaks English very well. He can be understood.

5. I don't have a lot of time. I can't go with you.

6. The dog is very tame. It can play with young children.

4. **Using** *too* **to show excess:**   *Too* indicates that there is an excess (more than is wanted), so that a particular result is impossible. In sentence E on page 319, *too difficult* means that the article is more difficult than desired, so it cannot be understood. In sentence F, *too quickly* means that the author moves from one idea to another more quickly than desired, so I cannot follow his ideas. What is the meaning of sentence G?

TOO

E. This article is **too difficult** *to understand.*

F. The author moves from one idea to another **too quickly** for me *to follow.*

G. There is **too much** technical **vocabulary** *to know* and there are **too few examples** *to help us.*

When *too* is used in a negative statement, it means that the result is possible.

> This article isn't too difficult to understand. (I can understand it.)

5. *Too* with adjectives and adverbs: *Too* is placed in front of an adjective or an adverb, and the result is expressed in an infinitive phrase that follows. If the subject of the infinitive phrase is different from the main subject, use a *for* phrase. Remember that the infinitive result phrase has a negative meaning.

	too	*Adjective or Adverb*	for *Phrase*	*Infinitive Phrase of Result*
I am	too	busy		to go right now. (I can't go right now.)
That problem is	too	difficult	for me	to do. (I can't do it.)
Janet speaks	too	softly	for us	to understand. (We can't understand her.)

6. *Too* with nouns: *Too* can also modify the quantity of a noun (plural count or noncount), as in sentence G. In such cases, *many*, *much*, *little*, or *few* must be placed before the noun.

> There is *too little time* to do all our shopping. (We can't do it all.)
> This is *too much work* for one person to do alone. (One person can't do it all.)
> We have *too few people* here to play a good game. (We can't play a good game.)
> He made *too many mistakes* to pass the final exam. (He didn't pass.)

Do not use *too* if you do not want to imply a negative result. Instead, use *very.*

Correct	*Incorrect*
The exam was *very* easy.	The exam was *too* easy.
They are *very* nice to me.	They are *too* nice to me.

7. Omitting the infinitve phrase: The infinitive phrase of result can be omitted after *enough* and *too* if the meaning is understood.

> Are you going this evening?
> > No, I don't have enough time. (to go)
>
> Can you carry that suitcase?
> > No, it's too heavy. (to carry)

In addition, a noun modified by *too* or *enough* can be omitted if the meaning is clear.

> Do you have any money?
> > Yes, but not *enough* to lend you any. (enough money)

8. Repeating the main subject: Do not repeat the main subject of the sentence in the infinitive phrase of result after *too* or *enough*.

Correct	*Incorrect*
This room is large enough to use.	This room is large enough to use it.
The coffee is too hot to drink.	The coffee is too hot to drink it.

EXERCISE 12.1-B COMBINING SENTENCES (ORAL)

too

Combine each pair of sentences into one sentence, using *too.*

> **Example:** He is very important. You shouldn't ignore him.
> > *He is too important for you to ignore.*

1.   The problems are difficult. You can't do them in your head.

2.   This book is very long. I can't read it in one night.

3.   Your report has a lot of mistakes. You shouldn't hand it in.

4.   The suitcase isn't heavy. She can carry it.

5.   There is a lot of information. I can't remember it.

6.   There is little time. We can't finish the report.

7.   He plays very poorly. He shouldn't be on the team.

EXERCISE 12.1-C CHECKING UNDERSTANDING (ORAL)

too and *enough*

In each sentence on page 321, is the result possible or impossible? State the result in a simple sentence.

Example: It's too late for us to go now.
We can't go.

1. The desk is too heavy for her to lift.

2. There is enough food for everyone to have a second helping.

3. He talked too softly for me to hear.

4. She gave them too many pages to read.

5. They came early enough to get good seats.

6. It was too crowded for us to get good seats.

7. George became too discouraged to continue.

SO AND *SUCH*

H. The weather is **so bad** *that our plane has been cancelled.*

I. It's snowing **so hard** *that the runways are unsafe.*

J. There's **so much snow** *on the ground* *that all flights have been delayed.*

K. **Such a large crowd** has gathered in the airport *that people have to sit on the floor.*

---

9. *So* and *such* to intensify: *So* and *such*, like *too*, can also be used to intensify another word. However, the result after *so* and *such* is expressed in a complete clause with *that*. In addition, the result does not have a negative meaning unless it is specifically stated. Examine sentence H. It means that the weather is very bad, and as a result, the plane has been cancelled. Sentence I means that it is snowing very hard, and hence the runways are unsafe.

10. *So* with adjectives and adverbs: *So* is used before adjectives and adverbs, as in sentences H and I. The *that* clause follows.

	so	*Adjective or Adverb*	that *Clause (Result)*
The temperature is	so	cold	that the water pipes have frozen.
The wind blew	so	violently	that trees fell over.

11. *So* and *such* with nouns: *So* can also be placed before a noun (plural count or noncount) with an expression of quantity, as in sentence J.

	so	*Quantity Expression*	*Noun*	that *Clause (Result)*
I have	so	many	assignments	that I can't possibly get them done on time.
There are	so	few	people here	that we should cancel the meeting.
She gave me	so	much	information	that I don't know where to start.
He has	so	little	money	that he can't pay the rent.

Such is used before an Adjective + Noun phrase that does not have an expression of quanitity, as in sentence K.

	such	*Adjective + Noun*	that *Clause (Result)*
This is	such	an easy course	that I hardly have to study for it.
Dr. Conrad gives	such	difficult exams	that half the class fails them.
She does	such	good work	that she will probably get a promotion.

12. Omitting *that*:   The word *that* can be omitted from the result clause after *so* or *such* with no change in meaning.

> This is such an easy course (that) I hardly have to study for it.

13. Using *enough*, *too*, and *so* with verbs: *Enough*, *too much*, and *so much* can also be used to modify a verb. Note that these expressions follow the verb.

> She *studied enough* to pass the exam. (She passed it.)
> Martha *complains too much*. (We don't want to be around her.)
> George *works so much* that he doesn't have any time for his friends.

14. Using the intensifiers: The same idea can often be expressed with *enough*, *too*, or *so/such*.

> This box isn't *light enough* for me to carry by myself.
> This box is *too heavy* for me to carry by myself.
> This box is *so heavy* that I can't carry it by myself.

EXERCISE 12.1-D COMBINING SENTENCES (ORAL)

so and *such*

Combine each pair of sentences into one sentence, using *so* or *such*.

> **Example:** She worked very quickly. She finished before anyone else.
> *She worked so quickly that she finished before anyone else.*

1. The weather is very warm. You don't need a coat.

2. We are having warm weather. You don't need a coat.

3. There are only three people here. We can't hold the meeting.

4. There are a lot of people here. We have to move the meeting to a larger room.

5. He's a very easygoing person. People feel comfortable around him.

6. The actors performed very well. They received a standing ovation.

7. The sun is very bright. I can't see.

EXERCISE 12.1-E COMBINING SENTENCES (ORAL)

so and *such*

Combine each pair of sentences into one sentence, using *so* or *such*. Make the main clause affirmative.

> **Example:** The roads are very slippery. We should stay home.
> *The roads are so slippery that we should stay home.*

1. He did his work very carelessly. He has to do everything over again.

2. I didn't find a lot of information. I'll have to choose a new topic.

3. She shook the box very hard. She broke it.

4. He has a lot of enemies. He has to be careful.

5. My neighbors made a lot of noise. I called the police.

6. She is a very fine teacher. Everyone wants to take her classes.

7. It was a very easy exam. I finished it in twenty minutes.

EXERCISE 12.1-F DISCRIMINATING FORM

too, enough, so, and *such*

Fill in each blank with *too, enough, so,* or *such*. Add articles and quantifiers (*many, much, few, little*) where necessary.

1. I ate _____ large breakfast that I think I'll skip lunch.

2. Your plans are _____ ambitious to be realistic. You'll never succeed.

3. She did _____ work to pass the course. She'll get an F.

4. These examples aren't clear _____ to demonstrate your meaning.

5. The children are screaming _____ loudly I can't hear myself think.

6. There isn't _____ information here. I'll need to ask some more questions.

7. _____ people came for everyone to get a seat. You'll just have to stand.

8. _____ students registered for the course that it will have to be cancelled.

9. He doesn't sing well _____ to join the choir.

10. I don't get _____ exercise. Perhaps I should start going to the gym.

11. Martha didn't participate _____ in class for the teacher to get to know her.

EXERCISE 12.1-G RESTATING INFORMATION

too, enough, so, and *such*

Summarize each situation, using *enough, too, so,* or *such.* More than one solution may be possible.

> **Example:** The weather is cold. You shouldn't wear your light jacket.
> *The weather is too cold for you to wear your light jacket.*

1. The work is very complicated. He'll never be able to understand it.

   _____

   _____

2. Professor Keller gave me some time. I should be able to complete the project.

   _____

   _____

3. This is a very complex issue. I need time to think about it.

   _____

   _____

4. Abby has an hour for lunch. She can eat at a restaurant in forty-five minutes.

   _____

   _____

5. George has ten boxes to move. He can fit only eight boxes in his car.

_____

_____

6. Gary has $15 with him. The book that he wants to buy costs $20.

_____

_____

7. That fence is more than twelve feet high. I can't climb over it.

_____

_____

8. It was a very simple question. Martha answered it without any trouble.

_____

_____

9. Enid doesn't have a lot of confidence. She's afraid to raise her hand.

_____

_____

EXERCISE 12.1-H COMPLETING SENTENCES

too, enough, **so**, and *such*

Complete each sentence with your own ideas.

1. I am too smart _____

2. I don't have enough money _____

3. The weather is so _____

_____

4. This is such _____ class that _____

_____

5. I have enough ambition _____

6. English is too _____

EXERCISE 12.1-I CORRECTING ERRORS

too, enough, **so**, and *such*

Each sentence on page 326 has one or more mistakes. Identify the errors, and write the corrected sentence on the line provided.

1. These questions are too difficult to answer them.

   _____

2. John hasn't been working enough hard to get a good grade.

   _____

3. She gave a such good argument that we couldn't turn her down.

   _____

4. We don't get enough exercise that we stay in good shape.

   _____

5. I am too tall to reach the top shelf.

   _____

6. He complains so much for us to take him seriously.

   _____

7. This car is large enough to fit in this small parking space.

   _____

SECTION 12.2   Comparatives

The comparative uses the words *more, less,* and *fewer* and the suffix *-er* to show relative differences between two items. Comparatives can be used with adjectives, adverbs, nouns, and verbs. A comparison is usually completed with *than* and a clause or a phrase.

COMPARATIVE ADJECTIVES AND COMPARATIVE ADVERBS

Adjectives

A. The Century Hotel is a **taller** and **more luxurious** building than the Plaza Inn.

B. But the staff is **less friendly**.

Adverbs

C. Martha usually works **harder** and **more efficiently** than George.

D. But she also works **less carefully**.

---

1. The comparative: Adjectives and adverbs are compared with either *more* or *-er* to show a higher degree. They are compared with *less* to show a lower degree. Look at the comparisons in sentences A and B. *Tall* is compared by means of the *-er* suffix, and *luxurious* by means of the word *more*, both to indicate the higher degree. *Less* is used with *friendly* to show the lower degree. How are the adverbs compared in sentences C and D?

2. The higher degree: Use the following rules to decide how to compare an adjective or an adverb in the higher degree.

Add *-er* to one-syllable adjectives and adverbs and to two-syllable adjectives that end in *y*, *ple*, or *le*.

>   big — bigger   simple — simpler
>   fast — faster   humble — humbler
>   happy — happier

Note that the final consonant is doubled in *bigger* and that the final *y* changes to *i* in *happier*. The spelling rules for adding the suffix *-er* are the same as those for adding the third person singular past tense *-ed*.

Use either *more* or the suffix *-er* for two-syllable adjectives ending in *ly*, *ow*, *er*, or *some*.

>   friendly — friendlier — more friendly
>   narrow — narrower — more narrow
>   clever — cleverer — more clever
>   handsome — handsomer — more handsome

Use *more* for other adjectives and for adverbs of two or more syllables. *More* should be used with all present participle adjectives and all past participle adjectives.

>   useful — more useful
>   interesting — more interesting
>   honored — more honored
>   arrogant — more arrogant
>   easily — more easily
>   quickly — more quickly

Do not use both *more* and *-er* together.

>   *Correct*   *Incorrect*
>
>   more clever   more cleverer
>   happier   more happier

A few adjectives and adverbs have irregular comparative forms.

>   good — better
>   bad — worse
>   well — better
>   badly — worse
>   far — farther (more often used for distance in space)
>   far — further (more often used for distance in time or to mean ''additional'')

3. The lower degree: *Less* is the only form used to show the lower degree with adjectives and adverbs. It is usually not used with one-syllable adjectives and adverbs. Instead, *not as . . . as* is used (see Section 12.3).

Correct	*Incorrect*
less useful	less good (instead, *not as good as*)
less quickly	less fast (instead, *not as fast as*)

EXERCISE 12.2-A CHECKING FORM (ORAL)

comparing adjectives

Compare the items in terms of the adjective in parentheses.

> **Example:** mathematics – chemistry (difficult for me)
> *Chemistry is more difficult for me than mathematics.*

1. London – New York (large)

2. the Empire State Building – the Eiffel Tower (tall)

3. Miami – Chicago (warm)

4. a scholar – an athlete (valuable to society)

5. English – [your native language] (easy to learn)

6. the news on television – a newspaper (reliable)

7. the flu – a cold (bad)

EXERCISE 12.2-B CHECKING FORM (ORAL)

comparing adverbs

Compare the items in terms of the adverb in parentheses.

> **Example:** wood – paper (burn easily)
> *Paper burns more easily than wood.*

1. a turtle – a cheetah (move quickly)

2. a Concorde – a Boeing 747 (fly fast)

3. [student A] – [student B] (talk quietly)

4. men – women (write clearly)

5. a bus – a small car (drive easily)

6. [student A] – [student B] (walk slowly)

7. [student A] – [student B] (go to the language lab often)

NOUNS
E. Janet has **more confidence** than her sister does.
F. But she has **less charm** and **fewer friends**.

4. Comparing nouns: Plural count nouns and all noncount nouns can be compared for quantity with *more, less,* and *fewer,* as in sentences E and F. Use *more* to show a greater quantity. Use *less* before noncount nouns (*less charm*) and *fewer* before plural count nouns (*fewer friends*) to show a smaller quantity.

> Bob had *more money* than I did, so he bought *more souvenirs*.
> I had *less money* than he did, so I bought *fewer souvenirs*.

5. *More* for "additional": *More* is sometimes used with the meaning of "additional."

> I need *more time* to finish the exam. (I need additional time to finish the exam.)

VERBS
G. David **studies** for this course **more** than I do.
H. But he **participates less** in class.

6. Comparing verbs: Verbs can be compared with *more* or *less,* as in sentences G and H. *More* and *less* should be placed after a direct object, if there is one.

Correct	*Incorrect*
She drives the car more than I do.	She drives more the car than I do.

7. Intensifying comparisons: Comparisons can be intensified with *much, many,* and *a lot. Much* and *a lot* are used before comparisons of adjectives, adverbs, verbs, and noncount nouns. *Many* and *a lot* are used before comparisons of countable nouns. *A lot* is conversational and should be avoided in formal writing. Examples are on page 330.

Adjectives

The first exam was *a lot easier* than the second one.
This lab experiment is *much more interesting* than the one we did last week.
The new master plan is *much less comprehensive* than the original one.

Adverbs

You need to work *much more carefully* than you have in the past.
Let me type the letter for you. I can do it *a lot more quickly*.

Nouns

We spend *a lot more money* on entertainment than we used to.
Professor Fernandez gave me *much more information* than I can possibly use
    in my report.
He has had *many more problems* adjusting to college life than his brother.

Verbs

She used to *exercise a lot more* than she does now.
I *smoke a lot less* than my roommates do.

8. Reducing the *than* clause: A complete comparison consists of a full
clause after the word *than*. But as you have seen already, the clause is
frequently shortened.

> The first exam was a lot easier than the second exam was.
>> The first exam was a lot easier than the second.

> He works more efficiently than I work.
>> He works more efficiently than I do.
>> He works more efficiently than I.
>> He works more efficiently than me.

In the last example, either the subject pronoun (*I*) or the object pronoun
(*me*) can be used after *than* if no verb follows. The subject pronoun is
considered proper, but the object form is heard frequently and often sounds
more natural.

9. Using *those, that,* and *one* as pronouns: *Those, that,* and *the one* can be
used to refer to a noun in the second part of a comparison. Use *those* to
replace a plural count noun, *that* to replace a noncount noun, and *the one* to
replace a singular count noun.

> The students in the 8:00 class scored much higher on the exam than *those* in
>   the 10:00 class.
> The information in the appendix is more detailed than *that* in the first chapter.
> The latest news report gave more background information about the election
>   than *the one* we saw earlier in the day.

EXERCISE 12.2-C CHECKING FORM (ORAL)

● . . . .

comparing nouns and verbs

Listen to the statements about your classmates. Respond with a statement about yourself that compares the noun or the verb.

> **Example:** (Student X) has talked a lot in class today.
> *I have talked more than he has.*   OR
> *I have talked less than he has.*

1. (X) writes a lot of letters to her/his relatives.

2. (X) has a lot of confidence.

3. (X) talks on the phone a lot.

4. (X) goes to movies a lot.

5. (X) reads a lot of magazines.

6. (X) gives a lot of advice to other people.

7. (X) asks a lot of questions in class.

8. (X) volunteers answers a lot.

EXERCISE 12.2-D DISCRIMINATING FORM

● . . . .

comparative structures

Fill in each blank with the proper comparative form of the word in parentheses. A plus sign (+) means that you should show a higher degree, and a minus sign (−) means that you should express a lower degree. If there are two plus signs or two minus signs, add an appropriate intensifier (*much*, *many*, *a lot*) to the comparison.

1. The material that we have covered in the second half of this course has been _____ (*difficult*, +) than that in the beginning. In addition, there have been _____ (*assignments*, +), but with _____ (*guidance*, −) from the professor. I have never worked _____ (*hard*, +) in my life.

2. John's present plans for his trip are _____ (*complicated*, − −) than his earlier ones, so we should have _____ (*difficulty*, −) contacting him if there is an emergency. Now he intends to spend _____ (*days*, −) in the Midwest but _____ (*time*, +) on the West Coast. And he is _____ (*happy*, +) because he won't be gone as long.

3. Scientists are always looking for _____ (*good*, +) ways to explain natural phenomena. As our world becomes _____ (*mysterious*, −) to us, we have _____ (*opportunities*, + +) to control our environment and to create _____ (*comfortable*, +) lives for ourselves.

4. It has been _____ (*cold*, +), and there has been _____ (*precipitation*, −) than normal this summer. Farmers are hoping for _____ (*rain*, + +), but everyone else simply wants _____ (*warm*, +) weather with no increase in rainfall.

5. Martha seems to dislike Professor Taylor greatly; I've never heard her be _____ (*critical*, +) of a teacher. She claims that his lectures are getting _____ (*bad*, + +) as the term goes on and that _____ (*students*, −) attend his class each week. She talks about him _____ (*disparagingly*, +) every time I see her.

EXERCISE 12.2-E MODIFYING FORM (ORAL)

those, that, and the one to refer to a compared element

Substitute *those, that,* and *the one* for the second mention of the noun, as in the example.

> **Example:** Architectural styles that are found in the southern cities are more varied than the architectural styles found in the industrial Midwest.
>
> *Architectural styles that are found in the southern cities are more varied than those found in the industrial Midwest.*

1. The books on the top shelf are more difficult than the books on the other shelves.

2. The advice which Martha gave me yesterday was much better than the advice which other people have offered.

3. George's latest idea for his history project seems a lot more workable than the idea that he suggested initially.

4. A student who has a solid background in mathematics is more likely to do well in this course than a student who doesn't understand math fundamentals.

5. The drinking water in this area tastes much better than the drinking water in neighboring cities.

6. I practiced the dialogues in Chapter 1 more than the dialogues in the later chapters.

EXERCISE 12.2-F RESTATING INFORMATION

● ·

comparative forms

Write a comparative sentence using the information given in each item. Build your comparison around the word or phrase in parentheses. There may be several possibilities in some cases.

> **Example:** Arabic is spoken by 182 million people. Japanese is spoken by 123 million people. (people)
> *More people speak Arabic than Japanese.*   OR
> *Japanese is spoken by fewer people than Arabic.*

1. Russian is spoken by 287 million people. Spanish is spoken by 308 million people. (widely spoken)

    _____

2. American colleges and universities granted 88,161 bachelor's degrees in education in 1985. In the same year 233,351 degrees were conferred in the area of business and management. (popular major)

    _____

3. Colorado assesses a tax of 18 cents for each gallon of gasoline purchased. Georgia assesses a tax of only 7.5 cents per gallon. (low)

    _____

4. There are 27,000 farms in Colorado. There are 11,000 farms in Iowa. (farms)

    _____

5. The size of the average farm in Colorado is 1,259 acres. The average farm in Iowa is 312 acres. (small)

    _____

6. The average annual salary in the United States was $19,198 in 1985. It rose to $19,966 in 1986. (money)

    _____

7. The coastline of California is 840 miles long. The coastline of Florida is 770 miles long. (short)

    _____

8. Delaware was first settled in 1638. Connecticut was settled in 1634. (early)

    _____

EXERCISE 12.2-G EXPRESSING YOUR OWN IDEAS

● ·

comparative forms

Team up with a classmate from a different country to answer the questions on page 334. Then write sentences which compare the information you have gathered about your country and your classmate's.

1. What is the population of your country?

2. What is the average life span of people in your country?

3. What is the average annual income of a family in your country?

4. How many years of schooling do most people receive?

5. What percentage of the population farms?

6. _____

7. _____

8. _____

Examples: *(Country A) has a much smaller population than (country B).*
(Country A) has many fewer people than (country B).

EXERCISE 12.2-H RESPONDING TO INFORMATION

comparative patterns

Here is information about three countries: Indonesia, Japan, and Morocco. Read the data carefully. Then construct a quiz of eight comparative statements which are either true or false. Each of your statements should compare two of the countries in terms of one aspect, as in the example. Give your quiz to a classmate to take.

	Indonesia	*Japan*	*Morocco*
Population	174,900,000	122,200,000	21,750,000
Land area (sq. mi.)	735,268	143,574	172,414
Density (people/sq. mi.)	238	851	126
Capital city (population)	Jakarta	Tokyo	Rabat
	(7,636,000)	(8,386,000)	(556,000)
Percentage of land used for agriculture	9%	13%	19%
Life expectancy (female/male)	55/52	79/75	59/55

Examples: *The population of Indonesia is larger than that of Japan. (true)*
Morocco has more people per square mile than Indonesia. (false)

SECTION 12.3   More Expressions of Comparison

1. *The same as*:   *The same as* is used to express equality between two items, as in sentence A, where George's reaction is equal to my reaction. A noun or a

---

EXPRESSIONS OF COMPARISON

The Same

A. George's reaction to Martha's idea was **the same as** mine.

B. I had **the same** *objections to her idea* **as** George had.

C. And we both had **the same** *questions* about her ability to carry through her plan.

Similar

D. A refrigerator is **similar to** an air conditioner.

E. They work on **similar** *principles*.

Different

F. The new dean is very **different from** the former one.

G. They hold **different** *views* on the purpose of education.

Like and *Alike*

H. Dena is **like** her mother.

I. They even talk **alike**.

---

noun phrase can be placed between *the same* and *as*, as in sentence B. *The same* can also be used as an adjective before a noun, as in sentence C.

As is followed by a clause or a reduced clause.

> George's reaction was the same as *my reaction was*.
> George's reaction was the same as *my reaction*.
> George's reaction was the same as *mine*.

2. *Similar*:   *Similar* is followed by *to* if it is followed by the other item being compared, as in sentence D. Or it can be used as an adjective directly in front of a noun (sentence E).

3. *Different*:   *Different* is followed by *from* if it is followed by the other item being compared, as in sentence F. Or it can be used as an adjective directly in front of a noun (sentence G).

4. *Like* and *alike*:   *Like* is followed by a noun or a noun phrase, as in sentence H. *Alike* is used only if both items being compared are part of the subject of the sentence, as in sentence I. Both mean "similar to." *Like* and *alike* are often used with verbs other than BE.

> Bob and his brother *sound* very much *alike*.
> You *are acting like* a child.
> It *looks like* a nice day.

EXERCISE 12.3-A CHECKING FORM (ORAL)

expression of comparison

Compare each pair of items, using the expressions *the same, similar, different,* or *like/alike.*

> **Example:** a watch – a clock
> *A watch is similar to a clock.*   OR
> *A watch and a clock are similar.*

1. a dictionary – a thesaurus	**6.** a college – a university
2. a crocodile – an alligator	**7.** twelve – a dozen
3. eyeglasses – spectacles	**8.** H_2O – water
4. a fountain pen – a ballpoint pen	**9.** an apartment – a flat
5. jogging – running	**10.** a river – a lake

EXERCISE 12.3-B CHECKING FORM (ORAL)

the same . . . as

For each pair of sentences, use the expression *the same . . . as* with a noun to express the same relationship.

> **Example:** Towers Hall is five stories tall. So is Parks Hall.
> *Towers Hall is the same height as Parks Hall.*

1. George weighs 160 pounds. So does Paul.

2. This table is 36 inches wide. So is that table.

3. Mirror Lake is 75 meters deep. So is Hilliard Lake.

4. The bus is traveling at 55 miles per hour. So is the truck behind it.

5. Martha is five feet four inches tall. So is her sister.

6. This glass holds ten ounces. So does that glass.

AS . . . AS

J. George seems to be **as** *intelligent* **as** Martha.

K. But he doesn't learn languages **as** *quickly* **as** she does.

L. He studies **as** *many hours* every day **as** she does, but he doesn't make **as** *much progress*.

---

5. *As . . . as* for equality: The expression *as . . . as* is used to show equality between two items. It can be used with an adjective, as in sentence J, or with an adverb, as in sentence K. It can also be used with a quantity expression (*much*; *many*; *little*; *few*) and a noun, as in sentence L.

> He has *as little confidence in himself as* his sister does.
> She goes to *as few classes as* possible.

6. Negative statements: If *as . . . as* is used in a negative sentence, it shows inequality. The first item is *less* than the second.

> I'm *not as intelligent as* you are. (I am less intelligent than you are.)

The expression *as . . . as* can be stated as *so . . . as* in a negative sentence.

> I'm *not so intelligent as* you are.

7. Reducing the *as* clause: The final *as* and the clause or phrase following it can be omitted if the meaning is clear.

> Tomorrow's international festival should be similar to last year's, but it won't be as large. (It won't be as large as last year's festival was.)

EXERCISE 12.3-C CHECKING FORM (ORAL)

as . . . as

Use the expression *as . . . as* to express the relationship in each pair of sentences. You may have to make a negative statement in some cases.

> **Example:** You worked five hours last night. So did I.
> *You worked as many hours as I did.*   OR
> *You worked as long as I did.*

1. Gary's report is fifteen pages long. Julie's report is fifteen pages long.

2. My car is very fast. Your car goes the same speed.

3. Our new apartment doesn't have much space. Our old apartment was the same.

4. This table is thirty inches high. So is that one.

5. Our 10:00 class has only eight students. So does our 1:00 class.

6. Stella usually drinks three cups of coffee every morning. Stanley drinks the same amount.

7. George is very intelligent, but most people think Martha is more intelligent than he is.

EXERCISE 12.3-D COMPLETING SENTENCES

as . . . as

Complete each sentence, using *as . . . as.*

Example: Both classrooms are the same width. One is *as wide as the other.*

1. Our first exam was difficult. The second one wasn't any easier. It was _____ the first.

2. The population of the Soviet Union isn't _____ the population of China.

3. I only need an hour to finish my work today. I don't need _____ I needed yesterday.

4. The new dean seems friendly, but she isn't _____ the former dean.

5. It's important to study hard. You should always study _____ you can.

6. We had a terribly hot summer last year. I hope that this summer isn't

_____

7. He can't lend me any more money. He's already lent me _____ he can.

EXERCISE 12.3-E RESTATING SENTENCES

as . . . as and *the same . . . as*

Write a statement of comparison in the affirmative or in the negative about the information provided in each pair of sentences. Use *as . . . as* or *the same . . . as.* There may be more than one possible answer.

Example: My essay is five pages long. Your essay is five pages long.
My essay is as long as yours.   OR
My essay is the same length as yours.

1. The ten-speed bicycle costs $200. The twelve-speed bicycle also costs $200.

   _____

2. Everyone thinks that Janet is beautiful. Everyone thinks that Joan is equally beautiful.

   _____

3. The glass beaker holds one liter. The plastic one does, too.

   _____

4. John's parking fine was $20. Gary's was $15.

   _____

5. Professor Pendleton's class has made more progress than Professor Manley's class.

   _____

6. The island of Baffin is a little over 180,000 square miles in size. So is the island of Sumatra.

   _____

7. The St. Lawrence River and the Rio Grande are both approximately 1,900 miles long.

   _____

EXERCISE 12.3-F EXPRESSING YOUR OWN IDEAS

comparatives

Team up with a classmate to answer the questions. Then write sentences which compare the information you have gathered about you and your classmate. Use any of the comparative structures from Section 12.2 or Section 12.3. Try to express each comparative relationship in more than one way, as in the examples on page 340.

1. How old are you?

2. How tall are you?

3. How much do you weigh?

4. How far is your native country or your home city from here?

5. How long have you studied English?

6. How many siblings do you have?

7. How much money do you have with you right now?

8. How often do you go to a film?

9. How many hours do you study each night?

10. _____

11. _____

> **Example:** *I am older than (X).*   OR
>   *(X) is not as old as I am.*   OR
>   *(X) and I are not the same age.*

EXERCISE 12.3-G RESPONDING TO INFORMATION

comparatives

Here is information about four planets: Mercury, Mars, Earth, and Saturn. Read the data carefully. Then construct statements of comparison using the structures presented in Section 12.2 and Section 12.3 (*more/less/fewer/-er . . . than; the same . . . as; as . . . as;* etc.). Try to state each relationship in more than one way.

	Mercury	*Mars*	*Earth*	*Saturn*
Distance from sun (miles)	36 million	142 million	93 million	886 million
Diameter (miles)	3,100	4,218	7,926	75,000
Time to orbit sun (Earth days)	88	687	365	10,767
Number of moons	0	2	1	20
Time to rotate on axis [length of day] (Earth days)	59	1	1	0.4

> **Example:** *Earth is closer to the sun than Mars is.*   OR
>   *Mars isn't as close to the sun as Earth.*   OR
>   *Earth isn't as many miles from the sun as Mars.*

SECTION 12.4   Superlatives

The superlative uses the words *most, least,* and *fewest* and the suffix *-est* to show that an item is at the top or the bottom of a group of items with respect to a certain characteristic. Superlatives can be used with adjectives, adverbs, nouns, and verbs.

1. Superlatives: Adjectives and adverbs are made superlative with either *most* or *-est* to show the highest degree and with *least* to show the lowest degree. Look at the superlatives in sentences A and B on page 341. *Old* is made superlative with the *-est* suffix, and *restrictive* is made superlative with the word *most,* to show the highest degree. *Favorable* is made superlative with

---

SUPERLATIVES OF ADJECTIVES AND ADVERBS

Adjectives

A. This city's zoning laws are **the oldest** and **the most restrictive** ones *that I am familiar with.*

B. They are also **the least favorable** to builders and will continue to hurt the city's economy in the future.

Adverbs

C. Julie works **the hardest** *of all the students in this class.*

D. She studies **the most diligently** and complains **the least frequently**.

---

the word *least*, to show the lowest degree. How are the adverbs in sentences C and D made superlative?

2. The highest degree: The rules for choosing *most* or *-est* are the same as those for choosing *more* or *-er* for the comparative (see Section 12.2). The adjectives and adverbs that have irregular comparative forms also have irregular superlative forms.

> good — better — (the) best
> bad — worse — (the) worst
> well — better — (the) best
> badly — worse — (the) worst
> far — farther — (the) farthest
> far — further — (the) furthest

3. The lowest degree: *Least* is the only form for the lowest degree. One-syllable adjectives and adverbs are usually not used with *least*.

Correct	*Incorrect*
He is the shortest man here.	He is the least tall man here.
She runs the most slowly.	She runs the least fast.

4. *The* with the superlative: The superlative indicates that an item is at the top or the bottom of a group in some way. Therefore, the item is unique, and you should include the definite pronoun *the*.

5. Expressing the group: Superlatives are often completed with a phrase or a clause that defines the entire group of items that is being considered. In sentence A, the entire group is [the zoning laws] *that I am familiar with.* In sentence C, the group is *of all the students in this class.* In sentences B and D, the groups are understood, as they are in the following example.

English is the easiest language
{
in the world.
that I've ever studied.
of all the major languages.

EXERCISE 12.4-A CHECKING FORM (ORAL)

. . . .

superlatives of adjectives

Listen to each statement. Change the adjective to the superlative form, and add a phrase or a clause to define the entire group.

> **Example:** Jupiter is a very large planet.
> *It's the largest planet in the solar system.*

1. (X) is very tall.

2. The Nile is a very long river.

3. The blue whale is a very large animal.

4. (X) has a very good sense of humor.

5. (X) tells very bad jokes.

6. China is a very populous country.

7. The Soviet Union is a very large country.

EXERCISE 12.4-B CHECKING FORM (ORAL)

. . . .

superlatives of adverbs

Listen to each statement. Change the adverb to its superlative form, and add a phrase with *of* which defines the entire group.

> **Example:** The cheetah runs very fast.
> *It runs the fastest of all the animals in the world.*

1. (X) walks very quickly.

2. (X) sings very sweetly.

3. The Concorde flies very fast.

4. A kangaroo can jump very far.

5. (X) studies very hard.

6. (X) behaves very politely.

SUPERLATIVES OF NOUNS

E. Scott Labs has **the most equipment** and **the most workstations** *of all the laboratories on campus.*

F. But it has **the least storage space** and **the fewest private offices**.

6. Superlatives of nouns: Nouns can be made superlative for quantity with *most, least,* and *fewest,* as in sentences E and F. Use *most* before plural count nouns and all noncount nouns to show the highest degree. Use *least* before noncount nouns (*the least storage space*) and *fewest* before plural count nouns (*the fewest private offices*) to show the lowest degree.

SUPERLATIVES OF VERBS

G. *Of all the people I know,* Sam **cares the most** about doing a good job.

H. And he **worries the least** about what other people think of him.

7. Superlatives of verbs: Verbs can be made superlative with *most* or *least,* as in sentences G and H. *Most* and *least* should be placed after a direct object, if any.

Correct	*Incorrect*
Of all my friends, she calls her parents the most.	Of all my friends, she calls the most her parents.

EXERCISE 12.4-C CHECKING FORM (ORAL)

superlatives of nouns and verbs

Listen to each statement about your classmates. Respond with a superlative of the noun or the verb.

> **Example:** (Student X) talks a lot.
> *I agree. She talks the most of all the students in the class.*   OR
> *I disagree. She talks the least of all the students in the class.*

1. (X) reads a lot.

2. (X) drinks a lot of coffee.

3. (X) brags very little.

4. (X) volunteers a lot of answers.

5. (X) has a lot of confidence.

6. (X) exercises a lot.

7. (X) makes a lot of suggestions.

EXERCISE 12.4-D CHECKING FORM

superlative forms

Fill in each blank with the superlative form of the word in parentheses. A plus sign (+) means that you should show the highest degree, and a minus sign (−) means that you should express the lowest degree.

1. A lot of the students think that Professor Myers is _____ (*good*, +) sociology teacher in the department. They feel that her lectures are _____ (*interesting*, +) and _____ (*effectively*, +) organized. Even _____ (*motivated*, −) students enjoy her classes.

2. Topics which at first seem _____ (*promising*, −) can sometimes be developed into _____ (*originial*, +) essays. Writers who take _____ (*great*, +) chances and think creatively about an everyday topic often produce more effective pieces of writing than those who take _____ (*risks*, −).

3. George has _____ (*ambition*, +) of any person I know. Unfortunately, he also has _____ (*common sense*, −). Instead of working hard and behaving modestly, which might bring him _____ (*recognition*, +), he tends to brag about even _____ (*trivial*, +) accomplishments.

4. In last Saturday's debate, Martha argued _____ (*convincingly*, +) all of the participants and scored _____ (*points*, +) from the judges. Although she was probably _____ (*impressive*, −) person physically, her arguments were _____ (*well*, +) constructed and _____ (*passionately*, +) stated.

EXERCISE 12.4-E DISCRIMINATING MEANING

comparative forms and superlative forms

Fill in each blank space with the proper superlative form or comparative form of the word in parentheses. A plus sign (+) means that you should show the high degree, and a minus sign ($-$) means that you should express the low degree.

1. Tom's test scores are _____ (*high*, $+$) than most, but they are not _____ (*good*, $+$) in the class. He plans to work _____ (*hard*, $+$) from now on so that on the next exam he can get _____ (*high*, $+$) grade of all.

2. Denmark spends _____ (*money*, $+$) per capita on public health than Norway, but Sweden spends _____ (*large*, $+$) amount per citizen of all the countries in the world. Of the top twenty nations in terms of health care expenditures, Ireland spends _____ (*money*, $-$), approximately $260 per person each year.

3. Wheat was probably _____ (*early*, $+$) cultivated crop in the world. It has been grown by humans even _____ (*long*, $+$) than beans, which were first cultivated in about 6000 B.C. The potato is _____ (*recent*, $+$) of the major world crops. It was not cultivated until A.D. 200.

4. The eyesight of a dog is _____ (*poor*, $+$) than that of a human, but a dog's sense of smell is much _____ (*sensi-tive*, $+$). The dog has a superior sense of smell because it has many _____ (*smell-sensitive cells*, $+$) in its nose than a person does. German shepherds and bloodhounds have _____ (*accute*, $+$) senses of smell in the dog world.

EXERCISE 12.4-F RESTATING INFORMATION
• ·

comparative relationships and superlative relationships

Write a sentence expressing both a comparative and a superlative relation-ship for the facts given in each item. Build the relationship around the word or phrase in parentheses.

> **Example:** The Sears Tower is 1,454 feet tall. The World Trade Center is 1,377 feet tall. The Empire State Building is 1,250 feet tall. (tall)
> *The World Trade Center is taller than the Empire State Building, but the Sears Tower is the tallest of the three buildings.*

1. A cat can live to be 34 years old. A chimpanzee can live to be 50 years old. A horse can live to be 62 years old. (live long)

_____

_____

2. A butterfly's wings beat approximately 10 times per second. The wings of a bee beat 130 times per second. A mosquito's wings beat over 600 times per second. (beat quickly)

_____

_____

3. Lithium has an atomic number of 3. Helium has an atomic number of 2. Hydrogen has an atomic number of 1. (small)

_____

_____

4. An apple has 80 calories. An orange has 65 calories. A peach has 40 calories. (calories)

_____

_____

5. The Sahara covers 3,250,000 square miles. The Great Australian Desert covers 1,000,000 square miles. The Great Arabian Desert covers 900,000 square miles. (large)

_____

_____

EXERCISE 12.4-G EXPRESSING YOUR OWN IDEAS

superlative relationships

Then write sentences which express superlative relationships about the information you have gathered, as in the examples on page 347.

1. How old are you?

2. How tall are you?

3. How long have you been in the United States?

4. How far can you run?

5. How often do you cook dinner?

6. How many siblings do you have?

7. How many hours do you sleep each night?

8. How many languages do you speak?

9. _____

10. _____

Examples: *(Student A) is the oldest of the three/four of us.*
(Student C) speaks more languages than the rest of us.

EXERCISE 12.4-H RESPONDING TO INFORMATION

superlative relationships

Here is information about three countries in South America: Argentina, Chile, and Colombia. Write a superlative statement or a comparative statement about each information category.

	Argentina	Chile	Colombia
Population	31,500,000	12,400,000	29,900,000
Annual population growth (percent)	1.6%	1.6%	2.1%
Percentage of population that is urban	84%	83%	65%
Land area (sq. mi.)	1,027,067	292,132	455,355
Density (people/sq. mi.)	29.3	42.4	65.7
Gross national product (billions)	$76.2	$17.5	$29.0
Annual exports (millions)	$8,396	$3,825	$3,552
Annual imports (millions)	$3,814	$3,007	$4,131
Per capita income	$2,390	$1,870	$1,430
Electricity production (billions of kilowatt hours)	44.9	13.5	27.8
Wheat production (metric tons)	13,000	988	76
Corn production (metric tons)	476	165	1,696
Rice production (metric tons)	9,500	7,024	874

Example: *Of the three countries, Chile has the smallest population.*   OR
Chile has the fewest people of the three countries.   OR
Chile has fewer people than either Argentina or Colombia.

13 Conditionals

This chapter reviews the various types of conditional sentences in English. In the first section you will examine conditions which are considered possible (real conditions). The second and third sections cover conditions that are considered contrary to fact or hypothetical (unreal).

SECTION 13.1   **Real Conditional Clauses**

SECTION 13.2   **Unreal Conditional Clauses in the Present or in the Future**

SECTION 13.3   **Unreal Conditional Clauses in the Past**

SECTION 13.1   Real Conditional Clauses

FACTUAL AND HABITUAL CONDITIONALS

A.   *If* you **heat** water to 100 degrees Celsius, it **boils**.

B.   *If* water **boils**, it **vaporizes** as steam.

C.   I **become** very irritable *if* I **don't get** enough sleep.

D.   *If* I **am** irritable, my friends **avoid** me.

---

1. Conditional clauses: An adverbial clause with *if* states a condition. The main clause of the sentence states a result that will occur if the condition is met. In sentence A, the condition is heating water to 100 degress Celsius. The result is that the water boils. What are the conditions in the other sentences? What are the results if the conditions are met?

2. Real factual conditions: The real conditions in sentences A and B present information which is considered factual. The simple present tense is used in the adverb (*if*) clause and also in the main (result) clause. This type of conditional statement is common in science; see the next page.

A body *continues* in a state of rest if no forces *act* on it.
Some forms of ocean life *live* to be over 100 years old if they *do not die* early
from disease or accident.

3. Real habitual conditions: The real conditions in sentences C and D present information about habitual activities or situations. Again, the simple present tense is used in both clauses.

If a lot of students *are* late, Professor Fujita *delays* the start of class.
An essay *is* more likely to be effective if it *has* a strong central idea.

4. Using *when* in conditional clauses: Conditional statements of fact or habit can be expressed with *when* rather than *if*. The meaning is the same.

When you heat water to 100 degrees Celsius, it boils.
My friends avoid me *when* I am irritable.

5. The placement of the conditional clause: As with all adverbial clauses, clauses of condition can come before or after the main clause. A comma should follow the *if* clause when it comes first in the sentence.

If George makes the effort, he gets good grades.
George gets good grades if he makes the effort.

EXERCISE 13.1-A CHECKING FORM (ORAL)
· ·

real factual conditions

Express the information in each item as a factual conditional.

Example: water become a solid – water freezes
Water becomes a solid if it freezes.

1.   your heart become strong – you exercise regularly

2.   lead melt – you heat lead to 327 degrees Celsius

3.   water expand – water freeze

4.   air rise – air become warmer

5.   you lose time – you fly east

6.   salt dissolve – you mix salt in water

7.   you gain time – you fly west

EXERCISE 13.1-B STATING RESULTS (ORAL)
· ·

real habitual conditions

What happens when the following conditions are true? Begin your response with *usually* or *generally*.

> **Example:** You drink a lot of coffee in the evening.
> *Usually, if I drink a lot of coffee in the evening, I don't sleep well.*

1. You don't get enough sleep.

2. You don't prepare well for a test.

3. The weather turns very cold.

4. Class is cancelled.

5. You receive money from home.

6. There is no rain for several months.

7. An earthquake occurs near a populated area.

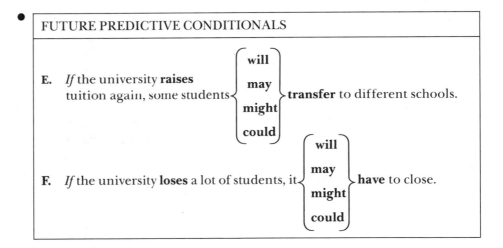

FUTURE PREDICTIVE CONDITIONALS

E. *If* the university **raises** tuition again, some students { **will** / **may** / **might** / **could** } **transfer** to different schools.

F. *If* the university **loses** a lot of students, it { **will** / **may** / **might** / **could** } **have** to close.

6. Future predictive conditions: Sentences E and F express conditions that predict *future* situations, not general facts or habits. These future conditions are called real because they are considered possible. In sentence E, the speaker believes that it is possible that the university will raise tuition again. The *if* clause expresses a time in the future, but it uses the *present* tense.

7. The result clause: The result clauses in future predictive conditional sentences use a modal with a simple verb (*will transfer*, etc.). *Will* shows that the result is certain if the condition is met. *May*, *might*, and *could* show that the result is possible if the condition is met. *Can* expresses ability, and *should* expresses advisability.

> If we begin to work on the project next week, we *might finish* it by the end of the month.
> George *will help* us if you ask him nicely.
> If you come this evening, you *should bring* a friend.
> They *can finish* the work tomorrow if they hurry.

The future with BE *going to* can also be used in the result clause.

> If I have enough money, I *'m going to go* to Europe this summer.
> We *'re going to be* late if you don't hurry up.

Remember not to use *will* in the *if* clause.

Correct	*Incorrect*
If you pass the final exam, you will pass the course.	If you will pass the final exam, you will pass the course.

EXERCISE 13.1-C ASKING QUESTIONS (ORAL)

Future predictive conditionals

Ask another student what will happen if the following possibilities become true in the future.

> **Example:** The instructor may be absent tomorrow.
> Student A: *What will happen if the instructor is absent tomorrow?*
> Student B: *If the instructor is absent tomorrow, class may (will/ might/could) be cancelled.*

1. Airline pilots might go on strike next week.

2. There may be a power outage this evening.

3. The instructor may give a long homework assignment for the weekend.

4. The university might raise tuition for English classes.

5. World population will continue to grow rapidly.

6. The government may ban the use of pesticides.

7. Mankind might not stop polluting the environment.

8. Women might not be given the same rights as men.

UNLESS AND *WHETHER OR NOT*

G. **Unless** the school gets more money from the state, it will be forced to increase student tuition substantially.

H. It may have to raise tuition, **whether or not** the state provides additional funding.

---

8. *Unless***:**   *Unless* has a meaning similar to *if . . . not*. Examine sentence G. Can you restate it using *if*?

> *Unless* the school gets more money, it will raise tuition.
> *If* the school does *not* get more money, it will raise tuition.

Not all conditional sentences with *if* can be restated with *unless*. However, it is important to understand the meaning of sentences with *unless*.

9. *Whether or not***:**   *Whether or not* has a meaning similar to *if or if . . . not*. Read sentence H. It means that the school may raise tuition in either of two cases: if the state provides more money or if the state doesn't.

> I will fail the exam if I study. I will fail the exam if I don't study. It doesn't matter.
>   I will fail the exam, *whether or not* I study.
>   I will fail the exam, *whether* I study *or not*.

Notice that the clause with *whether or not* is normally preceded by a comma, even when it occurs at the end of the sentence.

EXERCISE 13.1-D CHECKING FORM (ORAL)

using *unless*

Restate each sentence, using *if . . . not* rather than *unless*. Do not change the meaning.

> **Example:** Unless I run into some problems, I'll finish before five o'clock.
>   *If I don't run into any problems, I'll finish before five o'clock.*

1. We will arrive by noon unless the traffic is very heavy.

2. George will fail the course unless he passes the final exam.

3. Unless Martha gets some help, she may not be able to complete her report.

4. Unless we stop using fluorocarbons, the ozone layer will be destroyed.

5. Many endangered species will become extinct unless we take special precautions.

6. World hunger will continue unless population is controlled.

EXERCISE 13.1-E CHECKING FORM (ORAL)

using *whether or not*

Restate each situation using *whether or not.*

> **Example:** It doesn't matter if there is a storm. We will leave tomorrow anyway.
> *We will leave tomorrow whether or not there is a storm.*

1. It doesn't matter if John doesn't come. I'm going to go to the reception this evening anyway.

2. It doesn't matter if you aren't prepared. You will have to take the exam today anyway.

3. It doesn't matter if you have a good reason for being late. Martha will be angry at you anyway.

4. It doesn't matter if you don't approve. I'm going to go to Europe this summer anyway.

5. It doesn't matter if I don't get some financial aid. I can go to the university anyway.

6. It doesn't matter if the landlord doesn't raise the rent. I'm going to move to another apartment anyway.

EXERCISE 13.1-F DISCRIMINATING MEANING

if, unless,* and *whether or not

Fill in each blank with *if, unless,* or *whether or not.*

1. You can borrow my typewriter _____ yours is broken.

2. _____ the weather improves, we will have to postpone our camping trip.

3. The governor will be reelected _____ a strong candidate runs against him. He is unbeatable.

4. _____ the strike is settled, the factory will close down.

5. Martha will graduate _____ she passes this course. She already has enough credits for her bachelor's degree.

6. The tax rate will double next year _____ the bill to raise taxes is passed.

EXERCISE 13.1-G DISCRIMINATING FORM

● ·

verb forms in real conditional sentences

Fill in each blank with the proper form of the verb in parentheses. Some verbs must be made passive. In some main clauses, you will have to add modals.

1. Biotechnology companies are gambling that they will be able to obtain patents on the substances and life forms they create. For instance, if a company _____ (BE *able to*) create a breed of larger and faster-growing cows by manipulating the genetic code, farming _____ (*revolutionize*). But the company _____ (*receive*, negative) any money for its work unless it _____ (*hold*) a patent. And if companies _____ (*reward*, negative) for their efforts, they _____ (*stop*) investing money in bioengineering research in the future.

2. Psychologists have only recently begun to understand stress in the workplace. They have discovered that jobs _____ (BE) especially stressful if they _____ (*involve*) danger and extreme pressure. For example, if you _____ (*work*) as a policeman in a large city or as an air traffic controller, it is likely that you _____ (*suffer*) from stress at some point in your career. In addition, a job _____ (*carry*) stress if it _____ (*demand*) a lot of responsibility but _____ (*provide*) little control. Thus if you _____ (*hold*) a job such as waiter or secretary, you also _____ (*experience*) stress at some time in your life.

3. The cost of higher education in the United States has risen sharply, and many parents worry that they _____ (*have*, negative) enough money to send their children to college if costs _____ (*continue*) to increase. Now some states are offering tuition guarantees for their residents. Under these plans, if parents _____ (*invest*) a certain amount of money with the state while their child is still young, the state _____ (*guarantee*) the full cost of tuition when the child is ready to go to college. For instance, in Wyoming, if parents

_____ (*pay*) $9,617 for their third grader now, their child _____ (*receive*) four years of paid tuition at the University of Wyoming upon reaching the age of 18. The school's current tuition cost for four years is $13,760.

EXERCISE 13.1-H   EXPRESSING YOUR OWN IDEAS

future predictive conditionals

Write three predictions about your own life in the next few years. Then write three predictions about what might happen in your native country.

> **Examples:** *I will receive a degree in industrial design four years from now.*
> *My country may increase aid for education in the future.*

Predictions about Your Life

1. _____
2. _____
3. _____

Predictions about Your Country

4. _____
5. _____
6. _____

Now share your predictions with a classmate. You and your classmate should ask each other conditional questions about the possible results of each other's predictions.

> **Examples:** What will you do if your receive a degree in art education?
> What will happen if your country increases aid for education?

Now answer each other's questions, and report the information you gather from your classmate as conditional statements.

> **Examples:** *(X) will become a teacher trainer if he receives a degree in art education.*
> *If (X's country) increases aid for education, the literacy rate will increase and unemployment may decrease.*

EXERCISE 13.1-I   RESPONDING TO INFORMATION

factual conditionals

The charts on pages 357 and 358 provide guidance for certain spelling and pronunciation rules of English. Study the charts carefully. Then write conditional statements which express the information in the charts.

> **Example:** *If the verb ends with a consonant and the letter* y, *you should change the* y *to* i *and add* -ed.

Rules for Forming the Past Tense of Regular Verbs

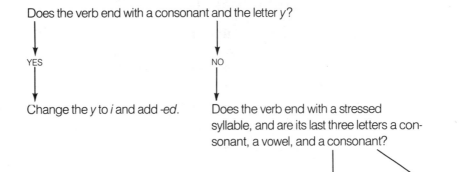

Does the verb end with a consonant and the letter *y*?

YES

NO

Change the *y* to *i* and add *-ed*.

Does the verb end with a stressed syllable, and are its last three letters a consonant, a vowel, and a consonant?

YES

NO

Double the final consonant and add *-ed*.

Add *-ed*.

Rules for Forming the Third Person Singular Simple Present Tense of Regular Verbs and the Plural of Regular Nouns

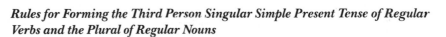

Does the word end with the letters *s, sh, ch, x,* or *z*?

YES

NO

Add *-es*.

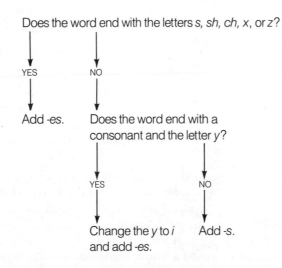

Does the word end with a consonant and the letter *y*?

YES

NO

Change the *y* to *i* and add *-es*.

Add *-s*.

Rules for the Pronunciation of the Past Tense Ending

Does the verb end with the sound /t/ or /d/?

YES   NO

Add the sound /ld/.   Does the word end with a vowel sound
or with a voiced consonant sound?

                                   YES   NO

                                Add the sound /d/.   Add the sound /t/.

SECTION 13.2   Unreal Conditional Clauses in the Present or in the Future

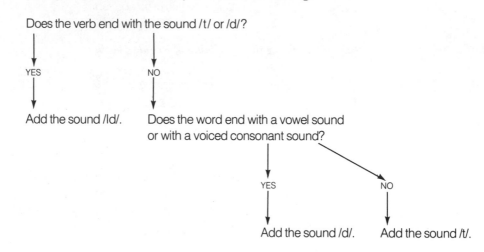

HYPOTHETICAL CONDITIONALS

A. *If* a woman **became** president, national priorities { **would** **could** **might** } **change.**

B. *If* more women **were elected** to Congress, we { **would** **might** } also **see** changes.

1. Unreal conditions: Sentences in which the condition is considered unlikely or contrary to fact are called unreal. In unreal conditional sentences, the result is also considered unlikely or contrary to fact. Unreal conditions can be in the present, in the future, or in the past.

2. Hypothetical conditionals: Unreal conditions in the future that the speaker considers unlikely to happen are called hypothetical. Examine sentence A. The speaker thinks that it is unlikely that a woman will become president; therefore, the result (a change in national priorities) is also considered unlikely. Notice that the verb in the *if* clause is in the simple past tense even though it refers to a future time. The result clause uses a modal (*would, might, could*) and the simple verb. Although the result clause refers to the future, it does not use *will, can,* or *may.*

3. Comparing real and unreal conditionals: Hypothetical conditionals are unreal because the speaker feels that the condition is unlikely to happen. Another speaker might feel that the same condition is likely to happen and use a real conditional clause instead (Section 13.1). Notice the different verb forms that are used in the *if* and result clauses.

Unreal Conditional (Present or Future)

If a woman *became* president, national priorities *would change*. (The speaker thinks that a woman will not become president.)

Real Conditional (Future Predictive)

If a woman *becomes* president, national priorities *will change*. (The speaker thinks that a woman may become president.)

4. The verb BE: When the *if* clause contains the verb BE, *were* is used for both singular and plural subjects except in informal speech and writing.

If he *were* granted a scholarship, he wouldn't have to take a part-time job.
If I *were* given the opportunity to travel extensively, I would take it.

5. *Would*:   *Would* is used in the result clause of an unreal conditional sentence (instead of the modal *will*) to indicate that the result is also unreal. Do not use *would* in the *if* clause. *Would* is commonly contracted with a pronoun subject or with *not*.

I would	=	I'd	would not	=	wouldn't
you would	=	you'd			
he would	=	he'd			
she would	=	she'd			
we would	=	we'd			
they would	=	they'd			

EXERCISE 13.2-A STATING RESULTS (ORAL)

●. . . . .

real and unreal conditionals in the present or in the future

Do you think that each situation on page 360 is likely or unlikely to happen? Respond with a real conditional statement or an unreal conditional statement, depending on your point of view.

Example: Class will be cancelled tomorrow.
If class is cancelled tomorrow, I will sleep until noon.   OR
If class were cancelled tomorrow, I would sleep until noon.

1. You will win a million dollars in the lottery.

2. You will get an A in this course.

3. You will miss class tomorrow.

4. You will go out with some friends this evening.

5. Someone will invite you to a movie tonight.

6. You will have an exam tomorrow.

7. Your landlord will raise your rent.

8. There will be a snowstorm tomorrow.

CONTRARY-TO-FACT CONDITIONALS

C. *If* people **were** more trusting, nations **wouldn't have to arm** themselves.

D. *If* nations **didn't spend** so much money on defense, they **could spend** more on social welfare programs.

---

6. Contrary-to-fact conditions: Some conditions are unreal because they are contrary to present fact rather than unlikely to occur in the future (hypothetical). Examine sentences C and D. In each of these sentences, the *if* clause states an untrue, or contrary-to-fact, situation or event in the present. In sentence C, the speaker implies that people are *not* trusting. In sentence D, the speaker implies that nations *do* spend a lot of money on defense.

A contrary-to-fact condition is usually in the present, and the result may be expressed in the present or in the future. Contrary-to-fact conditionals are identical to hypothetical conditionals in form. The only difference is that the condition is impossible rather than unlikely.

> If Thomas Edison *were* alive today, he *would be* amazed by our advanced technology. (The condition is contrary to fact; Edison is not alive today.)
> If you *went* to the science exhibit, you *would be* amazed by the technological demonstrations. (The condition is hypothetical; it is unlikely, though still possible, that you will go to the exhibit.)

7. Unstated conditions: A conditional result can be expressed without stating the condition in the same sentence. The condition can be implied, or it can be stated at the beginning of a paragraph, with several results following.

What would you do if you taught this class?

> I'*d try* to be more understanding when the students have problems. And I *wouldn't give* homework on weekends or over holidays.

If you were an astronaut returning from a prolonged space flight, you would find that you were taller at the end of your journey than at the beginning. You *would be* taller because the cartilage disks in your spine would expand during your period of weightlessness. Your height *would increase* up to two inches, but it *would* soon *return* to normal after a few days back in the earth's gravity.

EXERCISE 13.2-B STATING RESULTS (ORAL)

contrary-to-fact conditionals

Factual situations are stated. What would be the result if each situation were contrary to fact?

> **Examples:** Napoleon is not alive today.
> *If Napoleon were alive today, he might control Europe.*
>
> College tuition is expensive.
> *If college tuition were not expensive, more lower-income people could obtain a college education.*

1. Nations fight among themselves.

2. People still smoke cigarettes.

3. Industry pollutes the environment.

4. People speak many languages.

5. You are not a native speaker of English.

6. Child care is expensive.

7. The United States and the Soviet Union have huge nuclear arsenals.

8. Learning English isn't easy.

EXERCISE 13.2-C FOCUSING ON VERB FORMS

unreal conditions in the present and in the future

The conditional statements on page 362 are all unreal in the present or in the future. Fill in each blank with the correct form of the verb in paren-theses. You will have to add a modal to the result clause. You will also have to make some verbs passive.

1. The Historical Museum does not have enough money to expand its exhibits. If sufficient funds _____ (BE) available, the museum _____ (increase) the space devoted to early Indian history. The collection of Indian artifacts _____ (increase), and a display of modern Indian art _____ (add). And if the public _____ (express) interest, the museum _____ (host) several artists in residence.

2. Over 60 million animals are used in scientific research in the United States alone every year. If scientists _____ (BE able to, negative) use these mice, rats, rabbits, dogs, and other animals, medical research _____ (come) to a halt. It _____ (BE) impossible to test the effectiveness and the safety of new drugs, and the cause of diseases _____ (BE) more difficult to determine. But some people feel that the use of animals for scientific research is wrong. If these people _____ (have) their way, science _____ (have to) do without laboratory animals.

3. It is unlikely that people will ever be willing to conform to the speed limits on our nation's highways. However, if all people _____ (obey) the 55-mph laws, thousands of lives _____ (save) each year. In addition, because cars are more efficient at lower speeds, drivers _____ (use) much less gasoline. And if people _____ (mix, negative) alcohol and driving, the savings in human life _____ (BE) even greater.

SUMMARY OF CONDITIONAL CLAUSES IN SECTIONS 13.1 AND 13.2

	Verb in if Clause	Verb in Result Clause
Real Conditions		
1. Present fact or habit	Simple Present	Simple Present
2. Future predictive	Simple Present	Modal + Simple Verb (*will, may, can, might, could, should*)
Unreal Conditions		
3. Present or future (hypothetical or contrary to fact)	Simple Past	Modal + Simple Verb (*would, might, could*)

EXERCISE 13.2-D FOCUSING ON THE VERB

real conditionals and unreal conditionals in the present and in the future

These conditional sentences are both real and unreal. Read them carefully, and fill in each blank with the correct form of the verb in parentheses. You will have to make some verbs passive.

1. The weather may not be clear tomorrow. If it _____ (*rain*), we _____ (*postpone*) our field trip.

2. Bob isn't free this evening. But if he _____ (BE), I'm sure that he _____ (*enjoy*) meeting you.

3. My typewriter is broken. If it _____ (*work*), I _____ (BE) happy to let you use it.

4. Several new drugs for heart disease seem very promising. If these drugs _____ (*show*) to be effective, thousands of people _____ (*give*) a chance to lead longer lives.

5. Air travel is relatively safe. If it _____ (BE, negative), people _____ (*fly*, negative).

EXERCISE 13.2-E RESTATING RELATIONSHIPS

unreal conditions in the present and in the future

Read each situation carefully. What would be the result if the condition were not true?

> **Example:** Martha doesn't have class tomorrow, so she can join us.
> *If Martha had class tomorrow, she couldn't join us.*

1. The extremely rich soil in this area allows farmers to grow crops intensively.

    _____

    _____

2. John is a very good friend, so I don't resent his criticism of my work.

    _____

    _____

3. I don't think the exam will be difficult, so I won't study very hard.

    _____

    _____

4. None of the classrooms is air-conditioned, so summer classes are unbearable.

    _____

    _____

5. Dolphins are able to make distinctive underwater sounds, which enables them to send sophicated messages to one another.

    _____

    _____

6. Both the sun and the moon exert a gravitational pull on the earth, which causes the oceans to move in tides.

    _____

    _____

EXERCISE 13.2-F EXPRESSING YOUR OWN IDEAS

unreal conditions in the present and in the future

Pair up with a classmate and discuss the city or town you are now living in. Consider different aspects of your city, such as transportation, education, entertainment, shopping, housing, services, and government.

How could your city be improved? What would be the results of the improvements you suggest? With your classmate, decide on six changes that you think would improve your city. Write your suggestions in the form of unreal conditional sentences.

> **Examples:** *If (name of city) expanded its highway system, traffic could move more quickly.*
> *If the stores and restaurants in (name of city) stayed open later at night, more people would go downtown in the evenings.*

EXERCISE 13.2-G RESPONDING TO INFORMATION

unreal conditionals in the present and in the future

In Section 9.3 you read about the earth's ozone layer and how chlorofluoro-carbons threaten its existence. Here we trace the sequence of events that would probably occur if the ozone layer were destroyed. Write a paragraph reporting this information, using the unreal conditional. Remember that you do not have to state a condition in every sentence.

The ozone layer disappears.

Ultraviolet radiation is no longer blocked by the ozone layer.

Ultraviolet radiation reaches the surface of the earth.

The number of cases of skin cancer increases:
    500,000 new cases each year in the United States alone
    20,000 deaths each year in the United States

The incidence of cataracts increases.

Most microscopic life forms die.
    Higher organisms that depend on microscopic life forms perish.
    Larger sea and land animals die.
    The food chain is destroyed.

SECTION 13.3 Unreal Conditional Clauses in the Past

UNREAL CONDITIONALS IN THE PAST

A. *If* I **had gotten** better grades last year, I { **would** **might** **could** } **have received** a scholarship from the university.

B. *If* the university **had given** me a scholarship, I **wouldn't have had** to take a part-time job in the evenings.

1. Past unreal conditionals: Past unreal conditionals are contrary to fact. That is, the *if* clause states an untrue situation or event in the past. The results of past unreal conditions are also contrary to fact. Examine sentence A on page 365. *If I had gotten better grades last year* means that I did not get grades that were good enough, and thus I did not receive a scholarship. In sentence B, *If the university had given me a scholarship* means that the university did not give me one, and so I had to take a part-time job.

> If you had come earlier, you could have met Professor Franz. (You didn't come earlier, and therefore you didn't have the opportunity to meet him.)
> George would have graduated last year if he hadn't failed the required science course. (He did fail the science course, and so he didn't graduate last year.)

2. Verb forms in past unreal conditionals: Notice the verb forms used in sentences A and B. The past perfect tense (*had* + Past Participle) is used in the *if* clause. A modal perfect (*would/might/could* + *have* + Past Participle) is used in the result clause.

3. Questions: The main clause (result clause) of a conditional sentence can be made into a question.

> If you hadn't been admitted to this school, what *would* you *have done*?
> What *would have happened* if CFCs had been banned ten years ago?

EXERCISE 13.3-A STATING RESULTS (ORAL)

unreal conditionals in the past

Consider the statements to be factual events or situations in the past. What would have been the result in the past if each event or situation were contrary to fact?

> **Example:** You had class yesterday.
> *If I hadn't had class yesterday, I would have slept until noon.*

1. There wasn't anything interesting on television last night.

2. You were admitted to this school.
    If I hadn't admitted to this school, I would have been working.

3. You came to the United States to study.
    If I hadn't come to the U.S. to study, I wouldn't learn English.

4. You had to study last weekend.
    If I hadn't had to study last weekend, I would have gone to Theater.

5. You had enough money to pay your rent last month.

6. The Red Cross was founded in 1864.

7. The United States won its independence from Great Britain over 200 years ago.

8. The Organization of Petroleum Exporting Countries (OPEC) was formed in 1960.

SUMMARY OF CONDITIONAL CLAUSES IN CHAPTER 13		
	Verb in if Clause	Verb in Result Clause
Real Conditions		
1. Present fact or habit	Simple Present	Simple Present
2. Future predictive	Simple Present	Modal + Simple Verb (will, may, can, might, could, should)
Unreal Conditions		
3. Present or future (hypothetical or contrary to fact)	Simple Past	Modal + Simple Verb (would, might, could)
4. Past (contrary to fact)	Past Perfect	Modal + have + Past Participle (would, could, might)

Examples

1. If water *is* boiled, it *turns* to steam.
   If it *rains*, I usually *get* a ride with George.

2. If I *score* over 500 on the TOEFL next week, I *will begin* academic study next term.
   If he *has* enough money, he *will pay* me back at the end of the month.

3. If I *scored* over 500 on the TOEFL next week, I *would begin* academic study next term.
   If he *had* enough money, he *would pay* me back at the end of the month.

4. If I *had scored* over 500 on the TOEFL last year, I *would have begun* academic study last term.
   If he *had had* enough money, he *would have paid* me back last month.

EXERCISE 13.3-B FOCUSING ON THE VERB PHRASE

past unreal conditionals

These conditional statements are all unreal in the past. Fill in each blank with the correct form of the verb in parentheses.

1. If the university _____had not received_____ (receive, negative) very large donations from corporations and alumni over the past decade, the new

library and the student center ___would not have been built___ (*build*, negative). The minority student scholarship program ___wouldn't have been created___ (*create*, negative), and hundreds of minority students ___wouldn't have been able___ (BE *able to*, negative) enroll.

2. The city's task force on housing has been highly successful since it was established ten years ago. If the task force ___had not been created___ (*create*, negative), there ___would not have been___ (BE, negative) an organized effort to rehabilitate inner-city buildings that were decaying. The unacceptable housing alternatives for the poor ___would have remained___ (*remain*) unchanged, and middle-class families ___would have moved___ (*move*) to the suburbs in much greater numbers.

3. The interstate highway network was initiated in the 1950s in order to link cities by means of the best possible modern roads. If billions of dollars ___had not been spent___ (*spend*, negative) to develop the interstate highways, it ___would have been___ (BE) impossible for the United States to develop its efficient system for the distribution of agricultural products and manufactured products. In addition, without these highways, we ___would have had___ (*have to*) rely much more heavily on railways and air transportation for business travel and personal travel.

EXERCISE 13.3-C DISCRIMINATING FORM

real conditionals and unreal conditionals

These conditional sentences are both real and unreal, in the present, the future, and the past. Read them carefully, and fill in each blank with the correct form of the verb in parentheses. In some cases, you will have to make the verb passive.

1. If polio vaccines had not been developed in the 1950s, many thousands more cases of the disease ___would have occurred___ (*occur*).

2. If a safe vaccine against AIDS were developed today, the current epidemic ___would end___ (*end*).

3. If the economy ___continues___ (*continue*) to improve, the unemployment rate will begin to drop.

4. This year's harvest ___will be___ (BE) disappointing if we don't get rain within the next few weeks.

5. Martha wouldn't have bought you the gloves if she ___had known___ (*know*) they were the wrong size.

6. Most journalists will not report an event if they _____*are not*_____ (BE, negative) sure that their sources are accurate.

7. If geothermal energy _____*were use*_____ (*use*) more widely, pollution from the buring of fossil fuels would decrease.

8. Many lives _____*would have been saved*_____ (*save*) during medical procedures in the past if the importance of hygiene had been known.

9. World tensions would be even higher than they are today if organizations such as the United Nations _____*didn't exist*_____ (*exist*, negative).

10. The modern theory of continental drift would not have been proved if scientists _____*had not study*_____ (*study*, negative) the magnetism of rocks in the 1950s and 1960s.

EXERCISE 13.3-D RESPONDING TO SITUATIONS

past unreal conditionals

Respond to each situation or event with advice in the form of a past unreal conditional.

> **Example:** George failed the grammar test last week.
> *If he had studied harder, he might/would not have failed the test.*

1. John's car ran out of gas on the highway.

_____*If he had filled out the tank, he would not have ran out gas on the highway.*_____

2. Henry did the wrong exercises for homework last night.

_____

3. Martha paid more than necessary for her new car.

_____*If she had waited for any good special, she wouldn't paid more for her new car.*_____

4. Jeannette got terribly sunburned at the beach yesterday.

_____*If Jeannette had not gone to the beach, she gotten have a terribly sunburned*_____

5. Gary got lost driving to Minneapolis last week.

_____

6. Julie slept late and missed her class this morning.

_____

_____

7. Dena got a speeding ticket on Route 315 yesterday.
   If she had not been speeding, she would not have gotten the ticket.

EXERCISE 13.3-E EXPRESSING YOUR OWN IDEAS

past unreal conditionals

Pair up with a classmate, and list several famous historical figures from each of your countries. Discuss why these people are still remembered.

If you had been these people and had been in their situations, what might you have done differently? What would you have done the same? Report your ideas in past unreal conditional statements.

Examples: If I had been Lyndon Johnson, I wouldn't have expanded American involvement in Vietnam.
If I had been Franklin Roosevelt, I would have introduced Social Security as he did.

EXERCISE 13.3-F RESPONDING TO INFORMATION

past unreal conditionals

On April 14, 1912, the new ocean liner *Titanic* hit an iceberg off the southeastern tip of Greenland. The ship sank in less than three hours, and over 1,500 lives were lost. Many people say that the tragedy should never have happened and that a series of mistakes led to the disaster. Read the following information. What would have happened if the conditions had been the opposite?

The *Titanic* was warned about icebergs in the area less than an hour before it hit one.

The *Titanic* radio operator was overburdened with messages from the passengers.

He didn't pay attention to a warning about icebergs from a nearby ship, the *Californian*.

He never learned the location of the danger.

1. *If the* Titanic *radio operator hadn't been overburdened with messages from the passengers, he might have paid attention to the warning from the* Californian.

2. _____

   _____

   The ship *Californian* was less than ten miles away from the *Titanic* when it hit the iceberg.

   > The *Californian* radio operator left his post at 11:30 P.M. and turned the radio off.
   >
   > The *Californian* did not hear the *Titanic*'s signals of distress.
   >
   > ↓ The *Californian* did not come to the *Titanic*'s rescue.

3. _____

   _____

4. _____

   _____

   The captain of the *Titanic* sent a series of rocket flares into the air as a call for help. Officers aboard the *Californian* saw the flares.

   > The officers on the *Californian* thought that the *Titanic* was unsinkable.
   >
   > They couldn't believe that the flares were a distress signal.
   >
   > ↓ They weren't aware that the *Titanic* was in trouble.

5. _____

   _____

6. _____

   _____

14   Noun Clauses

With noun clauses, you can report information that you have heard or read. This chapter examines the different types of noun clauses—those that begin with *that* and those that are derived from questions. It also examines *that* clauses after the verb *wish*.

SECTION 14.1   *That* Clauses

SECTION 14.2   *That* Clauses after *Wish*

SECTION 14.3   Embedded Question Clauses

SECTION 14.1   *That* Clauses

NOUN CLAUSES WITH *THAT*
A.   The workers at the McGee Company heard **some rumors.**
B.   They heard **that their factory might close down.**
C.   Now they fear **that they will all lose their jobs**.

1. Noun clauses: A noun clause is a dependent clause that functions as a noun in a sentence. Read sentence A. The object of the sentence is a noun, *rumors.* In sentence B, a noun clause, *that the factory might close,* functions as the object. The noun clause has a subject and a verb. It begins with the word *that.* Analyze sentence C. What functions as the object of the sentence?

Subject	Verb	Object
The workers	heard	some rumors.
They	heard	that the factory might close down.
They	fear	that they will all lose their jobs.

2. *That* clauses: We will use the term *that* clause for a noun clause that begins with *that.* Actually, the word *that* is usually optional when a noun clause functions as the object of a sentence.

I didn't realize that you were speaking to me.
I didn't realize you were speaking to me.

However, because the word *that* is sometimes required, it is better to include it at all times.

3. Verbs which are followed by *that* clauses: *That* clauses are frequently used after the following verbs.

assume	fear	notice
believe	figure out	observe
claim	find out	prove
conclude	forget	read
decide	guess	realize
deny	hear	remember
discover	imagine	say
doubt	know	think
expect	learn	understand

Here are some examples of verbs followed by *that* clauses:

We *expect* that the roads will be crowded tomorrow.
George *understood* that he had made a mistake.

4. Verbs which must have an object before a *that* clause: *That* clauses are also common after another group of verbs. However, with these verbs it is necessary to state another object before the *that* clause.

assure	notify	tell
convince	persuade	warn
inform	remind	

Notice the objects between these verbs and *that* clauses:

Martha *assures us* that she will finish by midnight.
My instructor *persuaded me* that I should revise my paper.

Notice that *tell* requires an object before the *that* clause but *say* does not.

Environmentalists *tell us* that we must find cleaner sources of energy.
Environmentalists *say* that we must find cleaner sources of energy.

5. Sequence of tenses: When the main verb of the sentence is in the present, the verb in the *that* clause can be in the future, the present, or the past.

I *think* that tomorrow's exam *will be* (*is going to be*) easy.
I *think* that George *is taking* an exam now.
I *think* that Professor Askew's exams *are* always easy.
I *think* that George *has* already *taken* his exam.
I *think* that last week's exam *was* easy.

If the main verb of the sentence is in the past, use *was/were going to* or *would* in the *that* clause if it expresses a later activity. Use the past tense if the activity in the *that* clause is at the same time. And use the past perfect tense if the activity in the *that* clause is at an earlier time.

> I *thought* that the exam the next day *would be* (*was going to be*) easy.
> I *thought* that George *was taking* an exam then.
> I *thought* that Professor Naumoff's exams *were* easy last term.
> I *thought* that George *had* already *taken* his exam.
> I *thought* that the exam the week before *had been* easy.

However, if the activity in the *that* clause is still clearly in the future, after the time of speaking or writing, the future with *will* or BE *going to* can be used even though the main verb is in the past tense.

> Professor Naumoff *told* us that the exam tomorrow *is going to be* (*will be*) easy.
> Martha *said* that she *will call* (*is going to call*) us next week.

Likewise, if the information in the *that* clause indicates habitual activity or a state of mind that will probably continue in the future or if it indicates a general truth or a fact, the simple present tense can be used even though the main verb is in the past tense.

> Professor Naumoff *told* us that she *jogs* every day.
> Martha *said* that falling barometric pressure *means* bad weather ahead.
> Lisa *said* that she *is* extremely happy in her new job.

EXERCISE 14.1-A CHECKING FORM (ORAL)

● ·

that clauses

Report the information in each statement in the form of a *that* clause.

> **Example:** The workers will go on strike. I assume this.
> *I assume that the workers will go on strike.*

1. The TOEFL will be given at the end of the month. I believe this.

2. We had been treated unfairly. John claimed this.

3. They wouldn't take the exam. The students decided this.

4. Martha had been cheated. She discovered this.

5. I will receive a reply from Dena soon. I imagine this.

6. Tuition is going to increase next term. We learned this.

7. You spoke to my roommate last week. I understand this.

8. English is a difficult language to learn. I am beginning to realize this.

9. The cost of living rose again last month. I read this.

10. My flight was cancelled. I found this out.

EXERCISE 14.1-B CHECKING FORM (ORAL)

tense usage in *that* clauses

Change the main verb of each sentence from the present tense to the past tense. Change the verb tense in the *that* clause as necessary.

> **Example:** Henry claims that the package was delivered already.
> *Henry claimed that the package had been delivered already.*

1. I think that my friends will arrive soon.

2. I think that my friends just arrived.

3. I realize that you are going to ask for some help.

4. I guess that my answer is wrong.

5. I remember that you asked me that question already.

6. I assure you that the office will be ready.

7. I believe that you are telling the truth.

8. I believe that you told me the truth.

9. I believe that you will tell me the truth.

EXERCISE 14.1-C ANSWERING QUESTIONS (ORAL)

***that* clauses**

Answer each question, using a *that* clause in your response.

> **Example:** What do you think about this class?
> *I think that it is very difficult.*

1. What do you predict about the weather tomorrow?

2. What do you think about this English class?

3. What have you learned about Americans?

4. What have you decided about your career?

5. What do you imagine about wars in the future?

6. What do you predict about computers in the future?

THAT CLAUSES AFTER ADJECTIVES AND *BE*

D. The workers are **afraid** *that the rumors are true.*

E. They are **worried** *that they will have trouble finding other jobs.*

F. The problem **is** *that the local economy is depressed.*

---

6. Adjectives followed by *that* clauses: *That* clauses frequently follow certain adjectives, as in sentences D and E. Adjectives that are commonly followed by *that* clauses include the following.

afraid	glad	proud
annoyed	happy	sorry
aware	irritated	sure
certain	pleased	surprised
disappointed	positive	worried

Here are some examples:

The workers are *certain* that the factory will close.
They are *aware* that other jobs are scarce.

7. *That* clauses after BE: A *that* clause can also follow the verb BE, as in sentence F.

The fact *is* that many area companies are closing.
The reason *is* that production costs are too high.

EXERCISE 14.1-D CHEKCING FORM (ORAL)

● . . . .

that clauses after adjectives

Report the information in each statement in the form of a *that* clause.

Example: Tuition will be raised next year. I am afraid of this.
I am afraid that tuition will be raised next year.

1. This is the last chapter in the text. I am happy about this.

2. Nobody would help me. I was irritated about this.

3. I did well on my last exam. I was proud of this.

4. Class has been cancelled for tomorrow. I am positive about this.

5. I have to take more English. I am disappointed about this.

6. You can't come with us. I am sorry about this.

7. You didn't call me. I was surprised.

8. Some of the students are unhappy. I am aware of this.

EXERCISE 14.1-E ANSWERING QUESTIONS (ORAL)

that clauses after BE

Answer each question, using a *that* clause in your response.

> **Example:** What is one advantage of living close to campus?
> *One advantage of living close to campus is that you don't need a car.*

1. What is one advantage of living in a large city?

2. What is one disadvantage of living in a large city?

3. What is one advantage of living in a small town?

4. What is one disadvantage of living in a small town?

5. What is one advantage of being an only child?

6. What is one disadvantage of being an only child?

7. What is one reason for taking public transportation?

8. What is one problem with taking public transportation?

THAT CLAUSES AS SUBJECTS AND DELAYED CLAUSES WITH *IT*

G. *That the workers may lose their jobs* seems unfair.

H. **It** seems unfair *that they may lose their jobs*.

I. *That some jobs will be saved* is possible.

J. **It** is possible *that some jobs will be saved*.

---

8. *That* clauses as subjects: A *that* clause can function as the subject of a sentence as well as the object. In sentence G, the clause *that the workers may lose their jobs* serves as the subject. *That* clauses which act as subjects must include the word *that*. Examine sentence I. What is the subject of this sentence? Is the word *that* necessary?

When a *that* clause serves as the subject of a sentence, it is singular in number. The main verb of the sentence will be in the third person singular, as in sentences G and I.

9. Delayed clauses with *it*: In many cases, a *that* clause subject is moved to the end of the sentence, and the world *it* is substituted in the subject position, as in sentences H and J. This is especially common after the following expressions with the verb BE.

a fact	a shame	a pity
the truth	the case	true
strange	irritating	apparent
unfair	surprising	(im)probable
(un)fortunate	too bad	(un)likely
interesting	possible	

Notice how the subject of the *that* clause is moved to the end of this example:

> That the university is in financial trouble is *a fact.*
> *It* is *a fact* that the university is in financial trouble.

EXERCISE 14.1-F CHECKING FORM (ORAL)

delaying a *that* clause subject

Substitute *it* for the subject of each sentence, and move the *that* clause to the end.

> **Example:** That languages are difficult to learn is a fact.
> *It is a fact that languages are difficult to learn.*

1. That John stole the money cannot be true.

2. That George asked for help is surprising.

3. That you had to cancel your trip is unfortunate.

4. That Laura is ill again is a pity.

5. That it will rain tonight is possible.

6. That Tim lost his job is unfair.

7. That Mike lied is the truth.

8. That our contract will be renewed is unlikely.

EXERCISE 14.1-G DISCRIMINATING TENSES

tense usage in *that* clauses

Fill in each blank with the correct tense of the verb given in parentheses.

1. Martha assured me that she _____
   (*make*) the plane reservations earlier that morning.

2. I now realize that I _____ (BE *able to*, negative) graduate at the end of this year.

3. We were disappointed when you said that you _____ (*join*, negative) us later in the day.

4. It's obvious that you _____ (*study*, negative) very hard for the exam last week.

5. The electric company notified us that it _____ (*receive*, negative) our payment for the previous month.

6. Some experts claim that the ozone layer _____ (*continue*) to thin in the future.

7. When they spoke to the press last week, the president's advisers claimed that he _____ (*veto*) the tax bill the next day.

8. That there _____ (BE) a discussion of the plan earlier in the week was denied by everyone involved.

EXERCISE 14.1-H COMPLETING SENTENCES

· ·

that **clauses**

Complete each sentence with a *that* clause. Use your own ideas.

1. It's a shame that _____

_____

2. Most of the students in this class think that _____

_____

3. Yesterday I heard that _____

_____

4. When I was a child, my parents told me that _____

_____

5. No one has ever been able to convince me that _____

_____

6. I am proud that _____

_____

7. Scientists predict that _____

_____

EXERCISE 14.1-I EXPRESSING YOUR OWN THOUGHTS

that **clauses**

Work with a classmate to prepare eight interview questions to ask each other. You may want to use some of the suggested topics that follow, or you may decide to use other topics of your own choosing.

> An early childhood event that you remember well
> A future scientific discovery that you predict
> A serious problem that may occur in your country in the future
> The most significant political event in your country in the past twenty-five years
> An important American social custom you have learned
> A personal accomplishment in which you take pride
> A possible future event that worries you
> An aspect of American society that surprises you

Take notes as you and your classmate interview each other. Then write a complete sentence expressing the information you have gathered from each question. Begin your sentences with expressions such as *(name of classmate) remembers/predicts/is proud that* . . .

> **Example:** *Nancy remembers that her family lived in Boston when she was very young.*

EXERCISE 14.1-J RESPONDING TO INFORMATION

that **clauses**

The following chart provides information about the number of Americans who are considered "older," that is, who are at least 65 years of age. Examine the chart carefully, and be sure that you understand the information. Notice that the predicted average life expectancy is not given for the years 2000 and 2030. What do you think it will be?

Year	Percentage of People 65 or Older	Number of People 65 or Older	Average Life Expectancy
1900	4.1%	3,100,000	50.0
1940	6.8%	9,000,000	62.9
1980	12.0%	25,700,000	73.7
2000	13.0%	34,900,000	?
2030	21.2%	64,600,000	?

Answer the following questions about the information provided in the chart. Use a *that* clause in each answer. Use the underlined word in the main clause of your answer.

1. What does the chart <u>indicate</u> about the percentage of older Americans during the past century?

   _____

   _____

2. What does the chart <u>predict</u> about the percentage of older Americans in the future?

   _____

   _____

3. What does the chart <u>suggest</u> about the number of older Americans?

   _____

   _____

4. What does the chart <u>tell</u> you about the average life expectancy of Americans?

   _____

   _____

5. What do you <u>think</u> will happen to the average life expectancy of Americans in the future?

   _____

   _____

6. What are some of the <u>possible</u> changes in American society that will occur as the percentage of older Americans increases in the future?

   _____

   _____

SECTION 14.2 *That* Clauses after *Wish*

· ·

●
HOPE AND *WISH*
A. Martha **hopes** *that she can earn enough money to pay tuition next term.*
B. She **wishes** *that school costs were not so high.*

1. *Hope*:   The verb *hope* indicates that an event or a situation is possible, at least in the mind of the speaker. A *that* clause is frequently used as the object of the verb *hope*, as in sentence A. According to this sentence, Martha believes that it is possible for her to earn enough money to pay tuition.

2. *Wish*:   When the verb *wish* is followed by a *that* clause, it indicates that the event or the situation is considered unreal (either hypothetical or contrary to fact). Examine sentence B. Martha knows that school costs are high; she wishes for the opposite. Notice that the past tense is used in the *that* clause, although the meaning is in the present.

3. Choosing *hope* or *wish*:   The choice of *hope* or *wish* may depend on the speaker's outlook.

> George *hopes* that he can begin a graduate program next year. (He thinks that it is possible.)
> George *wishes* that he could begin a graduate program next year. (He thinks that it is unlikely to happen.)

WISHES FOR THE FUTURE

C.   I *wish* that the university **weren't going to raise** tuition. (It is going to raise tuition.)

D.   I *wish* that it **wouldn't increase** class sizes. (It will increase class sizes.)

E.   I *wish* that the school **could afford** to offer all classes every term. (It can't afford to offer them each term.)

---

4. A wish for the future: To express a wish for the future, use *were going to*, *would*, or *could* in the *that* clause, as in sentences C through E.

5. The form of BE: In writing, use *were* after *I*, *he*, *she*, and *it*. In informal conversation, *was* is sometimes used.

> I wish that I *were* (or *was*) going to go with with you.
> I wish that John *weren't* (or *wasn't*) going to leave tomorrow.

6. Omitting the verb: If the verb is understood, only the auxiliary needs to be used.

> I can't go with you this evening, but I wish that I *could*.
> Sara won't come tomorrow. I wish that she *would*.
> Joe is going to quit school. I wish that he *weren't going to*.

EXERCISE 14.2-A CHECKING FORM (ORAL)

wishes for the future

On page 384, wish for the opposite of each situation in the future.

> **Example:** Our instructor won't accept late papers.
> *I wish that she would accept late papers.*

1. Our trip is going to be delayed.

2. We are going to leave town for the holidays.

3. We can't get tickets for the theater tomorrow.

4. The governor will resign his office next month.

5. The new library isn't going to open next term.

6. Student aid is going to be reduced next year.

7. I can't get a room in the dormitory for the fall term.

8. Our final exam is going to be at eight in the morning.

WISHES FOR THE PRESENT

F. Mary *wishes* that she **were** a talented student. (She's not very talented.)

G. She *wishes* that she **didn't have** trouble organizing her time. (She has trouble organizing her time.)

H. She *wishes* that she **had** good study skills. (She doesn't have good study skills.)

I. She *wishes* that she **could stop** worrying about her grades. (She can't stop worrying.)

---

7. A wish for the present: To express a wish for the present, use the past tense, the past continuous tense, or *could* in the *that* clause, as in sentences F through I. Remember that wishes for the present are contrary to fact.

8. Omitting the verb: If the verb is understood, only the auxiliary needs to be used.

> John doesn't call us very often. I wish that he *did*.
> Helen lacks motivation. I wish that she *didn't*.

EXERCISE 14.2-B CHECKING FORM (ORAL)

wishes for the present

Wish for the opposite of each situation in the present.

> **Example:** The airport isn't convenient from where I live.
> *I wish that it were convenient.*

1. This old building is drafty in the winter.

2. The library isn't open on Saturday mornings.

3. I can't find a book I need for my report.

4. I have difficulty learning new vocabulary.

5. George gets nervous when he speaks in front of a group of people.

6. My typewriter doesn't work properly.

7. Martha works in a dangerous neighborhood.

8. My friend isn't coming with us.

WISHES FOR THE PAST

J. I *wish* that our final exam **hadn't been** comprehensive. (It was comprehensive.)

K. I *wish* that the essay questions **hadn't asked** for so many details. (They asked for a lot of details.)

L. I *wish* that we **had had** enough time to do a good job. (We didn't have enough time to do a good job.)

---

9. A wish for the past: To express a wish for the past, use the past perfect tense in the *that* clause, as in sentences J through L. Remember that past wishes are always contrary to fact.

10. Omitting the verb: If the verb is understood, only the auxiliary needs to be used.

> Dena didn't request a refund, and now she wishes that she *had*.
> Tim ate three helpings at dinner, and now he wishes that he *hadn't*.

EXERCISE 14.2-C CHECKING FORM (ORAL)

wishes for the past

On page 386, wish for the opposite of each situation in the past.

> **Example:** I lost my notes yesterday.
> *I wish that I hadn't lost them.*

1. My friends didn't call last night.

2. Mary's plane was delayed for several hours.

3. John learned about the surprise.

4. The library wasn't open yesterday.

5. I didn't go anywhere during my vacation.

6. My landlord raised my rent last month.

7. Most of the students weren't able to do the assignment.

8. George wasn't feeling well last night.

EXERCISE 14.2-D DISCRIMINATING FORM

verb forms after *wish*

Fill in each blank with the correct form of the verb in parentheses.

1. Your paper has a lot of mistakes. I wish that you _____ (*proofread*) it more carefully before you turned it in.

2. John wants to stay home this evening and watch television. I wish that he _____ (*go*) to the concert with us instead.

3. The Walcutts aren't happy with their new apartment. They wish that it _____ (BE) larger and _____ (*have*) air conditioning.

4. I wish that you _____ (*tell*, negative) me the bad news yesterday. I was up all night worrying about it.

5. Sara doesn't mind having a morning class this term, but she wishes that it _____ (*start*, negative) so early.

6. Campbell Hall is a beautiful old building. I wish that the college _____ (*tear*, negative) it down next summer.

7. I won't be able to move all this furniture by myself tomorrow. I wish that somebody _____ (*help*) me.

EXERCISE 14.2-E DISCRIMINATING FORM

auxiliary forms after *wish*

In each blank on page 387, write the correct auxiliary form, rather than the complete verb form.

1. I signed up for an eight o'clock class, and now I wish that I _____*hadn't*_____.

2. Henry is going to drop his history course, but I wish he _____

3. Susan doesn't try very hard to get good grades. I wish that she _____

4. Not many people volunteered to help. I wish that more people _____

5. Robert didn't ask for an extension for his biology project, but now he wishes that he _____

6. The university doesn't offer a major in political science. I wish that it _____

7. Professor Duffy can't attend the orientation program for new freshmen. I wish that she _____

EXERCISE 14.2-F RESPONDING TO SITUATIONS

that clauses after *wish*

Write a one-sentence reaction to each situation. Use *wish*, followed by a *that* clause.

> **Example:** Enid bought an inexpensive typewriter without any advanced features.
> *She wishes that she had gotten a better one.*   OR
> *She wishes that she hadn't been so cheap.*   OR
> *Now she wishes that she had a better one.*

1. Kathy just ran out of gas on the highway.

   _____

2. Karl doesn't feel prepared for his chemistry examination.

   _____

3. Laura doesn't like the way her new car stalls in the cold weather.

   _____

4. Andy can't get into his car. He locked his keys inside.

   _____

5. Michael and Ann are at their favorite restaurant. They will have to wait an hour to get a table.

   _____

6. Professor Romstedt is upset. Her husband is being transferred to Fort Wayne.

   _____

7. Howard is usually a good student, but he failed his physics course last term.

   _____

SECTION 14.3 Embedded Question Clauses

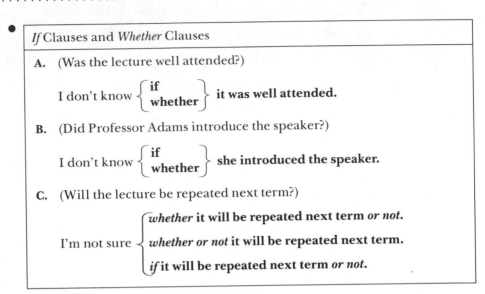

If Clauses and *Whether* Clauses

A. (Was the lecture well attended?)

I don't know { **if** / **whether** } **it was well attended.**

B. (Did Professor Adams introduce the speaker?)

I don't know { **if** / **whether** } **she introduced the speaker.**

C. (Will the lecture be repeated next term?)

I'm not sure {

whether it will be repeated next term *or not.*

whether *or not* it will be repeated next term.

if* it will be repeated next term *or not.

}

1. *If* clauses and *whether* clauses: A second type of noun clause is the *if* clause or *whether* clause. These clauses are embedded yes-no questions. In sentence A, the clause *if/whether it was well attended* refers to the yes-no question *Was the lecture well attended?*

The embedded yes-no question can begin with either *if* or *whether.* There is no difference in meaning. However, *whether* is considered somewhat more formal and is more common in writing than in speech.

2. Word order: Notice that question word order is not used in the *if* clause or *whether* clause. The question word order is changed to the statement word order.

Yes-No Question	*Embedded Yes-No Question* (*if or* whether *Clause*)
Is Mary coming tonight?	No one told me if she is coming.
Has the concert been cancelled?	I don't know if it has been cancelled.
Does the office open at 8:00?	We are not sure if it opens at 8:00.

3. *Or not*: The phrase *or not* can be added to an embedded yes-no question, as in sentence C. When the clause begins with *whether,* the phrase *or not* can be placed immediately after *whether,* or it can be delayed until the end of the clause. When the clause begins with *if,* the words *or not* must be placed at the end of the clause.

EXERCISE 14.3-A CHECKING FORM (ORAL)

if clauses and *whether* clauses

Answer each question about your classmates with an *if* clause or a *whether* clause. Begin your answer with *I don't know, I'm not sure,* or the like.

> **Example:** Does Martha write home often?
> *I don't know if she writes home often.*

1. Does (X) live in a dormitory?

2. Has (X) lived here very long?

3. Did (X) study English before coming here?

4. Is (X) an only child?

5. Has (X) ever been to Europe?

6. Was (X) a good student when she/he was young?

7. Will (X) study here next term?

8. Is (X) going to study this evening?

WH CLAUSES

D. (What causes acid rain?)
Scientists don't understand **what causes acid rain**.

E. (Why does it harm plant life and animal life?)
They know **why it harms plant life and animal life**.

F. (How is it produced?)
But they aren't sure **how it is produced**.

---

4. WH clauses: A third type of noun clause is the WH clause. These clauses are embedded WH questions. In sentence D, the clause *what causes acid rain* refers to the WH question *What causes acid rain?*

5. Word order: Embedded WH questions begin with the WH question word (*who; whom; what; why; when; where; how;* etc.). The words that follow are in statement word order, not question word order. In sentence D, the question has a subject focus, so there is no change in word order in the WH clause. However, in sentence E, the question has a predicate focus, so the word order must be changed in the WH clause. Examples follow.

Subject Focus Question (no change in word order)

Who delivered the package?	I don't know who delivered the package.
What is making that noise?	I don't know what is making that noise.

Predicate Focus Question (word order must change)

Who(m) is George talking to?	I don't know who(m) George is talking to.
What did Martha find out?	I don't know what Martha found out.
Why was the concert cancelled?	I don't know why the concert was cancelled.
When does Laura's plane arrive?	I don't know when Laura's plane arrives.
Where has our meeting been scheduled?	I don't know where our meeting has been scheduled.
How old is Gary?	I don't know how old Gary is.

EXERCISE 14.3-B CHECKING FORM (ORAL)

WH clauses

Answer these questions about your classmates, using a WH clause in your response. Begin each answer with *I don't know*, *I'm not sure*, or the like.

> **Example:** Where does George live?
> *I'm not sure where he lives.*

1. How old is (X)?

2. What does (X) like to do in his/her spare time?

3. Where does (X) usually eat lunch?

4. Why did (X) decide to come here to study English?

5. Where was (X) born?

6. Who is (X's) best friend?

7. How long has (X) studied English?

8. How does (X) get to class every day?

WH INFINITIVE PHRASES
G. We haven't been told **where we can register for classes**.   Can you tell us **where to register**?
H. I don't know **whether I should take more English or not**.   Can you help me decide **whether to take more English**?
I. George isn't sure **how he should prepare for classes**.   Can you tell him **how to prepare**?

6. WH infinitive phrases: WH clauses and *whether* clauses can sometimes be reduced to infinitive phrases. In sentences G, the WH clause *where we can register for classes* has been reduced to the infinitive phrase *where to register*. The meaning is the same. What is the reduction in sentences H and I?

The meaning of WH infinitive phrases often involves obligation or desirability (*should*) or, less frequently, possibility or permission (*can* or *could*).

EXERCISE 14.3-C CHECKING FORM (ORAL)

WH infinitive phrases

Restate each sentence, changing the WH clause to an infinitive phrase.

> **Example:** I don't know what I should do.
> *I don't know what to do.*

1. I can't remember where I should go.

2. Can you tell me whom I should talk to?

3. George can't decide whether he should leave early or not.

4. The directions don't explain where we should exit from the highway.

5. Martha already told me what I should expect.

6. I'm not sure whether I should ask for an extension or not.

7. Your invitation didn't say when we should arrive.

8. This article explains how you should prepare for an interview.

SUMMARY OF NOUN CLAUSES

that *Clauses (Embedded Statements)*

John will come tomorrow.	I think that John will come tomorrow. I thought that John would come the next day.
The results are available.	I assume that the results are available. I assumed that the results were available.
We passed the exam.	I hope that we passed the exam. I hoped that we had passed the exam.

that *Clauses after* **wish** *(Embedded Statements)*

John will not come tomorrow.	I wish that John would come tomorrow.
The results are not available.	I wish that the results were available.
We didn't pass the exam.	I wish that we had passed the exam.

if/whether *Clauses (Embedded Yes-No questions)*

Will John come tomorrow?	I don't know if/whether John will come tomorrow.
Are the results available?	I don't know if the results are available.
Did we pass the exam?	I don't know if we passed the exam.

WH *Clauses (Embedded WH Questions)*

Who can come tomorrow?	I'm not sure who can come tomorrow.
When will the results be available?	I'm not sure when the results will be available.
Why did you fail the exam?	I'm not sure why I failed the exam.

EXERCISE 14.3-D CHECKING FORM

forming *if* and WH clauses

Change each question into an embedded question clause (*if/whether* or **WH**).

1. What is the deadline for filing tax return forms?
   Does anyone know _____

   _____

2. How were the boys hurt?
The newspaper doesn't indicate _____

_____

3. Did the city council pass the antilittering ordinance?
Howard will know _____

_____

4. Who forgets to turn off the lights every evening?
We can't figure out _____

_____

5. How much will tuition be increased next year?
The administration hasn't determined yet _____

_____

6. Can textbooks be returned for a full refund?
The clerk isn't sure _____

_____

7. When does the next term begin?
Can you tell me _____

_____

EXERCISE 14.3-E CHECKING FORM
● ·

forming *that* clauses, *if* clauses, and WH clauses

Change each sentence into a noun clause (*that*, *if/whether*, or WH). Begin
your sentence with the phrase provided. Be careful to use the correct tense
in the embedded clause.

> **Examples:** The cause of the delay hasn't been determined.
> Yesterday's newspaper reported *that the cause of the delay
> hadn't been determined*.
>
> What did Dena tell you?
> I don't remember *what Dena told me*.

1. John's project wasn't successful.
John told me _____

_____

2. Was John's project successful?
Do you know _____

_____

3. How can the computer access codes be changed?
No one seems to understand _____

_____

4. Can the computer access codes be changed?
This manual doesn't say _____

_____

5. The final examination was comprehensive.
I wish _____

_____

6. The final examination was comprehensive.
Martha isn't happy _____

_____

7. Who is going to write the report?
I don't know _____

_____

8. What is Bob going to write?
I don't know _____

_____

EXERCISE 14.3-F EXPRESSING YOUR OWN THOUGHTS

noun clauses

Work with a classmate to prepare interview questions for each other about your families. First prepare five yes-no questions and five WH questions. Be sure to write down your questions.

> **Examples:** *Yes-No Question*
> Are the people in your family close to one another?
>
> *WH Question*
> How many brothers and sisters do you have?

Now interview your classmate. Ask the questions that you have prepared, and take notes as your classmate answers. Finally, report the questions that you asked and the answer that you received, as in the following examples.

> *I asked (X) if the people in his family are close to one another. He said that they have always been very close.*
> *I asked (X) how many brothers and sisters he has. He told me that he has two brothers and two sisters.*

EXERCISE 14.3-G RESPONDING TO INFORMATION

● ·

noun clauses

The following chart provides you with information about three precious gemstones: diamonds, emeralds, and sapphires. Examine the chart carefully, and be sure you understand the information. Notice that some information is missing.

	Diamonds	*Emeralds*	*Sapphires*
Where found	—	Colombia	Sri Lanka; India
Color	—	Green	Usually blue
Largest specimen ever found	Cullinan diamond (3,106 carats)	—	—
Principal mineral components	—	Beryllium aluminum silicate	Corundum
Folklore attached to gemstone	Makes people lucky in love; strong; courageous	—	Promotes peace and purity of the mind
Hardness (Mohs scale of 1-10)	10	—	—

Use WH clauses to report the type of information which the chart provides and does not provide about each gemstone. When the information is provided, also report the details with a *that* clause.

Examples: *The chart doesn't specify where diamonds are found.*
The chart indicates how hard diamonds are. It says that they measure 10 on the Mohs scale.

A Irregular Past Tense Forms and Past Participle Forms

Simple Form	Past	Past Participle
be	was/were	been
beat	beat	beaten
become	became	become
begin	began	begun
bend	bent	bent
bet	bet	bet
bind	bound	bound
bite	bit	bitten
bleed	bled	bled
blow	blew	blown
break	broke	broken
bring	brought	brought
build	built	built
burst	burst	burst
buy	bought	bought
catch	caught	caught
choose	chose	chosen
come	came	come
cost	cost	cost
cut	cut	cut
deal	dealt	dealt
dig	dug	dug
do	did	done
draw	drew	drawn
drink	drank	drunk
drive	drove	driven
eat	ate	eaten
fall	fell	fallen
feed	fed	fed
feel	felt	felt
fight	fought	fought
find	found	found

Simple Form	*Past*	*Past Participle*
fit	fit	fit
fly	flew	flown
forbid	forbade	forbidden
forget	forgot	forgotten
forgive	forgave	forgiven
freeze	froze	frozen
get	got	gotten
give	gave	given
go	went	gone
grow	grew	grown
hang (= suspend)	hung	hung
have	had	had
hear	heard	heard
hide	hid	hidden
hit	hit	hit
hold	held	held
hurt	hurt	hurt
keep	kept	kept
know	knew	known
lay	laid	laid
lead	led	led
leave	left	left
lend	lent	lent
let	let	let
lie (= recline)	lay	lain
light	lit/lighted	lit/lighted
lose	lost	lost
make	made	made
mean	meant	meant
meet	met	met
pay	paid	paid
put	put	put
quit	quit	quit
read	read	read
ride	rode	ridden
ring	rang	rung
rise	rose	risen
run	ran	run
say	said	said
see	saw	seen
seek	sought	sought
sell	sold	sold
send	sent	sent

Simple Form	*Past*	*Past Participle*
set	set	set
sew	sewed	sewed/sewn
shake	shook	shaken
shine (= give light)	shone	shone
shoot	shot	shot
show	showed	shown
shrink	shrank	shrunk
shut	shut	shut
sing	sang	sung
sink	sank	sunk
sit	sat	sat
sleep	slept	slept
slide	slid	slid
slit	slit	slit
speak	spoke	spoken
spend	spent	spent
split	split	split
spread	spread	spread
spring	sprang	sprung
stand	stood	stood
steal	stole	stolen
stick	stuck	stuck
sting	stung	stung
stink	stank	stunk
strike	struck	struck
swear	swore	sworn
sweep	swept	swept
swim	swam	swum
swing	swung	swung
take	took	taken
teach	taught	taught
tear	~~torn~~ tore	torn
tell	told	told
think	thought	thought
throw	threw	thrown
understand	understood	understood
upset	upset	upset
wake	woke	woken/waked
wear	wore	worn
weave	wove	woven
weep	wept	wept
win	won	won
write	wrote	written

Two-Word Verbs

The following list includes some common two-word verbs, both separable and nonseparable. The separable verbs are marked with an asterisk (*).

ask for	to request
blow up	to explode; to destroy by explosion*
break down	to stop functioning properly
	to analyze*
break in	to enter illegally
	to train (someone)*
break off	to stop or discontinue
bring about	to cause*
bring on	to cause or produce*
bring up	to introduce (something) into a discussion*
call off	to cancel (something)*
call on	to visit (someone)
	to ask (someone) to speak
call up	to telephone (someone)*
carry on (with)	to continue (with)
carry out	to fulfill or execute (a task)*
catch on (to)	to understand (something)
catch up (with)	to reach the same place or level
check into	to investigate
	to register at (a hotel)
check out	to investigate (something)*
check out (of)	to leave (a hotel)
clear up	to become fair weather
	to explain a problem or a mystery*
come about	to happen
come across	to find (something) by chance
count on	to rely on
cut in (on)	to interrupt
do away with	to eliminate; to throw away
do over	to repeat (something)*
drop in (on)	to visit (someone) without warning
drop out (of)	to leave; to stop attending
fall back on	to use (something) in an emergency
fall behind	to make less progress than expected

fall off	to decrease
figure out	to solve (something)*
fill in (for)	to substitute (for someone)
fill out	to complete (a form)*
find out	to discover (something)*
get along (with)	to be congenial (with someone)
get away (from)	to leave
get back (from)	to return (from somewhere)
	to receive (something) again*
get in/get out (of)	to enter/to leave (a room, a building, a car, or a taxi)
get on/get off (of)	to enter/to leave (a train, a bus, a subway, a plane, a boat, or a bicycle)
get over	to recover from (an illness or a loss)
get through	to finish (something)
get together (with)	to meet (with someone)
get up	to arise (from a bed or a chair)
give back (to)	to return (something) to (someone)*
give up	to stop trying*
go on (with)	to continue
go over	to look over or review
hand in	to submit (something)*
have on	to wear (something)*
hold on	to wait
hold up	to rob*
	to delay*
keep up (with)	to stay at the same place or level
leave out	to omit*
look after	to take care of
look for	to search for
look into	to investigate (something)
look out (for)	to be careful
look over	to examine*
look up	to find information in a reference book or directory*
look up to	to admire (someone)
make up	to invent*
pass out	to distribute (something)*
pick out	to choose*
pick up	to take (someone) along in a car*
	to take (something) in one's hand*
put off	to delay (something)*
put on	to dress in clothes*
put out	to extinguish (a fire)*
put up with	to tolerate or endure
run across	to find (something) by chance
run into	to meet (someone) by chance

run out (of)	to exhaust the supply of
see about	to consider (something)
show up	to appear
shut off	to stop (a machine, an appliance, or a light)*
shut up	to stop talking*
stand out	to be conspicuous or noticeable
take after	to resemble
take back	to return*
take off	to remove (clothing)*
	to leave the ground
	to not work for a period of time*
take out	to remove*
	to escort (someone) on a date*
take over	to assume control of*
take up	to consider or discuss*
	to begin (a new activity or habit)*
talk over	to discuss (something)*
throw away	to discard (something)*
try on	to test for fit or appearance*
try out	to test*
turn down	to decrease the volume or intensity of*
	to reject*
turn in	to submit (something)*
	to go to bed
turn off	to stop (a machine, an appliance, or a light)*
turn on	to start (a machine, an appliance, or a light)*
turn out	to extinguish (a light)*
turn up	to increase the volume or intensity of*
	to appear
wear out	to use (something) until it becomes useless*
	to exhaust or tire (someone)*
work out	to solve (something)*
	to exercise vigorously

C Verbs by Complement Pattern

Group 1 *Verbs Followed by an Infinitive*

Main Verb + *to* + Verb

I *decided to leave* early.

afford	fail	pretend
agree	happen	promise
appear	hope	refuse
arrange	intend	seem
consent	learn	struggle
decide	manage	swear
deserve	offer	wait
demand	plan	wish

Group 2 *Verbs Followed by a Gerund*

Main Verb + *Ving*

I *enjoy studying* English.

admit	dislike	miss
anticipate	enjoy	postpone
appreciate	finish	practice
avoid	(can't) help	quit
complete	imagine	recall
consider	involve	recommend
delay	keep (on)	report
deny	mention	resent
discuss	(not) mind	suggest

Group 3 *Verbs Followed by Either an Infinitive or a Gerund*

Main Verb + *to* + Verb/*Ving*

I *started to write* my report.

I *started writing* my report.

No Change in Meaning

attempt	like	regret
begin	love	(can't) stand
continue	neglect	start
hate	prefer	

Change in Meaning

forget	remember	stop

Group 4 *Verbs Followed by an Infinitive, with an Optional Second Subject*

Main Verb + (Second Subject) + *to* + Verb

I *asked to go.*

I *asked John to go.*

ask	expect	prepare
beg	get	want
choose	need	would like
dare		

Group 5 *Verbs Followed by an Infinitive, with a Required Second Subject*

Main Verb + Second Subject + *to* + Verb

I *persuaded Howard to join* us.

①advise	⑧force 강요하다	⑮persuade 설득하다
②allow 허가하다	⑨hire 고용하다	⑯remind 생각나게 하다
③challenge	⑩instruct 가르치다	⑰require 요구하다
④command	⑪invite	⑱teach
⑤convince 납득시키다	⑫order	⑲tell
⑥encourage	⑬pay	⑳urge 재촉하다, 주장하다
⑦forbid 금지하다	⑭permit 허가하다	㉑warn 경고하다

① I advised him to go to school.
② I allowed her to join the party.
③ He challenges adventure to climb the mountain.
④ He commands servant to clean the house.
⑤ I convinced him to work easily.
⑥ He encourages her to go to the trip.
⑦ My father forbid me to do something.
⑧ He forces him to work hard.
⑨ He hires him to work in the office.
⑩ She instructed me to study math.

⑪ I invite her to join the party.
⑫ I ordered steale to make a medium.
⑬ He paid money to buy a new car.
⑭ He permitted kid to play the game.
⑮ She persuaded him to go to the trip.
⑯ He reminds his cousin to the died.
⑰ The school required total to over the $50.
⑱ He teached math to study for me.
⑲ I tell him to run away from the hall.
⑳ He urges subject to plan the project.
㉑ He warned me to do not leave this room.

Group 6 *Verbs Followed by a Simple Verb or a Gerund, with a Required Second Subject*

Main Verb + Second Subject + Verb/*Ving*

I *felt the car go* out of control.

I *felt the car going* out of control.

feel	look at	overhear
hear	notice	see
listen to	observe	watch

Group 7 *Verbs Followed by a Simple Verb, with a Required Second Subject*

Main Verb + Second Subject + Verb

I *made the children quiet* down.

have	let
help (also uses infinitive)	make

D Irregular Plurals of Nouns

Singular	Plural
analysis	analyses
axis	axes
bacterium	bacteria
basis	bases
calf	calves
child	children
crisis	crises
criterion	criteria
datum	data
diagnosis	diagnoses
ellipsis	ellipses
foot	feet
goose	geese
half	halves
hypothesis	hypotheses
index	indices
knife	knives
leaf	leaves
loaf	loaves
man	men
medium	media
mouse	mice
nucleus	nuclei
oasis	oases
ox	oxen
parenthesis	parentheses
phenomenon	phenomena
self	selves
shelf	shelves
stimulus	stimuli
synthesis	syntheses
thesis	theses
thief	thieves
tooth	teeth
wife	wives
wolf	wolves
woman	women

Index